Pennsylvania CURIOSITIES

Praise for previous editions

"From Bird-in-Hand to Mars, Clark DeLeon takes you on a stylistic tour of the Keystone State, and introduces you to characters who could exist no place else. (Thank God.)"

—Stu Bykofsky, Columnist, *Philadelphia Daily News*

"Grab a bag of Snyder's and a six-pack of Yuengling! With Clark DeLeon as your guide you'll visit every oddball and oddity in the great Keystone State without ever leaving your rowhouse. The sage of Pennsylvania delivers laughs and insights, but this book is also a memoir of Clark's lifelong love affair with Pennsylvania."

—Steve Lopez, Columnist, *Los Angeles Times*

"Linking the anomalies of Pennsylvania's past and present, keen-eyed journalist Clark DeLeon takes readers on informative, amusing journeys throughout the common-wealth. An indispensable travel guide for anyone in search of the quaint and quirky in the Keystone State."

—Jack Severson, Executive Travel Editor, *Philadelphia Inquirer*

"From the story of our world-famous groundhog to the history of hoagies, *Pennsylvania Curiosities* covers it all with wit and charm. A delightful read for every Pennsylvanian with a sense of humor."

—Denise Remillard, Associate Publisher, *Central Pennsylvania Parent*

"*Pennsylvania Curiosities* is a great offbeat primer on Pennsylvania and its residents. Even lifelong Pennsylvanians can learn colorful history about the state they call home."

—Connie McNamara, Travel Editor, *Patriot-News*

Curiosities Series

Pennsylvania CURIOSITIES

Quirky characters, roadside oddities & other offbeat stuff

Fourth Edition

Clark DeLeon

Guilford, Connecticut

To Benjamin Franklin, who is not only a constant inspiration, but also the correct answer to at least 50 percent of any American history questions beginning with the words, "Who was the first to . . ."

To buy books in quantity for corporate use or incentives, call **(800) 962-0973** or e-mail **premiums@GlobePequot.com.**

The prices, rates, and hours listed in this guidebook were confirmed at press time. We recommend, however, that you call establishments to obtain current information before traveling.

All photos by the author unless otherwise noted.

Maps updated by Alena Joy Pearce © Morris Book Publishing, LLC

Project Editor: Lauren Brancato

Text Design: Bret Kerr

Layout Artist: Casey Shain

Library of Congress Cataloging-in-Publication Data is available on file.

ISBN 978-0-7627-7239-1

Printed in the United States of America

10 9 8 7 6 5 4 3 2 1

contents

★ ★

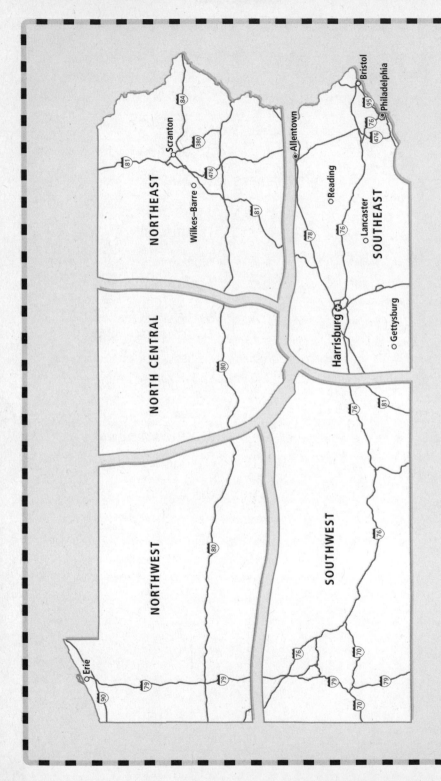

Pennsylvania

preface

★ ★

*B*ill Clinton was president when I started researching the first edition of *Pennsylvania Curiosities.* Thirteen years later this fourth edition of *Pennsylvania Curiosities* is being published the same year that Barack Obama begins his second term as president. This is a once-in-a-century year when the date of each of its 365 days ends with the number 13. If you haven't yet heard of the word "triskaideka-phobia" (the fear of the number 13, or more likely, the fear of being asked to spell "triskaidekaphobia" in a spelling bee) you will have by the end of the year 2013. My traveling companion on trips around the state from the first edition to the fourth has been our youngest daughter, Molly, who was a reluctant ten-year-old on summer break from fifth grade when we made our first journeys in the summer of 2000. Molly has blossomed into a beautiful and still reluctant twenty-three-year-old traveling companion entering her senior year at Temple University. Together we toured the Martin Guitar factory in Nazareth, saw a house shaped like a shoe near York, and found the heart-shaped tombstone of Hollywood blonde bombshell Jayne Mansfield in a frigid cemetery outside Pen Argyl. We also found a great coffee house in Pittsburgh's Strip district, a sandwich called The Growler in Lock Haven, a spooky "Gravity Hill" on a rural road outside New Paris (formerly Mudtown), and a Catholic church with stairs leading from the special parking area on the shoulder of the Pennsylvania Turnpike near New Baltimore.

Since the first edition of *Pennsylvania Curiosities*, the little town of Shanksville has become world famous as the site where forty Americans died in the first counterattack against the terrorists aboard hijacked Flight 93 bound for Washington, DC, on September 11. Pennsylvania's Governor Tom Ridge was named the first secretary of Homeland Security. Penn State football coach Joe Paterno set the new record for Division 1 college football victories a month before he was fired in a child sex scandal that has rocked the entire nation to its core. The Philadelphia Phillies won their second World Series championship and the Pittsburgh Steelers won their fifth and sixth Super Bowl victories. And in Punxsutawney every day is exactly the same for a groundhog named Phil.

preface

★ ★

Pennsylvania's population has increased by half a million people since
the first edition of *Pennsylvania Curiosities* and both the cities of Philadelphia and Pittsburgh reported population growth for the first time since
the 1950 census. Pennsylvania has become ground zero in the environmental debate over "fracking," the controversial natural gas drilling
technique that has made overnight millionaires out of rural landowners
who lease their land to gas drilling companies. Pennsylvania's dilemma
over the social and environmental impact of fracking is the subject of
two films, 2010's *Gasland,* a documentary, and 2013's *Promised Land,*
a major motion picture starring Matt Damon. In *Gasland* tap water from
the spigot of one homeowner actually catches fire. In *Promised Land* the
character played by Matt Damon is a gas company representative who
convinces Western Pennsylvania landowners to lease mineral rights on
their land for drilling gas wells. In the course of the movie Matt Damon's
character rebels against the gas company's devious and illegal methods
to convince landowners to sell. The film was shot entirely in Pennsylvania, most of it in Avonmore, Westmoreland County, a rural farming
community depicted as the fictional McKinley, Pennsylvania. Virtually
the entire state sits atop an ocean of natural gas embedded in a layer
of rock called the Marcellus Shale. Once again the boom is on—first it
was lumber, then hard hot-burning anthracite, then oil as green as tea,
and now natural gas extracted from rock—for what lies beneath the rich
soil of the Quaker State. In McKean County, where there are more than
ninety thousand oil wells drilled, you can see a working oil well next to
the drive-through lane at the McDonald's in downtown Bradford. Where
else can you get fries to go and a quart of 30-weight?

Pennsylvania: Where the curiosities never cease. Why do you think
Ben Franklin moved here?

introduction

*P*ennsylvania is the only state that begins with the letter *P*. It is one of only two states that starts with the same letter as its largest and second largest cities (Philadelphia, Pittsburgh). While you're trying to figure out the other state (hint: it also is the only state that begins with that particular letter in the alphabet) let's consider some of the many Pennsylvania curiosities hiding in plain sight. For instance, everyone knows that Pennsylvania is named in honor of its founder, William Penn, right? Wrong. William Penn was a Quaker. And a Quaker would never have been so publicly prideful as to name such a vast province after himself. Penn intended to call his "Holy experiment" of religious tolerance by the name Sylvania, which is Latin for "forest" from the Greek word meaning "woods." (It's been said that when William Penn first arrived in Pennsylvania in 1683, there were so many trees that a squirrel could run from Philadelphia to Pittsburgh without ever touching the ground.) But the king of England, Charles II, insisted that the colony be named in honor of Penn's father, Admiral William Penn. The father had lent the king the equivalent of thirty-five thousand dollars and when the admiral died, the king's debt was transferred to the son. The son was smart enough to ask for land in North America rather than cash. So for the amount of thirty-five thousand dollars the king of England gave William Penn forty-five thousand square miles of land in what is now the state of Pennsylvania. Do the math; it's a very good real estate deal.

By now you've probably figured out that there are no states that begin with the letters *B, E, J,* or *Q*. Not to mention *X, Y,* or *Z*. There are several states that begin with the same letter as their largest cities—New York, New York; Indianapolis, Indiana—it's that second largest city, that's the toughie. Keep working on it. Where were we? Oh, yes, everyone knows that Pennsylvania is called the Keystone State, but what's a keystone and why is Pennsylvania called that? A keystone is the stone at the top of an arch that holds the other stones in place. Without a keystone, the arch collapses. Pennsylvania is called the Keystone State because it locked in the thirteen original states. There are six states north of it and six states south of it. Pennsylvania was the only one of the thirteen to be landlocked without a coastline on the Atlantic Ocean.

Pennsylvania: A place full of history

★ ★

Do you need another hint? That other state is in the far west. Don't give up yet, you'll get it. The official State Insect of Pennsylvania is the firefly, which most Pennsylvanians call a lightning bug. Whether that has anything to do with the influence of Benjamin Franklin, I do not know. Speaking of which—now here's a curiosity—did you know that Benjamin Franklin was inducted into the International Swimming Hall of Fame in 1968? Among his lesser known inventions were swim fins. He designed them out of wood attached to both hands and feet. As a young man he was quite athletic and loved to swim. In fact, on frequent voyages to England, he would swim in the ocean alongside the ship. That's when he noticed that about three hundred miles off the American coastline the cold waters of the North Atlantic turned suddenly warmer. He began to track this warm river in the middle of the ocean, and wrote a scholarly scientific paper about it in 1768, but nobody took much notice at the time and not until years later was he given credit for identifying what Franklin called the Gulph Stream. I'm telling you, the guy was a mutant. He did everything and did it first. And he had a quirky sense of humor. Once he figured out how to electrify a fence, he would pull practical jokes on friends by asking them to touch it. He was the first world famous American. When he went to France as our ambassador during the Revolutionary War the French referred to him as *Monsieur Electrique*.

OK, one more hint. The other state is in the deep south. Far, far west and deep, deep south. This is the fourth edition of *Pennsylvania Curiosities* and as with the previous three editions, I am humbled by how much I didn't know about the state where I was born and have lived in and written about my entire life. What I wrote in the introduction to the first edition of *Pennsylvania Curiosities* twelve years ago is true for the fourth time. "What I didn't know about Pennsylvania could fill a book. This one." OK, time's up, we're running out of Introduction space. Last call. What's the name of the other state? Absolute final hint: far, far west; deep, deep south; and in the middle of the Pacific Ocean. Honolulu, Hilo, and Obama. *Aloha.*

Do Pennsylvanians Tawk Funny?

Pennsylvania is a lot like England and America, which Winston Churchill once described as "a great people divided by a common language." Yes, all or at least most Pennsylvanians speak English. But Pittsburgh speaks English its way, Scranton its way, Philadelphia its way, and, well, there's a reason that the Pennsylvania Dutch aren't called Pennsylvania English. The *New York Times* "language" columnist William Safire noted the differences between spoken Pennsylvanian and spoken English when in 1983 he wrote about a friend who "roots for a football team he calls the Iggles [and] talks in a patois so incomprehensible" that he asked for help in understanding "words and pronunciations peculiar to people from Philadelphia." Because I grew up in Philadelphia, I am more familiar with the "patois" Mr. Safire spoke of, although real Philadelphians don't use words like *patois*.

To speak proper Philadelphian, it helps to understand the following terms:

FLUFFYA: Ciddy of Brotherly Love

SENDA CIDDY: downtown Fluffya

KWAWFEE: what you buy at Dunkin' Donuts

WOODER: clear liquid that turns brown in kwawfee

WINDA: glass rectangle on the side of a house

WINDIZ: more than one winda

SHTREET: asphalt path used by cars

PAYMENT: concrete path used by people

CROWNS: those little wax sticks you get in Crayola boxes

KELLER: crowns come in different kellers

ACKAMEE: big supermarket

INKWIRE: Fluffya's morning newspaper

PIXTURE: painting or photo hanging on the wall

PURDY: good looking, as in "purdy as a pixture"

CHIMBLY: hole in the roof that lets the smoke out

YOUSE: second person singular, "Youse lookin' at me?"

YIZZ: plural of youse

YIZZLE: contraction of youse will, as in "Yizzle be comin' over tonight, won'tchizz?"

VETCH-T-BLS: t'maydahs and p'taydahs

BUDDER: something to put on p'taydahs or a samitch

WUNST: half of twiced

STRAWBIDJEZ: a department store now used as the newsroom of the Fluffya Inkwire

AKKROST: something you have to do to Fiff to get from Forf to Sixt Shtreet

AWN: opposite of awf

DINT: a denial, as in "I dint do it"; sometimes pronounced "ditt'n"

WOOTNA: would not have, "Hey, even if I cooda, I wootna done it."

SUMP'N: not nothin'

BERFDAY: have a happy one

POCK A BOOK: what a man wouldn't be caught dead carrying

TAL: cloth used to dry off after a shower

JAWN: a word unique to Fluffya but gaining popularity among urban hipsters around the country. Jawn is the same as a thingamajig or a whosywhatsis with fewer syllables. A jawn is anything or anyone you mean it to be. "Hand me that jawn, will you?" or "Check out that jawn." It can also be a messed up situation. "This is a heckuva jawn, ain't it?" (See photo next page.)

CHUMPIE: another word for jawn. "Look at the chumpie driving that jawn."

AST: to inquire in the past tense, as in "I ast Gloria for a date, and she tole me to go take a wawk."

WIDGES: in your company, as in "Hey, I'll go widges!"

HON: variation on Sir, Ma'am, or Miss as practiced in Philadelphia eating establishments, as in, "Yo, Hon, watches want with that hamburger?"

DOUNNASHORE: anywhere but here, a summer destination; the Lannick Ocean. You have to drive akkrost Jersey to get to it.

During the Occupy Philly demonstrations and encampment outside City Hall in the fall of 2011, this discarded sign shows how the all-purpose Philadelphia-born term "jawn" can mean anything you want it to mean.

GAWNA: to depart or proceed to, as in, "And to think I was gawna taker dounnashore."

SKOOK'L: name of a river that nobody can spell—S-C-H-U-Y-L-K-I-L-L—, means "hidden river" in Dutch

ADDYTOOD: cojones, huevos, what Fluffyans are proud to have, you got a problem widdat?

GAZ: expensive fuel that makes cars go, what you get from eating a bad hoagie, sometimes causes newborns to appear to smile

SPIGOT: where wooder comes out in the zink when you're making kwaffee; same thing as a faucet but people notice which word you choose—faucets think they're smarter than spigots.

Philadelphia and Pittsburgh share a heritage of nobody knowing what the heck people who come from either place are talking about. Is it the words we choose to speak, or how we say them, like what the people in Pittsburgh call their own city:

PIXBURG: Pennsylvania's second largest ciddy, where the Mon meets the Ohio

YUNZ: same as youse, only more nasal

WE'UNZ: first person plural, "We'unz were here first."

YINZER: native of Pixburg, a person who can speak perfect yunz

DAHNTAHN: sedda ciddy Pixburg, great view from the top of Coal Hill, also pronounced "dawn tawn"

DA BUCOS: once great National League baseball team, sometimes called "da Parrots"

DA STILLERS: two or more moonshiners, the greatest NFL team ever from Pennsylvania

GIANT IGGLE: Pixburg area supermarket chain, what Fluffya's NFL team would be called if it could win one stinkin' Super Bowl

STEEGLES: name of the NFL team representing Pittsburgh and Philadelphia during World War II

DA PENS: name of NHL team that defeated the cross state Flyers in order to meet Detroit in the 2008 Stanley Cup finals; what Redwings forwards would have worn underneath if they had to play the Flyers

DA IGLOO: where da Pens play

FARCE FAR: what Smokey da Bear says only yunz can prevent

IT'S A BURG THANG: Pixburg expression Fluffyans wouldn't understand

SLIPPY: what roads get when wet

AHT: opposite of in

SLIBERTY: slippy suburb section called East Liberty

SAHSIDE: Pixburg Dixie, south side of the Monongahela Rivers, working class and hipster neighborhoods with South Philly addytood

STILL MILLS: what Pixburg used to have a lot of, why it was called "The Still Ciddy"

JUMBO: a big baloney sangwich, a Pixburg hoagie

QUIT JAGGIN DAT JUMBO: stop playing with your food

POND: what 16 ounces equals, "Same as that beer in your hand, gimme one of those cold ponders."

DAWN: a masculine name, short for Dawnald

BAW KNEE: muy bonita, a feminine name, Scottish for "pretty," as in "baw knee lass"; male name of 1970s hit comedy cop show, "Baw-Knee Miller"

EYE SEE LITE: a cold bottle of beer, and not one of them boutique beers neither; what a broke customer tells his bartender at last call

POP: Coke, Pepsi, any carbonated beverage; quaint Midwestern term for what anyone east of Altoona calls "soda"

People from Pixburg call themselves Yinzers.

SPUTZIE: a noisy little bird

RADIO TOWER: steel-belted rubber around a wheel; cars use four at a time

IMP n ARN: a shot and a beer, Imperial and Iron Ciddy

GUM BANDS: what rubber bands are called in Pixburg

MOUNT WARSHINGTON: Coal Hill, best view of dahntahn, great place to watch da Stillers or da Parrrots play if you have a pair of binoculars

With a working knowledge of the dialects in Pennsylvania's largest cities on the state's southeastern and southwestern extremities, understanding Northeast and Central Pennsylvania—an area known as Coal Country—should be a piece of cake. But not necessarily. "Hayna," for instance, is an expression everyone up and down the line from Wilkes-Barre to Scranton uses or understands, but I have yet to meet someone who can explain it. "Hayna, you know, it means 'you know what I mean?'" an Old Forge resident told me. "Hayna or no." Make sense? OK, then you should have no problems with understanding northeast Pennsylvania speak:

HAYNA VALLEY: where people who say "hayna" live

WIXBERRY: what Scrantonyans call Wilkes-Barre, also Wuxe Bare

GIMME A STEG: I'll have a cold beer, please

MELK: white liquid kids drink before they're old enough for a Steg

PIGGIES: cabbage rolls that can be eaten with melk or beer

KUZZINTS: your aunt and uncle's childrens

ONNAKOWNA: reason something happened; "He was late to work onnakowna traffic."

BE'ENDAT: same as onnakowna; "Be'endat traffic was bad, he was late."

RUDE AIDY: east-west interstate highway; "Take rude aidy to get to Penn State."

LONN MORE: what you use to cut grass on your front lonn

CORPSE HOUSE: funeral parlor

TOCK: the act of speaking, what people do on the phone

I TOTSO: just as I suspected

HALUSHKI: cabbage again, sautéed with pasta

DA YOU: the University of Scranton

DEE ACKAMEE: same as in Fluffya; "Meet me at dee Ackamee."

MAYAN: ancient Mexican civilization; also, "that belongs to me"

LECKTRIC: Scranton is called the Lecktric City

BREFISS: first meal of the day

BAFF ROOM: where you go after eating brefiss

DRAFF: beer served cold from the tap

LIE BERRY: classy place with books

DINKYBANK: large pile of mine waste, usually slag; very pretty when covered with snow

SHENDO: Shenandoah, town surrounded by dinkybanks

ON TICK: running a tab, credit, the tick or checkmark entered in the record book of the store giving credit

CARLOAD OF ROCK: a bounced check, failure to pay the tick. Miners were paid by the carload—of coal. A carload of rock was worthless.

SCRA'UN: big city up the line from Wixberry

PROLLY: in all probability; quite likely

LEFT HANDERS: non-Catholics

PUBLICS: left handers attending non-Catholic school

PANKED DOWN: hair flattened on the head; hat hair

MEER: what people look in to make sure their hair isn't panked down

OVER TOWN: in the direction of downtown, as in "I'm going over town" when town is on the other side of the ridge, hill, or mountain

JAHAFTA: "Was that really necessary?"

BUGGY: cart to carry groceries at the Ackamee

BADEN SUIT: what you wear to go swimming

AFTERLATER: later than now, when I'm done here. "I'll go widges afterlater."

COUPLA: as few as two, as many as twelve, especially beers, as in "I stopped for a coupla." All depends on whether you go home afterlater.

AIN'T LEFT: not allowed, permission denied. "Left" is past tense of "let," as in "I'd like to come out tonight, but I ain't left." Usually applies in the wake of arriving home afterlater from a coupla.

BREFFISS: the most important meal of the day.

The Pennsylvania Dutch have added their own flavor to the Pennsylvania language stew. How else do you think Kutztown High School could come up with a cheer that goes, "Ring baloney once! Ring baloney twice! Hey, yah, Kutztown sure is nice!"

FIGHTIN' AMISH: oxymoronic nickname for Kutztown University's championship rugby team. Like the Fightin' Quakers of Penn.

GETT'N TO WET'N: looks like rain

LEP'NEN: county adjoining Lancaster; a type of baloney

STOP BEING SO SHUSSLY: can't you walk without tripping over your own feet?

OUTEN THE LIGHTS: don't waste electricity

THE BABY'S GREXY: my, what a cranky baby

FRESS: eatin' too much

RUTSCH AROUND: what squirmy little kids do; ants in your pants

SNAKE GUARDER: hovering insect, dragonfly

MULLI: baby frog, tadpole

STROOBLY: what you look like when you first wake up, disheveled

SCHMUTZ: a little kiss

SCHLECK: what you do to the glue on an envelope, to lick

SCHUSHLICH: how stroobly people tend to act, clumsy

KOTZ: what people who fress often do, to throw up

GEDUNK: what puts junk in your trunk, sweets

IT WONDERS ME: to contemplate, I wonder

I NEED JUMPED: "My car battery is dead, can you help a brother out?"

BRUTZ BABY: don't be one, crybaby

WOOTZ: a person who makes a pig of himself at dinner

RAISON STROP: Amish buggies don't have them painted on the sides, but hot rods do

FRESSING: indulging a sweet tooth, a wootz with candy

HURRIEDER: what you can't do in traffic stuck behind an Amish buggy

MISHTY: nickname for an Amish person

DIPPY X: flip those eggs over easy

CROTCH: enclosed place to park the car

THROW MAMMA FROM THE CAR A KISS: kiss me from the window

QUIT YER BRUTZIN: you're acting like a grexy

COME THE HOUSE IN: come on in, but wipe your feet first

TASTES LIKE MORE: are you serving seconds?

ROOCHY: restless sleeper, tossing and turning

SKOOTCHY: what the person lying next to a roochy usually does

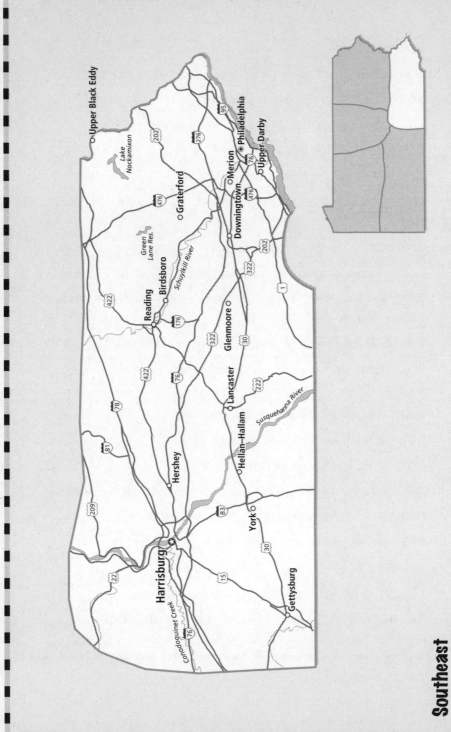

Upper Black Eddy

Lake
Nockamixon

Schuylkill River

202

276

95

Philadelphia

Merion

Downingtown

Upper Darby

76

476

202

Graterford

476

Green
Lane Res.

Birdsboro

322

1

422

Reading

176

Glenmoore

522

30

78

422

76

222

Lancaster

Susquehanna River

Hellan–Hallam

81

Hershey

209

83

York

30

Harrisburg

15

Gettysburg

22

Conodoquinet Creek

76

Southeast

1

Southeast

When you think of Pennsylvania, what do you see? Amish carriages? The Liberty Bell? Hershey chocolate? The bronze statue atop Philadelphia City Hall of William Penn (not Benjamin Franklin, as many visitors assume)? Rich rolling farmland? The battlefields of Gettysburg? The silent steel mill in Bethlehem that's now a casino? Billy Joel singing "Allentown"? Just about everything that immediately leaps to mind about Pennsylvania can be found in the Southeastern part of the state.

The Southeast stretches from the Delaware River (the same one Washington crossed to get to Jersey) on the east to just beyond the state capital of Harrisburg in the west (where in 2006 incumbent elected officials from all over the state were voted out of office by the dumpster load following an unannounced vote at two in the morning to raise their own pay). The Southeast's southern boundary with Maryland is the most famous border line in America, bearing the hyphenated name of its surveyors, Charles Mason and Jeremiah Dixon.

But the Southeast is also home to lesser known Pennsylvania curiosities including: the Curse of William Penn, the smallest church in the world, and the home of Pennsylvania's only president, James Buchanan, who was the only bachelor president and possibly gay. Two of America's canonized saints lived in the Southeast and you can see the mummified remains of one in a glass coffin in the basement of a Philadelphia church. The Southeast is a great place to start because, after all, didn't America start here?

William Penn Back Where He Belongs: Top of the World, Ma!

Beneath a clear blue 9/11 sky—it was almost too blue, like it was that Tuesday in September twelve years earlier—I climbed to the top of Philadelphia's (and Pennsylvania's) tallest office tower in search of an urban legend. I wanted to see with my own eyes what I had been telling people for years. Not that I ever doubted that the story was true. As we all know, William Penn works in mysterious ways. The story I tell is familiar to Philadelphians and delightful to visitors hearing it for the first time. For almost one hundred years the tallest man-made object in the City of Philadelphia was the bronze Quaker hat atop the head of Pennsylvania founder William Penn in the thirty-seven-foot-tall statue that crowns the top of City Hall Tower. At a height of 548 feet from street to hat, City Hall Tower was the tallest building in the world (briefly) until it was surpassed in 1889 by that Parisian erector set on steroids, the Eiffel Tower. City Hall Tower still retains the title of world's tallest "habitable" masonry structure, and its status as Philadelphia's tallest building was enforced for decades, not by law, but rather by an understanding, an unseen handshake between corporate and political leaders who agreed to abide by what was known as the "Billy Penn Hat Rule."

Looking at Center City's vaunted skyline today, where City Hall Tower is a slender, almost insignificant presence, it's hard to believe it once dominated the downtown, with the statue of William Penn ruling over the glass and stone buildings below him like a peaceful bronze colossus. All that changed in 1987 with the completion of One Liberty Place, the sixty-one-story blue glass Chrysler Building look-alike crowned with a steel spire that tops off at a height of 945 feet. If the massive bronze shoulders of William Penn weren't already in that position, he would have turned his back on the young upstart

The tiny statue of William Penn atop the Comcast Tower is 427 feet higher than the top of the huge bronze statue of Penn on City Hall Tower.

and all the other higher-than-thou-hat skyscrapers that popped up during the past two decades. And sometime during that first decade—no one is exactly sure when and the man responsible isn't talking—William Penn put a curse on Philadelphia and its ungrateful citizens. He wouldn't let any of the city's professional sports teams win a national championship.

He had his reasons beyond being upstaged in the skyline. In 1993 when the Phillies went to the World Series, the city put a big red Phillies hat on top of Billy Penn's bronze hat. The Phillies lost in six games. Lesson: Don't be mocking the man's hat. In 1997 when the Flyers went to the Stanley Cup finals, they put an orange hockey jersey on William

Penn. He's a Quaker, for crying out loud! The Flyers were swept in four games. Lesson: Don't be mocking a man's faith. In 2001 when the Sixers made it to the NBA finals, nobody did anything to William Penn but he still wouldn't let us beat the Lakers. Lesson: The man don't forget. But five years later, something Comcastic happened to the Center City skyline with the opening of Philadelphia's (and Pennsylvania's) tallest and greenest skyscraper in June of 2008. Months earlier during the topping off ceremony of the Comcast Center, along with the traditional evergreen tree and American flag, iron workers placed a small replica statue of William Penn on a steel I beam and hoisted it to the highest point on the tallest building in Philadelphia almost a thousand feet above street level, with William Penn now back on top. And guess who won the World Series that year? The Phillies. Lesson: At the end of the day, the man is still a fan.

Billy Penn was back where he belonged. Top of the world, Ma! "We know how to take care of our curses in Philadelphia," I like to tell out-of-towners, who invariably ask, "Is it still there?" To which, I happily reply, "Of course. Who would dare remove it?" Only an idiot. Possibly a New York Mets fan. But no properly loyal and reasonably superstitious Philadelphia sports fan would ever mess with William Penn again, right? But then I heard that some diabolical nitwit had stolen the statue of William Penn on top of the Comcast building. Say it ain't so! "It's true," said John Demming, senior director of corporate communications for Comcast. Demming discovered the theft when he was taking a camera crew to the roof a few years ago to shoot video of the statue. It fell to Demming to find a replacement statue, which wasn't so easy, but he was successful at last. And on September 11, 2012, he took me to the roof of the Comcast building to see with my own eyes. It's quite a schlep, incidentally, and it's not a tourist attraction. Guided by Kelly Argo of Liberty Property Trust, which owns and manages the building, Demming and I and three others rode a freight elevator to the fifty-sixth floor followed by four flights of stairs up to the unoccupied fifty-seventh floor. Then began

With South Philadelphia spreading out behind it, Billy Penn's hat is once again the highest point in the City of Philadelphia. The top of the spire of One Liberty Place behind it is 30 feet lower.

the seventy-five-foot climb up ten flights of stairs to the roof of the Comcast tower. And on the highest beam on the south side of the rooftop, stood a six-and-three-quarter-inch-tall bronze statue of William Penn, facing northeast, just like the larger Penn statue way, way below. What a view of the city. Never in my life have I seen City Hall look small. From up there it did. From the new top of the city where little Billy Penn reigns, and will continue to—"Oh, we've got him epoxied down on that beam," said Demming—I could see the cooling tower of the Limerick nuclear power plant forty miles away and miles beyond that. From up there, shoulder to shoulder with William Penn surveying his domain, Pennsylvania looked pretty darn good.

★ ★

Daniel Boone Was a Pennsylvania Kind of Guy
Birdsboro

"Daniel Boone was a man. Yes, a real man." So goes the theme song
to the old *Daniel Boone* TV show starring Davy Crockett (or was it
Fess Parker?). Daniel Boone was also a Quaker, or at least he started
life that way. Boone was born in 1734 in a log cabin in Berks County
in what is now called Birdsboro. There is a stone farmhouse where
his log birthplace once stood, but the original earth-floored cellar and
spring remain from the structure that Boone called home for the first
sixteen years of his life. That was about as long as the frontiersman
ever stayed in one place, because from the time he turned twenty-one
until his death at the age of eighty-five in Missouri in 1820, Daniel
Boone was a man on the move.

The Daniel Boone Homestead off Route 422 is a collection of eighteenth-century buildings maintained and operated by the Pennsylvania
Historical and Museum Commission. You can learn about Boone's
travels in a twelve-minute video in the visitor center. ("Them Boones
was always lookin' for more elbow room, if you know what I mean,"
says the colonially dressed narrator of the documentary.) Daniel was
the sixth of eleven children born to Squire Boone and his wife, Sarah.
The Boones were Quakers from Devonshire, England, who had come
to Pennsylvania seeking the religious freedom and opportunities promised by the commonwealth's proprietor, William Penn.

Young Daniel was a gun-toting Quaker. He became a proficient
shot with a long gun that would become famous as the Pennsylvania
rifle when he moved to Kentucky in later life. After Squire Boone had
a falling out with his fellow Quakers over the issue of one of his children marrying a non-Quaker, the family began a trek southward and
westward that would take them through Maryland and Virginia and
finally to North Carolina, where they settled when Daniel was sixteen.
At the age of twenty-one, Daniel married Rebecca Byrne, a woman
who would spend most of her life wondering where that husband of
hers had gotten himself this time—either being captured by Indians or

★ ★

leading a raiding party or exploring new territory and settling communities named in his honor, such as Boonesborough, Kentucky. Daniel was home enough to leave Rebecca with ten children, however.

Daniel Boone's Pennsylvania years were the stuff of storybooks, which means you could make up stories about them because so little is known about his youth. He did return to his birthplace twice, in 1781 and 1788, to visit relatives who had purchased the homestead from his father. Today the homestead is as much about the settlers who carved out a life in the sparsely populated wilderness of central Pennsylvania. There is a flintlock rifle range where specialty competitions are held on the 579-acre property that the state took over in 1938. There is a total of seven structures on the site, including a restoration of the original eighteenth-century smokehouse, blacksmith shop, and sawmill.

The Daniel Boone Homestead, on Daniel Boone Road in Birdsboro, is open year-round. Call (610) 582-4900 or visit their website at www .danielboonehomestead.org.

Where the Blob First Oozed
Chester County

POLICE LIEUTENANT DAVE: "Just because some kid smashes into your wife on the turnpike doesn't make it a crime to be seventeen."

That line from the 1958 movie *The Blob* should have been enough to alert viewers that this wasn't just another B horror movie; it was a teenage angst B horror movie. Why won't grown-ups listen when we tell them there's a flesh-absorbing ball of goo rolling around the Pennsylvania countryside?!

The Blob was Steve McQueen's first starring movie role and he played—what else?—a teenager who is on a lovers' lane with his girlfriend when a meteor crashes nearby. They go to investigate, but a hobo finds the crash site first. He pokes the meteor with a stick and it breaks open to reveal a clear gooey center, which quickly leaps onto the hobo's hand. That's when Steve McQueen and his girlfriend find him screaming on the side of the road. They rush him to the local

★ ★

doc, and soon the hobo, the doctor, and Nurse Kate have all been blobsorbed.

The rest of the movie consists of McQueen and his teenage buddies trying to wake up authorities to the otherworldly menace. By the time of the movie's climax, the rolling ball of blood-red silicone is as big as a house, or at least the Downingtown Diner, which the Blob is oozing over when McQueen discovers it can be stopped by cold. (In the end they parachute a crate holding the Blob onto an Arctic ice floe. The credits read "The End" with a big question mark.)

The Blob was one of the great horror classics of the late '50s. It was filmed entirely in Montgomery and Chester Counties by Valley Forge Films in Yellow Springs. Something of a Blob cult has formed and there are pilgrimages to famous Blob sites, such as the Downingtown Diner and the Colonial movie theater in Phoenixville, where the Blob oozed through the projectionist's viewing holes and gummed up the audience during the "Midnight Spook Show."

A few years ago, thirty members of the Horror and Fantasy Film Society of Baltimore took a Blob tour led by Wes Shank, a Montgom-ery County resident who purchased the actual Blob—a five-gallon container of red silicone used as an animated prop in the movie—from Valley Forge Films in 1965. In addition to the Colonial Theatre and the Downingtown Diner (the original has been torn down, but another was built on the same site), the Blob tourists visited what is now a Meineke Discount Mufflers shop in Phoenixville where the Blob ate a mechanic working under a car. Also on the tour was Jerry's Super-market (now the "I Got It at Gary's" drugstore) on Lewis Road in Royersford, where Steve McQueen and his girlfriend hid in the walk-in refrigerator to escape the Blob. "The average person probably thinks we're a bunch of crazed fanatics, which we probably are," said Wes Shank during the Blob tour. "But it's all in good fun."

Once Upon a Time in America

Gettysburg Battlefield

Gettysburg hasn't changed much in the last 150 years. Not the land-scape of the battlefield, anyway. From the crest of Little Round Top today you can still see the slaughter pens below—unnamed places that became famous. To the left is Devil's Den, with its illusion of shelter behind the stands of boulders that both Union and Confederate sol-diers used before killing each other at point blank range, or hand to hand with knives and bayonets. To the right is the Peach Orchard, an open space so exposed it almost makes you laugh at what New York's General Daniel Sickles was thinking when he ordered his men to advance. What were *they* thinking? In between is what the historical markers identify as the Valley of Death.

You have to experience the battlefield at Gettysburg to under-stand what I'm about to say. It is a holy place. There is a reverence and importance to the peaceful landscape that is both apparent and yet elusive. These soft hills and gentle countryside offer no clues. But somehow you know, you can feel something deep and personal, something that reveals itself silently and forever.

It has nothing to do with the monuments. And yet there are hun-dreds of them, all heartfelt, all specific to individual units and moments during the endless three-day battle that saved the Union, and perhaps the world, by preserving the reality of a nation, of a larger idea called the United States of America. Where would the world be without it?

Lofty words? Almost certainly. But before you dismiss them as mere sentiment, go to Gettysburg. Let the battlefield whisper its timeless truths. There was a moment in history when it all came down to this: these hills, that farm, this stand of trees, that split rail fence. America lives today because of the men, many of them boys, really, who sol-diered and suffered and cried out to their mothers through parched lips before dying alone and unheard amidst the hellish noise and heat and gunpowder haze that scorched their lungs in the unrelenting agony of their final breaths. Such a beautiful, beautiful place to die so

★ ★

Guided tours of the Gettysburg Battlefield are given
on foot, by bus and private cars, and more recently on
two-wheeled Segway personal transports.

horribly and so anonymously. The scale of the slaughter was epic and
unspeakable

And where there were no words, adequate or even possible, to
describe the ache of a nation, someone found them. And those words
addressed the futile nature of words themselves. After acknowledging
the fitting and proper purpose of the dedication of a cemetery to the
fallen at Gettysburg on November 19, 1863, the president said, "But
in a larger sense, we cannot dedicate, we cannot consecrate, we cannot hallow this ground. The brave men, living and dead, who struggled
here have consecrated it far above our poor power to add or detract."

It's impossible not to hear echoes of Abraham Lincoln's words while
touring the battlefield at Gettysburg either on foot, on a bus, in a
car or, increasingly, astride a Segway PT (personal transporter). (Hey,
if Segway tours can navigate Elfreth's Alley, why should Devil's Den

be off limits?) Lincoln is everywhere in Gettysburg, in spirit if not in bronze, a lot like Ben Franklin in Philadelphia.

Other than the battlefield, which continues in degrees measured by the National Park Service to return to its mid-nineteenth century appearance, much has changed at Gettysburg National Military Park since the last edition of *Pennsylvania Curiosities.* There is a new discreetly located (some would describe it as hidden) Visitors' Center that replaces the unsightly building and parking area on a hilltop that was visible from the town and within walking distance from the cemetery Lincoln's words immortalized.

Gone is the old-fashioned, low-tech (and much beloved) map room with its expanse of floor-mounted light bulbs that traced the approach of the Union and Confederate armies. It was corny forty years ago, but by 2005 its analog technology resembled a rotary dial on a cell phone. The new Visitors' Center opened in 2008 is located in a wooded hollow outside of town that would be impossible to find without directional signs (and even with them I got lost trying to find my way out of the parking lot. Twice. Seriously).

Instead of the kitschy map room at the old Visitors' Center, the must-see centerpiece of the new Gettysburg visitors' experience is a first-rate documentary about the causes of the Civil War—slavery, regional pride, and astonishing ignorance—narrated by the venerable actor Morgan Freeman (What? You never heard of the *March of the Penguins* to reinforce Vicksburg?). The documentary breaks no new historical ground, and is surprisingly not Battle of Gettysburg-centric, which makes perfect sense when you consider the rich history everywhere outside the Visitors' Center's doors. The documentary, shown in multiple movie theaters continuously every fifteen minutes or so, ends with the audience being directed immediately into hallways leading to an escalator that takes everyone to a large circular room with a viewing platform in the middle. This is the restored Cyclorama painting on canvas of Pickett's Charge, the climactic and failed Confederate attack into the middle of the Union lines on the third day of the battle.

The view from Little Roundtop today. It's hard to imagine that this peaceful green hillside is remembered with
names like the Slaughter Pen and Devil's Den.

Cycloramas were the IMAX theater equivalents of the late 1800s
and early 1900s. Epic moments of history—the *Crucifixion of Jesus,*
for instance—were painted on huge canvases and displayed in round
buildings that allowed a seamless 360-degree narrative of the events.
The Gettysburg battle cyclorama was painted over a period of eighteen
months by French artist Paul Philippoteaux and five assistants. The finished work debuted in 1884 in Boston where it was a major attraction
for almost a decade.

The current cyclorama canvas at Gettysburg has been restored three
times. It measures 27 feet high by 359 feet long. The painting has a

★ ★

three-dimensional effect caused by the way it is hung on the walls with the lower part sloping forward toward actual wooden wagons and barrels and fences. It's a powerful painting, and because the audience turns over every fifteen minutes, you can't really linger. They keep you moving.

On the first floor of the Visitors' Center and Museum are displays showing weapons from rifles to explosive ordnance, used by both sides to kill each other during the Civil War. What I found interesting and surprising was the state-by-state list of the number of soldiers who served for either the Union or Confederate armies from the same state. For instance, Kentucky, a border state, had 75,000 men serve in the Union army and 28,000 serving Confederate forces. Louisiana, which is about as southern as the South gets, had 29,000 men serve in the Union military, while 69,000 fought for the Confederates. Even Georgia, which provided 135,000 recruits to the Confederacy, couldn't stop 195 Georgians from sticking with the Union. Pennsylvania, New York, and Massachusetts provided almost a million men among them to the Union cause, and none to the Confederacy.

Near the main entrance to the Visitors' Center is a life-size bronze statue of Abraham Lincoln seated on a concrete bench with enough room for one person to sit next to him for a photo op. This Lincoln looks like he's fresh off the penny. In his left hand is a leather folder containing the famous speech he delivered at Gettysburg in November 1863. Perhaps he had just finished the address, because this bronze Lincoln looks a little pooped. He's removed his top hat, beaver I suspect, and it sits on the bench next to him with his right hand resting protectively on top.

During my visit I took photographs of the Lincoln statue and the different people who sat on the bench next to him. I noticed one dark-haired fellow with a ponytail engaged in what looked like a serious conversation with the Great Emancipator. He later identified himself as Rick Almeida, an American history enthusiast who works as a bartender in South Philadelphia. As I took pictures I edged closer

★ ★

Outside the Visitors' Center at the Gettysburg Battlefield is a bronze statue of Abraham Lincoln sitting on
a bench with a copy of the Gettysburg Address in his
hand. Philadelphian Rick Almeida sat next to Lincoln
and said, "No, Mr. Lincoln, you were wrong. The world
did note and long remember what you said here."

to eavesdrop on this intense one-sided conversation. "No, Mr. Lincoln, you were wrong," Almeida said. "The world *did* note and long
remember what you said here."

★ ★

The Little Church

Glenmoore

"What is it we're looking for, Dad?" asked my then ten-year-old daughter, Molly. "We're looking for the smallest church in the world," I told her. "What does it look like?" she asked. I hadn't a clue. In fact, I didn't know if it even existed. I had been told by a newspaper-delivery-truck driver about what he described as "the smallest church in the world" off Route 282 in Glenmoore, Chester County. "You can't miss it," the truck driver had told me.

Famous last words if ever I've heard them. The biggest church in the world, now maybe that you can't miss. I drove through Glenmoore the first time without realizing that that little cluster of buildings I passed awhile back was, in fact, a town. Then I went through it a second time (it looks different coming from the other direction).

Downtown Glenmoore consists of an intersection with no traffic light and one antiques shop next to a convenience store, where I stopped to ask for directions. "Excuse me, guys," I said to the two teenagers behind the counter, "there's supposed to be a really, really small church around here. Have you ever heard of it?" They both shook their heads. I was half backing out the screen door when one boy said, "You mean *really* small?" I nodded. He pointed down Route 282. "It's a couple of miles that way on your right. But be careful; it's real easy to miss," he said. "It's about as big as a car."

For the record it's about the size of a one-car garage or a big tool-shed, if toolsheds were made out of flagstone. Also for the record, the Little Church, as the sign outside describes it, is located in Cornog Crossing, another one-intersection town about two miles south of Glenmoore, where Marshall Road crosses Route 282. The kid at the convenience store was right: You'd pass right by it if you didn't know where it was. The Little Church is nestled under trees just six steps from the roadway. Whether it's the smallest church in the world is an issue best left to Mr. Ripley, but it's the smallest one I've ever seen—about big enough for three people plus an altar. It's big enough for

★ ★

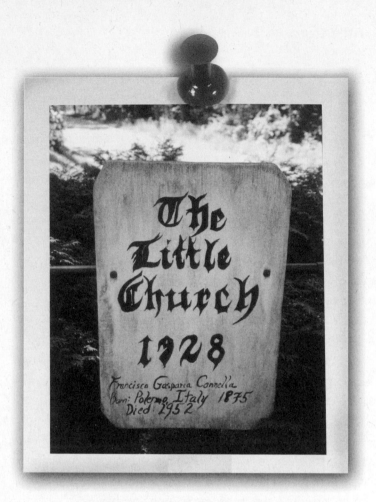

The little sign outside the Little Church is
almost as easy to miss as the church itself.

a really intimate wedding, which it has been used for on occasion,
according to Dorothy Lambert at the Exxon station across the street.

The sign outside the church reads: THE LITTLE CHURCH, 1928; FRANCISCO
GASPARIA CANNELLA; BORN: PALERMO, ITALY, 1875; DIED: 1952. The story
behind it is a sweet one. Francisco Cannella came here from Italy to
work the nearby quarry in the 1920s. Like many immigrants he left his
wife and children behind, determined to work and save until he had

★ ★

raised enough money to bring them all to America. Francisco went one better. He made a promise to God that he would go to church every day if God would allow him to bring his family from Italy. God and Francisco's hard work paid off. The only problem was that in order for Francisco to honor his pledge, he had to travel nine miles to the nearest Catholic church in Downingtown in all kinds of weather on a dangerously winding road. But the Italian stonemason was a man of his word, so he built the Little Church with his own hands, and each day until the day he died he went there to thank God for bringing his family to America.

Francisco's children still live in the house behind the Little Church. Upon hearing the inspiring story of a father's love and faith, my own darling child commented, "Can we go home *now?!*"

If the Shoe Fits, Live in It
Hallem

It's funny. I don't know how many times over the years during my travels around Pennsylvania that I've arrived in an unfamiliar town without a clue as to where I could find the person, place, or thing that is that town's claim to fame. Its *raison de moi*—the reason I had come. Its distinguishing something. The thing that makes it different than any other place. And just as often, when I stop and ask one of the locals, somebody sitting on a porch, someone walking out of a hardware store, "Do you know where such-and-such is?" the answer I get is, "Huh?" Or worse, a look that says, "What'chu talkin' 'bout, Willis?!" "You say that there's a famous bell? And it's got a big crack in it? And it's a symbol of liberty. And it's supposed to be right here in our town?" Sometimes it's almost like that. And that was the experience I had while in the town of Hallem in York County when I was looking for what has been for more than sixty years that town's most famous landmark—a house shaped like a shoe. Easy enough, right?

So I pull into a Sheetz convenience store/gas station off Route 30 in the borough of Hallem (which is surrounded by Hellam

Township—note the difference in spelling) and I ask the cashier if she knows where the shoe house is located. You would have thought I asked the correct spelling of Hallem. She calls over the manager who has heard of it. But his explicit directions were, "It's over there some-where [gesturing toward the north side of Route 30]. One of those streets."

Confident that there was no more exact information to be gained by further inquiry inside, I walked outside and asked a man pumping gas. He looked at me as though I had asked him if he *lived* in house shaped like a shoe. So I got back in my car and set out in the gen-eral direction of "over there." Within two blocks of the gas station I decided to follow a hunch. I turned left at the traffic light onto a street identified by the sign as Shoe House Road.

About a half mile up the winding road on the left was a house— osh kosh b'gosh!—shaped like a buff-colored shoe. More like a work boot, actually. In fact, it looked like a right shoe lost by a giant wear-ing a pair of dirty white bucks. This is the Haines Shoe House built in 1948 by a local shoe store magnate named Colonel Mahlon M. Haines, a man who knew a little something about self-promotion.

Haines owned forty shoe stores in Pennsylvania and Maryland and dubbed himself the "Shoe Wizard" in advertisements. The self-made millionaire had the house built on a hill overlooking what is now a major highway between York and Lancaster. The height of the house is twenty-five feet tall at the ankle, which tapers like a shoe to the toe forty-eight feet away. The wood and stucco house is seventeen feet across at its widest. There are eight windows on the ground (sole?) floor and three on the ankle floor where the two bedrooms are located. The kitchen is in the heel and the living room in the toe. No way a little old lady could have lived here with all of those children.

Colonel Haines lived here briefly. Then he moved across the street to enjoy the view and made the house available to lucky newlyweds and elderly couples on weekends (implied message: no children). The Shoe Wizard's image appears on the stained glass window in the front

Shoe Wizard Colonel Mahlon M. Haines built this
house shaped like a shoe in 1948 outside Hellam
as a honeymoon vacation site for newlyweds.

door (holding up a shoe in each hand) and every window features a
stained glass shoe. A brown shoe appears in the middle of every six-
foot section of the white fence surrounding the property.

The Haines Shoe House is one those wonders of sincere American
kitsch. Behind the house is a doghouse shaped like a shoe. Through
various owners and volunteers over the years (the "Colonel" died
in 1962) the house has been well maintained. Since 2004 the Shoe
House has been owned by Carleen and Ronald Farabaugh. For tour
information call (717) 840-8339.

★ ★

Chocolate City, USA
Hershey

What Philadelphia means to liberty, what Pittsburgh means (meant) to steel, what Heinz means to ketchup, the town of Hershey means to (a) kisses, (b) bars, (c) orphans, (d) chocolate. You have thirty seconds to answer. No, make that fifteen. In fact, time's up.

The answer, of course, is all of the above. Hershey symbolizes many things to many people, not the least of which is the bittersweet subject of orphans. And behind it all is the name Milton S. Hershey, the candy-making visionary who created a factory town and a product famous all over the earth.

The Hershey Bar is an American icon born and raised, like its inventor and namesake, in central Pennsylvania, just a stone's throw from the state capital, Harrisburg. Born in 1857 in the village of Derry Church to a devout Mennonite family, young Milton Snavely Hershey completed a formal education only through fourth grade. He worked first as a printer's apprentice and then as a candy maker's apprentice. At the age of eighteen, he moved to Philadelphia to open a candy shop, which failed after six years. Hershey moved to Denver, then Chicago, then New Orleans, then New York City, trying in each city to establish a successful candy-making business. In 1883 he returned to Lancaster, Pennsylvania, where he incorporated the candy-making techniques he had learned in his travels, key among them the use of fresh milk in the making of caramel. His Lancaster Caramel Co. was a success, and in 1893 he purchased new German-manufactured candy-coating machines, which he later used to manufacture his recipe for a milk chocolate candy bar he would name Hershey.

In 1900 Milton Hershey sold his caramel candy business for a tidy sum of $1 million. He used the money to move back to his birthplace of Derry Church, where he built the largest chocolate factory in the world. So successful was the Hershey Chocolate Co., and so generous and foresighted was Milton Hershey—he built employee housing of a quality-of-life design never seen before, as well as an inexpensive public transportation system to allow employees to live in nearby towns—that Derry Church was renamed Hershey.

In 1909 Milton Hershey and his wife, Catherine, who had no children of their own, established a trade school for orphaned boys. In 1918, three years after the premature death of his wife, Hershey placed his entire fortune of $60 million in a trust fund for the support of his school for orphans. Today the Milton S. Hershey School has a residential enrollment of fifteen hundred financially needy boys and girls between the ages of four and eighteen, no longer orphans necessarily, who live on a ten-thousand-acre campus. Milton Hershey, who lived to the ripe old age of eighty-eight, was technically penniless at the time of his death in 1945. Penniless but rich beyond measure, he had given away all his wealth and assured the future education of countless thousands. And it only gets better. In 1963 the Hershey School Trust donated $50 million to establish the Milton S. Hershey Medical Center and the Hershey College of Medicine, which opened in 1967.

Meanwhile, the business Hershey founded thrived, as did the city bearing his name. In the 1930s during the Great Depression, Milton Hershey launched a building program to make sure his employees still had work. They constructed a grand hotel, a sports arena, a community center, and a new corporate headquarters. Later, the gardens and public park and zoo that Hershey built with corporate funds were developed into one of the most popular theme parks in the United States. Hershey, Pennsylvania, is now a destination for families seeking fun and sweets, a chocolate Disneyland with streetlights that look like Hershey Kisses.

Hershey Bars may be an American icon, but the unlikely yarn of Milton Hershey, the kid with the fourth-grade education who persevered through failure to establish one of the great business and philanthropic empires in the United States, is a true Pennsylvania success story equal to that of Stephen Girard, John Wanamaker, and Andrew Carnegie. A sweet story about a sweet man, a nice guy who finished first.

Pennsylvania's Bachelor President
Lancaster

The only Pennsylvanian to become president of the United States is best remembered for being the chief executive who preceded Abraham Lincoln in the White House. Under James Buchanan, the United States inched inexorably toward civil war, even though he was considered a pro-South president. His one term in office was marked by the Supreme Court's dreadful Dred Scott Decision, which Buchanan considered binding as law. Dred Scott was a slave who escaped to a free state and who sought legal protection in the courts. Ultimately, the Supreme Court ruled that slaves had no rights as citizens, even on free soil. No historian ranks Buchanan among the nation's best presidents, and some would argue that he deserves to be listed among the worst. Perhaps it's only a coincidence, but in Buchanan's hometown of Lancaster, Buchanan Avenue begins where Lemon Street ends.

Buchanan was America's only bachelor president; his niece, Harriet Lane, performed the hostess duties of the First Lady. His failure to marry alone would be enough to start tongues wagging as to Buchanan's sexual preferences, although he has been "outed" in many gay publications in recent years because of his long-term relationship with William R. King, a senator from Alabama who died while serving as vice president of the United States under Buchanan's predecessor, Franklin Pierce. Buchanan and King shared a room at a Washington, DC, boardinghouse for several years while each served in Congress. One of President James Polk's law partners derisively labeled the two roommates "Mr. and Mrs. Buchanan." Several politicians referred to King as Buchanan's "better half," and President Andrew Jackson was known to call King "Miss Nancy" or "Aunt Fancy."

Buchanan's estate, Wheatland, is open for tours in the city of Lancaster. The grand brick Victorian country home is decorated with souvenirs from Buchanan's days as envoy to Russia and ambassador to Great Britain, including signed portraits of Queen Victoria and Prince Albert. Still intact at Wheatland is the back porch where Buchanan was

Wheatland, in Lancaster, home of Pennsylvania's only president, James Buchanan.

sitting in June 1856 when the news arrived that he had won the Democratic nomination for president. Fanning himself in the summer heat and sitting in shirtsleeves, Buchanan made a brief acceptance speech. Buchanan once wrote that the only reason he went into politics was "as a distraction from a great grief which happened at Lancaster when I was a young man." The grief was the death of his former fiancée, Anne C. Coleman, who died shortly after breaking off the engagement for unknown reasons.

Wheatland's hours vary by season. For the best information go to www.wheatland.org or call (717) 392-8721.

★ ★

At Long Last the Barnes Comes to Philadelphia

Merion and Philadelphia

For years the biggest story in Philadelphia's world of fine art was if and when the Barnes Foundation collection would move from the suburbs and join the famous Philadelphia Museum of Art and the Rodin Museum on the Benjamin Franklin Parkway, the premier showcase of the city's cultural treasures. The Barnes Foundation is one of the world's most valuable privately owned collections of French Impressionist, Post-Impressionist, and early modern paintings—not to mention important American paintings, African sculpture, Old Masters, and ancient Roman and Greek artwork. When the "if" was no longer the question, the "when" dragged on for years in courtroom litigation that became so contentious that the entire episode was the focus of a well received documentary called *The Art of the Steal,* in which the filmmakers sided with the traditionalists who wanted the priceless art to remain where it was in a private home on a leafy street in a quiet suburb.

The whole business was so thoroughly cantankerous—personally, politically, and judicially—that you can't help but imagine the foundation's namesake, Dr. Albert Barnes, looking down (or perhaps up) on the proceedings with a smile on his face.

By all reports and documentary evidence, Barnes was a cranky young man who grew into cranky old manhood while amassing a fortune with which he purchased artwork valued, conservatively, at $3 billion. Barnes grew up in Kensington, one of Philadelphia's crankiest working-class neighborhoods. He brought that chip on his shoulder and his collection of art to his stately home in Montgomery County, where it gave the art world and the neighborhood fits ever since the Barnes Foundation opened in 1922 at 300 North Latch's Lane in Merion.

Barnes was brilliant as well as ornery. He graduated from the University of Pennsylvania's Medical School in 1892 at the age of twenty. As a young man Dr. Albert Barnes developed a patent medicine called

★ ★

Argyrol, an antiseptic, which he manufactured and which made him a millionaire many times over. In 1913 Barnes began collecting art seriously. By 1920 he owned the largest collection of Renoirs outside of France, along with works by Cézanne, Matisse, Seurat, van Gogh, Picasso (stop me if your jaw hits the floor), Gauguin, Degas, Rousseau, Manet, Miró, Cassatt, Chagall, Pissarro, Titian, El Greco, Goya, Rubens, Delacroix, Daumier, Modigliani, van Goyen, and Toulouse-Lautrec, among others. Then Barnes hung his thousand paintings on the walls of his house—dozens of them per wall, stacked almost from floor to ceiling—and he placed his hundreds of pieces of sculpture in these same rooms. Then he dared anyone to actually come and see them.

At least that's the way it seemed to the art world that wanted to flock to the Barnes Foundation he created in 1922. Albert Barnes had his own ideas about how his art should be presented and who should see it. He wanted students, not critics or admirers. He had developed a scientific approach to the appreciation of art, and he wanted his art classes to reflect his theories. His classes were open to anyone, but his collection was not. You couldn't "drop by" the Barnes Foundation. And what you would find if you did were countless masterpieces unidentified by artist or period or subject but arranged on the walls to reflect the scientific principles of art—space, line, color, light, and focus—that Barnes wanted to express by his individual choices.

His last will and testament forbade any changes in the way his artwork was displayed, and after his death in a car accident in 1951 at the age of seventy-eight, several lawsuits were filed seeking greater public access to the priceless Barnes collection. In 1961 the lawsuits filed by the *Philadelphia inquirer* and the State of Pennsylvania were settled out of court, and the Barnes Foundation agreed to open its doors to the public—reservations were required months ahead of time—only two days a week.

Since then the collection has been made even more available to the public, which resulted in lawsuits brought by neighbors trying to prevent tour buses from parking with their engines idling in the quiet

★ ★

Main Line neighborhood. Even the board of the Barnes Foundation has gone to court seeking to overturn Albert Barnes's restrictive rules regarding how the art should be displayed. In 1992 a court ruling allowed a one-time world tour of some of the Barnes masterpieces to raise money for the upkeep of the collection.

Twenty years and endless court filings later the new home of the Barnes Collection opened to rave review in May 2012. The new cultural jewel on the Parkway replaces a juvenile prison on that site (good thinking on that original choice—build a prison next to the Rodin Museum! Sheesh.) On the outside the building is classic and modernistic, almost modest snuggled beneath the tall trees lining the broad boulevard directly across the street from the city's famous science museum, the Franklin Institute. Inside, however, a blindfolded Albert Barnes would have thought he'd walked into his own home. Curators meticulously recreated the art experience as envisioned by Barnes himself. The rooms are the same scale, if not dimensions, as the Barnes home. In each room of the museum, the art hangs exactly as it appeared in the original Barnes. Classic European masterpieces next to anonymous primitive African sculpture, industrial ironwork next to delicate furniture. Barnes saw connection between people and cultures, between art and function, between intentional placement and accidental insights. And he had a hidden sense of humor. There's one famous painting of nudes bathing with their voluptuous bottoms facing the viewer. Flanking them on the same wall are delicate yet functional brass strips used to hold and reinforce the sides and the hinged top of steamer trunks. The curved brass strips seem to form cupping hands on either side of the bathers . . . well, you get the idea. (And that's not me, that's pointed out in the audio narration on the individual headsets each visitor is issued.)

In the end the new Barnes is a win-win for the art world and for Philadelphia. More people will see it, more people will love it, and more people will appreciate the cranky genius of Dr. Albert Barnes.

Rocky's Back Where He Belongs

Philadelphia

Is it art? Who cares? The *Rocky* statue, depicting Sylvester Stallone as the million-to-one shot who made almost as many movie sequels, has found a permanent home in front of the Philadelphia Museum of Art, even if not at the top of the steps. Decried as a "movie prop" by art purists and hailed as an eight-foot, six-inch tall bronze symbol of Philadelphia by less-critical art and movie lovers, the statue by sculptor A. Thomas Schomberg was finally installed in front of the museum on Benjamin Franklin Boulevard in November of 2006, ending a twenty-four-year-long battle over where the statue belonged.

It all started in 1981 during the shooting of *Rocky III* when the Rocky statue was placed at the top of the art museum's steps, made famous by the original *Rocky* movie in 1976. The statue, like the steps, became a tourist attraction—and not because of the thousands of masterpieces inside the neoclassical building. At some point Stallone let it be known he wanted his gift to the city to remain where it was in perpetuity (remember, this was a few *Rocky* sequels ago). During the ensuing civic discussion, the statue was removed and placed in storage. Public opinion in Philadelphia seemed evenly divided among those who wanted the statue to remain at the top of the iconic steps and those who wanted it displayed in a more appropriate place, such as outside the Spectrum, where Rocky battled Apollo Creed for the heavyweight championship in the first two *Rocky* movies. This being Philadelphia, there was also a sizable minority who wanted the gift statue from a Hollywood star tossed into the Schuylkill River (the *nerve* of this guy!). Cooler heads prevailed. The statue was reinstalled at the top of the museum steps for a two-month period during the opening of *Rocky III* and then installed outside the front entrance to the Spectrum, where it remained until 1990, when it was returned to the top of the art museum's steps during the filming of *Rocky V,* renewing the statue-site controversy once again.

By 2006, the thirtieth anniversary of the original *Rocky* and the year of the release of fifth sequel, *Rocky Balboa,* resistance was futile.

Stand in the bronze footprints of Rocky Balboa at the top of the steps of the Philadelphia Museum of Art.

By now books had been written about the inspiration and personal impact that running up the Rocky steps had had on people from all over the world. The story of a club fighter from Philadelphia who wanted to prove he "weren't just another bum from the neighbor-hood" by going the distance with the champ had won the hearts of the world, not to mention the Fairmount Park Commission and the City Art Commission and every other commission whose approval

★ ★

was necessary to relocate the Rocky statute to a shady spot at street level in front of the Philadelphia Museum of Art just to the right of the Rocky steps. A pair of size-nine bronze footprints with the name "Rocky" beneath them remain embedded at the top of the steps where each year tens of thousands of visitors raise their arms in triumph and do a little victory dance. It's quite an amazing thing to see. And you don't even feel self-conscious if you find yourself doing it.

Rocky (Sylvester Stallone) leaped up and down in triumph here after running up the steps.

Stanley Kubrick, Arnold Toynbee, David Mamet, and Me
Philadelphia

If you were to Google my name and type *"Clark DeLeon Pennsylvania"* into the search field, one of the first things you'd see is an Amazon .com listing for *Pennsylvania Curiosities.* However, if you were to type *"Clark DeLeon Toynbee"* into the search field, you would find numerous stories of a true mystery, a concrete conundrum—one that grows curiouser and curiouser with each passing year. It/they are commonly called "Toynbee tiles," the UFOs (Unidentified Flat Objects) that appeared out of nowhere on crosswalks of busy urban intersections in Philadelphia and Pittsburgh—and New York and Baltimore along with Boston, Washington, Chicago, Atlantic City, St. Louis, Detroit, Cleveland, Columbus, and Toledo, not to mention Rio de Janeiro, Brazil, Buenos Aires, Argentina, and Santiago, Chile. These flat, colorful, license plate–size messages are made of a flexible linoleum-type substance that literally bonds to the asphalt and despite constant foot and car traffic remains legible, in some cases, for close to twenty years. And the repetitive message formed by hand-cut tiled letters is the same in every city with slight variations: TOYNBEE IDEA/KUBRICK MOVIE 2001/RESURRECT DEAD/ON PLANET JUPITER.

Curious yet? The Toynbee mentioned is English historian Arnold Joseph Toynbee (1885–1975), whose work may or may not have influenced filmmaker Stanley Kubrick (1928–1999), who did produce a science fiction movie called *2001: A Space Odyssey,* which may or may not have had something to do with resurrecting the dead on the planet Jupiter because, to this day, no one can really explain what that movie is about. At the end of *2001,* there is a big fetus floating in space that looks like the lead character, Keir Dullea—who hasn't been seen since, incidentally—and resurrecting the dead on planet Jupiter probably made as much sense as any other explanation.

But no one has been able to explain the Toynbee tiles. Who is responsible? Is it the work of a cabal or of a lone tiler behind the grassy knoll? In Cincinnati the Toynbee tiles were dubbed "graffiti from Mars" by a Scientologist, and they became an issue in the 2001 mayor's race when the Democratic incumbent refused to comment about them to a reporter, and a Republican city councilman admitted he didn't know much about them other than "I'm happy someone is paving the streets around here." In a 1999 *New York Times* article, the Toynbee tiles were described as "public displays of paranoia" perhaps because of tiles like the one imbedded in Forty-ninth Street and Fifth Avenue, which carried the additional message, MURDER EVERY JOURNALIST I BEG YOU.

In newspaper stories and websites (www.toynbee.net, www .resurrectdead.com) devoted to the Toynbee tiles, which made their first appearance on Philadelphia streets sometime in the late 1980s, the trail starts, or ends, with me and playwright David Mamet. In 1983 Mamet wrote a short one-act play called *4 A.M.* about an all-night talk radio host who gets a strange call from a guy who wants to talk about Arnold Toynbee, Stanley Kubrick, and the possibility of resurrecting human life on the planet Jupiter. Mamet, whose works include *American Buffalo* and *Glengarry Glen Ross,* has said he made up the entire story as "an homage to Larry King," who used to have an all-night talk radio show.

But the Rosetta Stone of the Toynbee tiles ends up being my column in the *Philadelphia Inquirer* on March 13, 1983. I wrote a daily column in the *Inquirer* from 1974 to 1994 called "The Scene," and on that day I wrote the following, under the headline, "Theories: Wanna Run That by Me Again?":

> Call me skeptical, but I had a hard time buying James Morasco's concept that the planet Jupiter would be colonized by bringing all the people of Earth who had ever died back to life and then changing Jupiter's atmosphere to allow them to live. Is this just me, or does that strike you as hard to swallow too? Morasco says he is a social worker in Philadelphia and came across this idea while reading a book by historian Arnold Toynbee, whose theory on bringing dead molecules back to life was depicted in the

movie 2001: A Space Odyssey. "There are no scientific principles I've found that can make this possible," Morasco said, "especially colonizing the planet Jupiter, which has a very poisonous atmosphere. The possibility of giving that planet an oxygen atmosphere is beyond even science fiction writers' imaginations."

Now that quote may sound as if Morasco doesn't believe it can be done, but that's not true. He thinks that between Toynbee and Stanley Kubrick there is a way to pull it off. That's why he's contacting talk shows and newspapers to spread the message. He's even founded a Jupiter colonization organization called the Minority Association, which he says consists of "Me, Eric, Eric's sister who does the typing, Frank . . ."

You may be hearing more from Morasco. And then again, you may not.

I have no idea of the real name of the man I spoke to on the phone in March 1983, but his name probably wasn't James Morasco. The only James Morasco living in Philadelphia died at the age of eighty-eight in 2003. He was a carpenter by trade, not a social worker, and he would have had to have been an especially spry seventy-something-year-old to have tiled Philadelphia—let alone New York, Baltimore, and Pittsburgh—during the first heyday of the Toynbee-tile era from the late 1980s through the mid-1990s. But a new wave of Toynbee tiles, with subtle but distinctive differences in size and wording, began in (gulp) 2001. In September 2006 National Public Radio aired a five-minute piece about the Toynbee-tile phenomenon featuring www.resurrectdead.com creator Justin Duerr, David Mamet, and me. As recently as November 2007, a new Toynbee tile appeared at the intersection of Thirty-eighth and Walnut Streets in West Philadelphia on the University of Pennsylvania campus. Meanwhile, in Buffalo, New York, a mutant form of the message tiles called House of Hades has appeared on downtown streets featuring specific language (KILL MEDIA and HELLION JEWS) peculiar to the more paranoid versions of the Toynbee tiles.

A typical "old school" Toynbee tile embedded in Chestnut Street in Center City Philadelphia.

In 2011 Justin Duerr and cinematographer John Foy earned a prestigious "competition documentary" slot at the Sundance Film Festival where their Toynbee-tile documentary *Resurrect Dead* debuted. Although the review in the *Hollywood Reporter* was less than enthusiastic, calling the search for the creator of the tiles "a diverting if rather inconsiderable urban mystery." I, for one, loved it. My name is all over that jawn. Although I do agree with the reviewer for the movie industry's premier trade news source that Duerr's enthusiasm for the project "comes across as a touch too absorbed with the subject matter." Much like the original Toynbee tiler. *Resurrect Dead* is available on Netflix.

A Tale of Two Ps

Pennsylvania is among the handful of states (along with New York, California, Texas, and Florida) that can claim to be home to seven major-league sports franchises among the Big Four—NFL, MLB, NBA, and NHL. But Pennsylvania is the only state with two Major League Baseball teams that have used the same letter—*P*—as the club logo for more than a century. In the west there is the spartan yellow or black P of the Pittsburgh Pirates and in the east there is the swirly white or red P of the Philadelphia Phillies. Both teams play in the National League. And that is where the similarities end.

The Phillies P may as well stand for "perpetual." It is the only team in Major League Baseball that takes its name directly from the name of the city it represents. The Philadelphia Phillies joined the National League in 1883 and is the oldest team in the senior circuit that has never changed names or city of origin.

Pittsburgh entered the National League in 1887 as the Pittsburgh Alleghenys, or more correctly, the Allegheny Alleghenys, since the team played on the north side of the Allegheny River in the city of Allegheny, which didn't become part of Pittsburgh proper until 1907. The proud Pirate nickname was first attached to the franchise in 1890 as a term of derision by other teams because of the robber baron mentality of ownership and the team's propensity to steal the best players from other clubs, most famously second baseman Lou Bierbauer of the Philadelphia Athletics. Pittsburgh fans and players embraced the pirate insult the way the 2004 Red Sox adopted the self-description "idiots." The Pirate patch didn't officially appear on the Pittsburgh uniform until 1912, but they were commonly referred to as brigands, pirates, and buccaneers by 1903, when Pittsburgh represented the National League in the first World Series, won by the Boston Red Sox in the eighth game of a best-of-nine.

The last time the Phillies won the World Series was 2008. Before that it was 1980. The time before that was . . . well, there was no time before that. Phillies fans have come to look at those two lonely championship rings the way a bride and groom look at their wedding bands —"forsaking all others, until death do us part." Pittsburgh Pirates fans could wear a different World Series championship ring for every finger on their left hands. The Pirates' five World Series titles are the second most in the National League, behind the eleven wins by the St. Louis Cardinals.

As for memorable World Series moments, the Pirates are remembered for being the first team to win a championship on a ninth-inning home run. It happened in 1960 when second baseman Bill Mazeroski won the seventh game with a walk-off home run against the Yankees, a team that had outscored Pittsburgh thirty-eight to three in the three Yankee victories. The last time a World Series was decided by a ninth-inning home run was 1993. With the Phillies leading the Blue Jays six to five, Philadelphia closer Mitch "Wild Thing" Williams gave up a three-run blast to Joe Carter in Toronto. That was the same series where the Phillies led the Blue Jays fourteen to nine in the seventh inning of game four at Veterans Stadium, only to lose fifteen to fourteen in a record-setting slugfest that Philadelphia fans immediately dubbed the Greatest Game That Ever Sucked.

In fairness it should be noted that the Pirates haven't appeared in a World Series since 1979. Since then the Phillies have had a ticket to the Big Dance four times, winning in 1980 and 2008, and falling to the Baltimore Orioles in 1983 before giving Canada its second consecutive World Series championship in 1993. In fact, since the Pirates, at the time boasting Barry Bonds, Bobby Bonilla, and Andy Van Slyke, won their third straight National League East division title in 1992, the once-proud Pittsburgh franchise hasn't enjoyed a single winning season. When my daughter, Molly, and I visited Pittsburgh in the last week of June 2007, the last-place Pirates were on a five-game losing streak on the West Coast, and the newspaper sports pages were bristling with stories of a planned fourth-inning mass walkout by Pittsburgh fans when the Pirates returned home

to play the Washington Nationals at PNC Park. "Fifteen years of losing baseball is enough," was the protest slogan of disgruntled fans.
The Pirates players responded by winning seven of their next ten.
In August Pittsburgh actually won more games (nineteen) than they
lost (fifteen). But in September the Pirates walked the gangplank and
played like they had eye patches over both eyes, losing thirteen of
their final fifteen.

Amazingly, on the other side of the Allegheny Mountains, the Phillies were doing the exact opposite, winning thirteen of their final sixteen, and winning the Eastern Division on the last day of the season,
their first division pennant since 1993. The victory was all the sweeter
for Pennsylvania baseball fans because, like a hound dog chasing an
escapee from a chain gang, the Phillies had run down the season-long
first-place team from the city called New York. The Mets' collapse
during the last two weeks of the 2007 season was both epic and
delightful. The Phillies swept the Mets in New York in mid-September
starting the New Yorkers into a five-to-twelve tailspin, bringing joy
into the hearts of Pirates and Phillies fans alike. The only major-league
team fans in both cities hate more than the Mets are the Yankees. And
the Rangers. The Giants, of course. The Knicks. We hate pretty much
every New York team except the Jets, who we don't really care about.
When was the last time the Jets beat an NFL team from Pennsylvania
in an important game? I rest my case. The Yankees, however, continue
to beat the Phillies when it matters most. After a magical 2008 season
when the Phillies won their second World Series championship, the
Phils repeated as National League champions only to lose in six games
to the Yankees in the World Series. In 2010 the Phillies lost to the San
Francisco Giants in the National League championship series and in
2011 the Phillies won a major league best 102 games before losing to
the St. Louis Cardinals in the first round of the playoffs. In 2012 . . .
we Phillies fans don't like to remember the 2012 baseball season. In
fact, I've forgotten it already.

★ ★

Why He's Called Penny Benny
Philadelphia

When Benjamin Franklin died at the age of eighty-four, he was argu-
ably the most famous American in the world. He was known in the
capitals of Europe as a statesman, inventor, writer, raconteur, and, yes,
ladies man. His experiments with electricity and the invention of the
lightning rod led to his fame as "the American Prometheus" because
he had harnessed fire from the sky. His funeral in 1790 drew the largest crowd in the history of the continent. Twenty thousand people
lined the streets of Philadelphia to pay tribute to America's oldest and
most prolific founding father. Not only did he found a new nation,
during his lifetime Franklin founded the country's first volunteer fire
company, first fire insurance company, first magazine, first university,
first law school, first hospital, and first subscription library.

Today visitors gather around Franklin's gravesite in Christ Church
Burial Ground on the southeast corner of Fifth and Arch Streets in
Philadelphia's historic district where they continue to pay tribute—
literally—one penny at a time. Why do people throw pennies on
Benjamin Franklin's grave? It's because of what he said about pennies
in his famous *Poor Richard's Almanack,* the most read publication
in colonial America other than the Bible. The almanac contained a
number of Franklin's well known aphorisms and witty sayings, such as
"Keep your eyes wide open before marriage, half shut afterward" and
"Three may keep a secret, if two of them are dead." But perhaps his
most enduring (not to mention profitable) saying was "A penny saved
is a penny earned."

Or is it "A penny tossed is a penny lost?" Every day thousands of
pennies are tossed on top of Franklin's gravestone by tourists and
locals alike. He has earned more pennies in death than he ever did in
life. Last year more than $4,000 worth of pennies was thrown on his
grave. The pennies are swept up every couple of hours and the money
is used for the maintenance of Christ Church Burial Ground where
more signers of the Declaration and Constitution are buried than any

★ ★

Groundskeepers at Christ Church Burial Ground sweep up the pennies tossed on Benjamin Franklin's grave several times a day.

cemetery in America. Now there is a belief in Philadelphia that if a newlywed bride throws a penny on Benjamin Franklin's grave and it lands heads up, that means she will have a good marriage. And if it lands tails up? Best out of three, best out of five. Whatever it takes, brides keep tossing pennies. And the supply is inexhaustible because the United States Mint is located directly across Arch Street from the gravesite.

★ ★

It's Always Funny in Philadelphia

Philadelphia

One of the darkest hit comedy series on cable TV in the last decade has been the FX network's *It's Always Sunny in Philadelphia,* which its creator, Philadelphia-born and St. Joseph's Prep graduate Rob McElhenny, described as "*Seinfeld* on crack." The series centers around four friends in their thirties (McElhenney, Glenn Howerton, Kaitlin Olson, and Charlie Day) and Danny DeVito, who plays the biological father of one of "the gang," born out of wedlock, as well as the divorced father (but not biological) of two others. Think of *Sunny* as a *Friends,* in which everyone is stabbing each other in the back, and the Philadelphia bar they run called Paddy's Pub as *Cheers,* where everybody knows your name and Social Security number and has cleaned out your savings account.

The show is wickedly funny and totally without redeeming social value. In fact *It's Always Sunny in Philadelphia* is gleefully psychopathic, as if the cast consisted of Hannibal Lecter, John Wilkes Booth, Lucrezia Borgia, Carrot Top, and the Sweathogs from *Welcome Back, Kotter.* When they find a healthy baby in a dumpster, DeVito's character says, "Put it back where you found it." The characters not only sleep with each other but with each other's parents. One character shows up at an AA meeting insisting he's not an alcoholic and carrying a beer. Other characters take drugs—Whatcha got?—crack, ecstasy, steroids. They burn down buildings and set each other on fire, they slip knockout drops to priests and then taken obscene photos of them when they pass out, they run for political office so they can take bribes, they sell drugs for the mob, and they're shallow, criminal, vain, sexist, insincere, racist, and dumber than a bag of hammers. There is no motive too shallow, no scheme too stupid, no morality untrampled upon. And not only is it hilarious in a way that creeps you out for laughing, but it's a big hit in Ireland and Sweden as well.

The original pilot was shot on a digital camcorder by McElhenney, Day, and Howerton, who claimed the total budget for the original

★ ★

episode in August 2005 was two hundred dollars, although DeVito told David Letterman on his late-night show on September 6, 2007, that the bottom line was actually eighty-five dollars. The show is shot in California with occasional on-location Philadelphia scenes with cast members. Like its Scranton counterpart, *The Office* on NBC, *It's Always Sunny in Philadelphia* opens with establishing shots of Philadelphia landmarks like South Street, Boathouse Row, the Ben Franklin Bridge, Logan Circle, and Thirtieth Street Station. *Sunny* is the kind of show that would do a city proud, so long as the mayor of that city was Jerry Springer.

The actual Paddy's Pub, the inspiration for the show's own Paddy's Pub, is located on Race Street between Front and Second Streets almost in the shadow of the Ben Franklin Bridge. In fact, the view of the bridge from the real Paddy's is used as an establishing shot in the show. Since going into syndication *Sunny* airs daily in Philadelphia and other markets. From the very first show of the first season viewers were alerted that this show wasn't what its title suggested. The opening and closing credits of *It's Always Sunny in Philadelphia* showing the skyline, the stadiums, and South Street were all shot at night.

A Milestone for the *L* Word
Philadelphia

Ironically, the Philadelphia Phillies almost-championship season in 2007 (they won the National League East Division over the Mets on the last day of the season and proceeded to get swept in three games in the first round of the National League playoffs by the Colorado Rockies) came during the same season as an embarrassing and much-publicized major-league sports milestone. By dint of perseverance, longevity, bad luck, and decades of indifferent and tightfisted management, the oldest continuous franchise in Major League Baseball did what no other team in any professional sport has ever done in recorded history, including the smackdowns between Rome and Carthage during Punic War League seasons.

It happened on April 15. It was a Sunday. The Phillies were hosting the world champion St. Louis Cardinals in the final game of a three-game weekend set at Citizens Bank Park in South Philadelphia. The Phillies were on a three-game winning streak and enjoying the rarefied statistic of being two games over .500, something the long-suffering franchise has enjoyed infrequently at any given time during 124 base-ball seasons. A sellout crowd of 44,872 enthusiastic fans had gathered to see if their Fightin' Phils would win their fourth in a row or make history. No one had left by the ninth inning when that question had long been answered. The Phillies were down to their last batter, trailing the Cardinals ten to two. The crowd was on its feet and cheering when the reigning major-league MVP, Ryan Howard, struck out and made it official. The Phillies had become the first professional sports team to lose ten thousand games.

Woo-*hoo!* We're Number *ONE!!* Phillies fans had been anticipating, dreading, or ignoring this day for more than a year. Although it was as obvious as global warming, many chose to embrace denial. At the start of the 2007 season, the Phillies needed forty-five losses to hit the magic ten-thousand-loss milestone; some fans mused, "Maybe the Braves (the second-losingest MLB team) will lose 350 in a row while we go undefeated for the next two years." It was not to be. Fans of the only team with two numerals before the comma in the loss column greeted the accomplishment with signs reading, TEN THOUSAND LOSSES FOR OUR PHILLIES AND I WAS HERE! or ZERO TO GO, or a variation on a famous try-try-again quotation by Thomas Edison: I HAVE NOT FAILED. I'VE JUST FOUND 10,000 WAYS THAT WON'T WORK. In a weird way, understandable only by lifelong fans of Philadelphia sports teams, we appreciated the Phillies staving off the ignominious moment until they could do it so spectacularly at home.

Most baseball fans don't know that the stylish Phillies logo worn by current players is a retro throwback to the swooshy-font "Phillies" logo worn by players on the ill-fated 1964 Phillies team. That team broke the hearts of millions by losing ten out of twelve in the final two

★ ★

**Dreadful Baker Bowl was home of the
Phillies during their worst years in the 1920s
and 1930s when they routinely lost 100 games
a season. One night a fan snuck in and painted
the words "And they still stink!" under the
"Phillies Use Lifebuoy" ad on the outfield wall.**
PHOTO COURTESY PHILADELPHIA PHILLIES

weeks of a season during which they seemed destined for a World
Series until the last day. What's interesting about the Phillies uniform
jersey logo is that it splits down the middle with the zipper. Unzipped
it reads "PHIL" on the right panel and "L . . . LIES" on the left. What's
the extra *L* stand for? Don't ask. A team doesn't lose ten thousand
times without becoming painfully familiar with the *L* word. Consider
what it takes to lose that many times: To match that record, a team
founded today would have to lose one hundred games a year for one
hundred years. That's pretty impressive stuff.

The late James Michener, the best-selling author and lifelong Phillies fan who grew up in suburban Bucks County, lived to see every one of the Phillies' then-five World Series appearances, including the first championship in 1980. But that took him ninety years on earth, eighty-five of which were object lessons in "next year" and usually much worse. Michener described the loony hope of the diehard Phillies faithful in a verse that goes like this: "Garland them with timeless lilies! Although they are a bunch of dillies, Who give honest men the willies. We love them for their sillies. Hail, The Phillies."

Perhaps this was the same sentiment, if not the poetic wording, that led a fan to sneak into Baker Bowl, the dilapidated North Philadelphia ballpark where the Phillies played for fifty-one and a half seasons, but never so dramatically and dreadfully as between 1918 and 1938. During those twenty years the Phillies enjoyed one winning season (two games over .500) and ten last-place finishes, averaging ninety-nine losses a season. During those two decades the dominant feature of the ballpark was a humongous sixty-foot-high right-field wall along Broad Street (by comparison, Boston's "Green Monster" in Fenway Park is only thirty feet high). Covering most of the wall was an advertisement for deodorant soap that declared in huge white block letters against the green backdrop, THE PHILLIES USE LIFEBUOY. The sneaky fan, bearing a bucket of white paint and big brush, added the words, AND THEY STILL STINK! In Philadelphia that's what we call "addytood."

Lonely Days, Lonely Nights, and Al Capone: America's First Big House
Philadelphia

It started, as did most new ideas that turned into reality in those days, in Benjamin Franklin's living room. It continues to stand today like an ominous medieval ruin in the middle of a lively city neighborhood, where it is a major tourist attraction and, during the Halloween season, the world's largest haunted house surrounded by thirty-foot-high stone walls enclosing eleven acres.

By the end of the 1800s Eastern State Penitentiary was so crowded a second tier of cells was added.

The story of America's first Big House—its first humane prison called a "penitentiary," its first modern architectural wonder that provided convicted criminals with hot water, central heating, and flush toilets before those same amenities were enjoyed by the resident of a different big house, a white one, occupied by the president of the United States—began the same year as the US Constitution was adopted.

In 1787 Benjamin Franklin hosted a meeting in his home of men who wanted to make a difference in society by improving the lives of those condemned by law to be denied liberty. Today we would call such men do-gooders. Which they were. But they were also practical. What good is sending men or women to prison if they emerge the same, or worse, people than before they entered? How can that result serve to better society?

These are exactly the same questions being asked today, but these men were among the first to ask them. They formed the Philadelphia Society for Alleviating the Miseries of Public Prisons, and by diligence and persistence they succeeded in convincing Pennsylvania to build the

Eastern State Penitentiary architect John Haviland's spokes-of-a-wheel cell block design was copied by three hundred prisons worldwide.

most expensive public building ever. They called it Cherry Hill at first because that was the name of the farm on the site chosen for Eastern State Penitentiary on a lovely hilltop overlooking the distant city.

Today the faux-Gothic-fortress turreted facade of Eastern State overlooks rowhomes across Fairmount Avenue near 21st in what has become a hip, gentrified, former working-class neighborhood in North Philadelphia. Tour buses make regular stops to drop off visitors interested in exploring the prison that changed the world. They tour the cell blocks and grounds while listening on headphones to an audio story of the prison narrated by actor Steve Buscemi, who discovered Eastern State, he explains, while scouting sites for a movie. Buscemi has the perfect voice for such a tour, as matter of fact and familiar as the unseen inmate in the next cell. It sounds like Mr. Pink from *Reservoir Dogs* or Nucky Thompson from *Boardwalk Empire* giving you the lay of the land.

The important thing to remember while walking through the "stabilized ruin" that is Eastern State is that these walls held prisoners as early as 1829 and as late as 1971. It opened as an architectural wonder designed around a Quaker principle that punishing a man is meaningless unless that man understands what he has done wrong. Unless he is genuinely sorry for his deeds. Unless he is penitent in the eyes of God.

To that end the reformist penal philosophy of what became known as the Pennsylvania System involved complete isolation of convicts from other human beings. New arrivals' heads were covered with a hood at the prison gates and then they were led to the their individual cells, equipped with running water and flush toilets and an outdoor exercise yard the size of their solitary cell. Here they would spend their entire prison sentence in private contemplation without hearing another human voice. Guards actually wore woolen socks over their shoes to muffle the sounds of human activity. Meals were shoved wordlessly through corridor slots. With no other company than a Bible, for those prisoners who could read, common sense of the progressive

★ ★

sort concluded that solitary confinement would lead to inevitable con-
trition and lifelong resolve to perform useful labor.

What were they thinking?

As revolutionary as the humanitarian and philosophical goals of the
Pennsylvania System were, the architectural innovations devised to
accommodate those goals changed the way prisons were built long
after the concept of true penitence was more of a wistful notion than
an expectation. The hub-and-spoke design of long cell blocks radiating
from a central circular command center was first conceived by Eastern
State's architect, John Haviland, in 1821. Since then that basic design
has been adopted by more than three hundred prisons worldwide.

By the 1840s, Eastern State's mission and design were the talk
of civilized society in Europe and beyond. Before his famous visit
and extensive tour of the United States in 1842, Charles Dickens
announced that the two places he wanted to see most in America
were Niagara Falls and Eastern State Penitentiary. His published
description of the latter seems both reasonable and prescient: "I am
well convinced that it is kind, humane, and meant for reformation; but
I am persuaded that those who designed this system of Prison Discipline, and those benevolent gentleman who carry it into execution, do
not know what it is that they are doing," Dickens wrote. "I hold this
slow and daily tampering with the mysteries of the brain to be immea-
surably worse than any torture of the body; . . . therefore I the more
denounce it, as a secret punishment in which slumbering humanity is
not roused up to stay."

Dickens's fear of prolonged solitary confinement driving inmates
nuts proved accurate yet academic within a decade when Eastern State
started doubling up inmates in cells designed for one. Over the late
1800s several new cell blocks were added, built with two tiers. By the
time Al Capone was arrested in Philadelphia and sentenced to a year
at Eastern State in 1929, the former experiment was now one hundred years old. Capone lived large during his celebrated stay at Eastern
State, his concrete cell floor covered by a Persian carpet.

Visitors to Eastern State will experience the eerie lighting from overhead skylights as they walk through the cell blocks.

Another notorious criminal who served time at Eastern State was prison escape artist and bank robber Willie Sutton, whose probably apocryphal answer to a reporter's question, "Why do you rob banks?" was famously answered, "Because that's where the money is." In 1945, Sutton made it outside the walls in a short-lived escape through a tunnel dug by others. In the 142 years that Eastern State was an operating prison in Pennsylvania, more than one hundred inmates escaped beyond the walls. But only one was never caught and returned to the original Big House on Fairmount Avenue. His name was Frederick Tenuto, a hired gun for the mob. He escaped in 1945 using the same tunnel as Willie Sutton. Tenuto was recaptured in Brooklyn two months later, but he escaped from custody and was never seen again. Today Eastern State remains one of Philadelphia's most popular tourist attractions. It is open daily for visitors from 10:00 a.m. until 5:00 p.m. From mid-September through early November Eastern State becomes what must be the world's largest haunted house in a nightly program called Terror Behind the Walls, which attracts round-the-block lines of eager visitors willing to pay good money to have the stuffing scared out of themselves. For more information, visit www.easternstate.org.

Eastern State resembles a medieval fortress in the middle of a city neighborhood. But those turrets are a non-functional decoration added years later to make the penitentiary appear more imposing.

★ ★

Living History That Doesn't Hurt
Philadelphia

No words cause the eyes of members of the Tweet, Twitter, Tweetest short-attention-span generation to glaze over faster than *United States Constitution.* Your typical teenager reacts to a discussion about the Constitution with a sort of catatonic despair. "You're not going to talk about that thing, are you?" "That thing" is the oldest existing national governing document on earth, a system of laws and agreements in principal created by parties who barely agreed on anything except that this so-called Constitution that they had hammered out would have to do "for now." Like attendees at a doomed marriage on the wedding day, many of the founding fathers gave the new Constitution "six months, tops." Little did they dream that more than two hundred twenty-six years later, this government "conceived in liberty and dedicated to the proposition that all men are created equal" would not have perished from the earth. Nor would they imagine that such a successful document would be so taken for granted, unappreciated, and misunderstood by the very people who enjoy its protections—or, some would say, suffer its inadequacies—generations after it was written.

On July 4, 2003, the long-awaited, and even longer under construction, National Constitution Center at Sixth and Arch Streets on Independence Mall in Philadelphia opened with a bang . . . well, more like a thud, actually. In truth, it was a near disaster. Supreme Court justice Sandra Day O'Connor was at the microphone at the conclusion of the grand-opening remarks. Selected members of the audience stood nearby holding on to long ribbons that were supposed to break and officially open the new facility. The ribbons were attached to a large wooden framework over the stage. Justice O'Connor gave the signal. The audience members pulled the ribbons. But the ribbons didn't break. Instead the large wooden framework that was improperly anchored to the floor fell forward like a fourteen-foot-tall doorjamb. The top part missed Justice O'Connor's head by inches, and several dignitaries, including Mayor John Street and National Constitution

★ ★

Benjamin Franklin is the most recognizable Founding Father among the bronze statues of the Pennsylvania delegation on display at the National Constitution Center.

Center president Joseph Torsella, got clobbered. "We all could have been killed!" a stunned Justice O'Connor said into the microphone.

The mayor and new center's president were taken to local hospitals. Mayor Street emerged with his arm in a sling and Torsella was treated for a lump on the noggin. It was an inauspicious, not to mention nearly catastrophic, opening for a national museum dedicated to celebrating and understanding an architecturally brilliant document with serious structural flaws.

★ ★

Much like the US Constitution itself, the National Constitution Center survived the shaky start and has already become one of the most frequently visited sites in Independence National Historical Park, which includes the new Liberty Bell Center and Independence Hall. Before touring the interactive video and computer exhibits in the Constitution Center, visitors first experience a lively and inspirational pep talk in a twelve-minute multimedia presentation hosted by a live actor and augmented by images projected on the walls of the intimate theater. These performances begin every thirty minutes, fifteen times a day during daily operating hours, and they emotionally prepare visitors for the exhibitions depicting the powerful and often startlingly contradictory meanings people have taken from the same words in the Constitution throughout American history.

Fortunately there are plenty of gizmos, computers, videos, and fun displays to keep kids and adults interested during the tour as the deeper significance of the historic document sinks in painlessly. Kids can see themselves on a video monitor sworn in as president of the United States, and adults can compare their height and paunch with the roomful of life-size bronze statues of the delegates to the Constitutional Convention in 1787. It is a brilliantly rendered and marvelously designed experience that brings life and modern meaning to words etched on parchment more than two centuries ago.

Visit www.constitutioncenter.org for more information.

Pennsylvanians in Heaven

Philadelphia

There are only four Americans officially canonized as saints in the Catholic Church, and two of them are from Philadelphia.

Saint John Neumann was the bishop of Philadelphia and the founder of the parochial school system in the United States. You can see him in the flesh, so to speak, in a glass coffin in the lower church of St. Peter's Church at Fifth Street and Girard Avenue in North Philadelphia. His remains were moved there in 1963 after the Pope

★ ★

declared him "Blessed," which is the last step before sainthood. Saint John Neumann was canonized by Pope Paul VI in Rome in 1977, one hundred and seventeen years after his death in 1860. The Shrine of St. John Neumann, which houses his remains, includes a small museum that tells the story of his life. Also on display are various instruments of self-mortification worn by the saint during his life on earth, such as a hair shirt of coarse fibers that made every movement uncomfortable, and a "discipline" collar with sharp edges that made every turn of his head excruciating.

Mother Katherine Drexel, who was canonized on October 1, 2000, is entombed in Bensalem, Bucks County, inside the convent of the Sisters of the Blessed Sacrament, the religious order she founded in 1891. She died in 1955 at the age of ninety-six. Her path to sainthood was much faster than Saint John Neumann's primarily because of the miracles attributed to her intercession in the relatively few years after her death. In 1974 Robert Gutherman, an altar boy who assisted in serving Mass at the convent, was diagnosed with a debilitating disease that doctors said would leave him deaf for life. Two bones in his right ear had literally dissolved. The Sisters of the Blessed Sacrament told his parents to pray to Mother Katherine Drexel. That night in the hospital, fourteen-year-old Robert heard a voice calling his name, heard it in his deaf ear. The next day the amazed doctor found that his ear bones were regenerating spontaneously. There was no medical explanation, although the family knew the reason.

The second miracle attributed to Mother Katherine Drexel also involved the deafness of a Bensalem child. Amy Wall was one year old when she was diagnosed as incurably deaf. Her parents, who had seen a TV show about the Gutherman miracle, obtained a piece of cloth from the habit worn by Mother Katherine, placed it on the child's ear, and prayed. Four months later, Amy Wall began hearing for the first time in her life. When asked before the canonization of Saint Katherine Drexel why she had been chosen for the miracle, Amy (then age seven) said, "Because God loves me and I love God."

★ ★

The glass coffin containing the remains of Philadelphia's
Bishop John Neumann, America's first male saint.

The lives of Philadelphia's two saints could not have been more
different in origin or more similar in purpose. The "Little Bishop," as
Neumann was affectionately known (he stood five feet, three inches),
was born in Bohemia in 1811. He immigrated to America seeking to
serve immigrant Catholics and, after being ordained a Redemptorist

priest, was assigned a parish on the frontier of Niagara, New York, where there were many German immigrants. Later he served as rector at St. Philomena's Church in Pittsburgh and St. Alphonsus in Baltimore before being consecrated Bishop of Philadelphia in 1852. As bishop he ministered to the Irish immigrants in Coal Country (he spoke Gaelic and seven other languages) and the Italian immigrants of South Philadelphia, establishing the first Italian parish, St. Mary Magdalene de Pazzi, after he purchased a former Methodist church. Neumann became an American citizen in 1848, and he established the first system of diocesan schools in his new country after he arrived in Philadelphia in 1852. On January 5, 1860, Bishop Neumann suffered a stroke while walking on the street not far from Philadelphia's new Cathedral of SS Peter and Paul on Logan Square. He died before last rites could be administered, but there is no doubt where his soul dwells.

Katherine Drexel was a socialite from one of the richest families in Philadelphia in the late 1800s. Her father, Francis Drexel, was a banker and business partner with J. P. Morgan. The Drexels were wealthy but charitable, and they opened their home three days a week to distribute food, clothing, and money to needy people. After entering the convent at the age of thirty, Katherine used her inheritance of $20 million to establish twelve schools for American Indians and more than one hundred rural and inner-city schools for black children. Among the thousands of children her religious order helped over the years was basketball legend Kareem Abdul-Jabbar, then a fourth-grader known as Lew Alcindor. He attended Holy Providence School in Bensalem in 1956 when it was called a mission school for "Indians and Colored People." The experience may have influenced Jabbar's later life, because in 2000 he wrote a book about his experiences as a volunteer high school basketball coach on the White Mountain Apache reservation in Arizona. You could say that Mother Drexel works in mysterious ways.

The Shrine is open every day from the beginning of the first daily mass at 7:30 a.m. until the end of the last daily mass at 5:30 p.m.

★ ★

One Hundred Years of Mummery
Philadelphia

The Mummers Parade on New Year's Day is Philadelphia and Pennsylvania's gift to the world. The gift comes wrapped in spangles and feathers and banjoes and saxophones, and it takes the better part of ten hours to unwrap.

A cold-weather Mardi Gras—that's the best description I can come up with to describe the indescribable, a parade of ten thousand performers stretching for miles from South Philadelphia to Center City, strutting, marching, and cakewalking from dawn to dusk and into the night. It is a Philadelphia institution, a parade that comes but once a year and is the focus of thousands of families in neighborhoods around the city and suburbs for the entire year leading up to it.

So what's a Mummer? Fair question with a long answer, the end of which still doesn't answer the question adequately. *Mummer* is a word of German origin that means "disguise." The original Philadelphia Mummers didn't even call themselves mummers. They called themselves shooters, because it was their tradition from colonial days to celebrate the new year by dressing up in costume and firing guns in the air. To this day the official name of the organization is the Philadelphia Mummers and Shooters Association, although guns have long since been holstered.

The ancient tradition of dressing up in elaborate costumes to celebrate the new year, or the return of the sun after the winter solstice, dates back to the Roman Saturnalia, when kings would dress as beggars and beggars would dress as kings. The whole concept of role reversal was key to the all-male (until the late 1970s) Mummer tradition: men dressed as women, called "wenches" in Mummerspeak. And until 1964, when the use of blackface was banned in the parade because of offensive minstrel racial stereotypes, white men would dress as black men in fancy top hats and canes, calling themselves "dudes."

Dudes and wenches were the heart of the Comic Clubs, one of the four divisions in the Mummers Parade (comics, fancies, string bands,

REAL MEN WEAR DRESSES **reads one Mummer's Parade fan's sign as a "wench brigade" passes on Broad Street during the annual New Year's Day "cold weather Mardi Gras."**

and fancy brigades). The parade today is far different from that first city-sponsored march "up the street" in 1901 to dedicate the new City Hall. For years the Mummers clubs would march informally up and down streets in "the Neck," the South Philadelphia neighborhoods situated on the neck of land between the Delaware and Schuylkill Rivers. The clubs would perform to the delight of spectators and homeowners who would voluntarily—and sometimes not so voluntarily—invite the well-armed Mummers into their houses for hot pepper pot soup or, better yet, hot cider or whiskey. Occasionally, well-lubricated Mummers clubs would confront each other while marching down the same street from opposite directions; these chance meetings frequently

★ ★

turned cranky rather than collegial. Alcohol and firearms have a way of mixing poorly.

In fact, it was the city's desire to control the violence on New Year's Day in South Philadelphia that led to the organized parade with the line of march uniformly north toward City Hall, where judging would be done and prizes awarded. To this day the intense rivalry between Mummers clubs is the competitive fuel that drives individual clubs

On New Year's Day members of the fancy division of the Mummers Parade march up Broad Street with elaborate one-man floats like this dazzling butterfly and these delicate feathered backpieces.

to outdo each other each year, especially the string bands and fancy brigades, whose elaborate choreography, costumes, and musicianship rise to utterly more improbable levels of ingenuity and excellence every New Year's Day. In fact, that is the source of continuing friction among the Mummers. The comics contend that they are the heart of the parade, and they will march in any and all weather. The string bands and fancy brigades have hundreds of thousands of dollars invested in their elaborate satin and feathered "suits" and props, which would be ruined by rain or high winds. Thus, a number of parades have been postponed in the last thirty years, which has caused ill will among the already fractious Mummers clubs and the loyal fans who line Broad Street sidewalks six deep to watch the parade.

The Mummers Parade returned to its South Philly roots and its historic Broad Street route north to City Hall on January 1, 2004, during what Mummers and tens of thousands of spectators universally hailed as the best parade in twenty years. The weather was more than cooperative; it was perfect—brilliant sunshine, temperatures in the high forties, and the merest hint of a breeze, which caused sequins to shimmer, banners to wave, and plumes to fan. The sidewalks on the parade route through Center City were eight and ten people deep with spectators, and sidewalks were gridlocked by a new generation of Mummers fans in strollers. On this, the first New Year's parade up Broad Street in the new millennium, a century-old Philadelphia Mummers tradition was restored.

For all things Mummer, visit www.mummers.com.

The Frogs of Two Street

Philadelphia

James "Froggy" Carr was a tough little kid with an improbably deep voice (hence the nickname) from Second Street in South Philadelphia. The area is known affectionately as Two Street and is home to the majority of Mummers clubs, including the James "Froggy" Carr NYB (New Year's Brigade). The Frogs, as they are known, is an old-school

The Frogs of Two Street frolic on South Broad Street
with the New Year's Mummer's Parade finish line—
Philadelphia City Hall—visible in the background.

comic club—all wenches all the time—that was formed by Froggy Carr's buddies after he died from a freak injury while playing a pickup game of tackle football in 1970. He was twenty years old at the time.

Froggy would have been sixty-two on New Year's Day 2013. Outside the Froggy Carr Clubhouse on Second Street in South Philadelphia, men, boys, and even a few women dressed as wenches began gathering about 8:00 a.m. under brilliant sunshine. In an ancient rite of mummery, men helped men with their makeup or helped zip up a friend's dress from behind. There was nothing metrosexual about it. This is as tough a group of working-class guys dressed up as women as you'll ever see. And there are a lot of them—more than eight hundred, the largest wench brigade in the Mummers Parade.

The Frogs' trademark chant "Who dat? Who dat? Who dat Froggy Carr?!" could be heard from blocks away as they marched up Broad Street, creating a buzz of recognition and appreciation among veteran Mummers Parade spectators. Despite their numbers and enthusiasm, the Frogs generally finish out of the money, if not actually in jail. One year Frogs Captain Mike Renzi ended up in police custody when Renzi protested the police confiscating dozens of cases of beer from the Frogs' support truck. This happened the first year the parade route was switched to Market Street. The leaderless Frogs responded with a spontaneous sit-down strike on Market Street, which prevented the parade from moving past them. Forty-five minutes later the police arrived with flashing lights and sirens to return the Frogs captain so the parade could continue. Even tough Philadelphia cops don't want to tangle with several hundred guys in dresses having a bad-hair day.

City of the Dead
Philadelphia

Philadelphia has its share of prominent and architecturally significant cemeteries, none more so than Laurel Hill Cemetery on the edge of North Philadelphia. Overlooking the Schuylkill River, Laurel Hill's seventy-eight acres are laid out like a promenade for the living rather than a resting place for the dead. Designed by Scottish architect John Notman, upon opening in 1836 Laurel Hill immediately became a destination for city-bound Philadelphians seeking a rural retreat, a place to picnic and stroll among the marble monuments.

Located three and a half miles from Center City, Laurel Hill's landscaping set the tone for later development of Fairmount Park, which

Size Matters

The population of the city of Philadelphia has been shrinking almost since the day I was born. In 1950 Philadelphia was the third-largest city in America and home to more than two million people. Since then the city has lost one quarter of its population—more than 500,000 people—most of whom moved to its suburbs in Pennsylvania and New Jersey. Today Philadelphia is America's fifth largest city, with a population of just over 1.5 million. The 2010 Census showed that the city actually gained population for the first time in sixty years. If you add the population of the three adjoining Pennsylvania counties (Bucks, Montgomery, and Delaware), the southeast Pennsylvania metropolis is well over three million people.

Including the suburbs in the city population may seem like fudging the statistics. However, in this case it is more than fair because Philadelphia is America's "smallest big city," literally. Of America's ten largest cities, Philadelphia is the smallest in area. Philadelphia has 135 square miles, compared to New York's 303, Los Angeles's 469, Chicago's 227, and Houston's awesome 579. Philadelphia's last growth spurt took place in 1854, when the city and county eventually spread to its very gates. Within the cemetery, which was declared a National Historic Landmark in 1998, are hundreds of exquisitely sculpted monuments, such as the tomb of William Warner, young son of William and Anna Catherine Warner, who died on January 20, 1889. The tomb shows a woman pulling aside the top of a stone sarcophagus, allowing a spirit, a face shrouded by wings, to soar

consolidated to its present size. Before that the city limits were within the boundaries of what is now called Center City, a twelve-block-by-twenty-block rectangle from Vine Street to South Street, from the Delaware River to the Schuylkill.

As a Philadelphian it bugs me to see cities with three times the area taking our top-city ranking, census after census. In 1960 Los Angeles surpassed Philadelphia, knocking us to fourth place. In the 2000 census Houston hopped over Philly, sending us to fifth place. In the 2010 census sixth-place Phoenix made a run for the top five with 1.4 million people within city boundaries filling 474 square miles; seventh place San Diego (1.3 million people) has 324 square miles. Running neck and neck is San Antonio with 1.3 million people in 407 square miles. And in ninth place is Dallas, which is named after a former Philadelphia mayor, George Dallas, and has a population of 1.2 million people within 342 square miles. Getting knocked out of the top five is gonna happen sooner or later. Philadelphia is like a mom-and-pop-size hardware store with four Home Depots competing for its sales. Meanwhile, Philadelphia gives Pennsylvania what only one other state on the East Coast has—a city of more than one million people. Shrinking

★ ★

to heaven. Over the years this striking work has been vandalized (both of the woman's arms are missing), but like a Venus de Milo of the departed, her serenity is enhanced by the loss of her extremities.

On the back of the tomb is the monument maker's signature, "A. Calder, Philadelphia." That would be Alexander Milne Calder, the artist

Baltimore (620,000) and Boston (617,000), formerly No. 17 and No. 20 respectively, were knocked out of Top 20 status by the 2010 Census. Booming Atlanta, number thirty-nine, has about the same area as Philadelphia and a population of 432,000. Only enormous Jacksonville, Florida, number eleven, with 757 square miles and 827,000 people, seems likely to pass a million in the next ten or twenty years.

New York, New York—let's give the devil his due—is in a league of its own. "There are eight million stories in the Naked City," began the epilogue of a famous TV crime show in the '60s. There are still eight million, despite a temporary dip to 7.3 million in 1990. There is a telling difference between New York State and Pennsylvania, though. New York State has a population of nineteen million, and almost half of those people live in New York City. Pennsylvania has a population of twelve million, and approximately 12 percent of those folks live in Philadelphia.

Still, Philadelphia dominates Pennsylvania's population like the Big Pretzel. You'd have to take the combined populations of responsible for the huge bronze statue of William Penn and the other 250 pieces of statuary adorning City Hall. The date of young Warner's death reveals that Calder was in the middle of the forty-year-long project that was the design and construction of City Hall when he accepted the commission to sculpt this grave monument. As you can

thirty-six of the state's next largest cities and towns—in order of ranking: Pittsburgh, Allentown, Erie, Reading, Scranton, Bethlehem, Lancaster, Harrisburg, Altoona, Wilkes-Barre, York, State College, Chester, Bethel Park, Norristown, Williamsport, Monroeville, Plum, Easton, New Castle, Lebanon, McKeesport, Johnstown, Hazleton, West Mifflin, Pottstown, Baldwin, Murrysville, Wilkinsburg, Carlisle, Chambersburg, West Chester, Hermitage, Lansdale, Sharon, and Greensburg—to surpass the population of Pennsylvania's largest city. However, excluding Philadelphia, if you added up the populations of the seventy-one Pennsylvania municipalities with populations of 10,000 or more, you'd get a little over two million people. Add Philadelphia to that, and you get 3.5 million. That means the vast majority—more than 70 percent—of Pennsylvania's twelve million people live in small towns.

Curious, no?

★ ★

see, the artist did not treat this stunning work with any less attention than he devoted to the statues on City Hall.

Among the better-known Philadelphians buried in Laurel Hill Cemetery are Anna Jarvis, the founder of Mother's Day; George Meade, the victorious Union general at the Battle of Gettysburg; and Owen Wister, the author who wrote the first "western" novel, called *The Virginian*. Laurel Hill is open daily for tours.

To learn more, visit www.thelaurelhillcemetery.org.

Armless woman raises the coffin lid to allow the soul of the departed to rise to heaven at a grave site at Laurel Hill Cemetery in Philadelphia.

The Schuylkill:
A Spelling Bee of a River

Most rivers in Pennsylvania have names of Indian origin: Susquehanna, Allegheny, Monongahela, Lehigh, Lackawanna. Even the Delaware, which is not an Indian name (it takes its name from the English Lord De La Warr), became the name commonly used to identify the Indian tribe known as Lenni Lenape.

The Schuylkill, however, is of Dutch origin (the word, not the river). There are many regular commuters on the expressway that bears the river's name who will swear that the word *Schuylkill* in any language means "this lane ends suddenly." But in Dutch it means "hidden river," which, in fact, makes the term Schuylkill River as redundant as Rio Grande River.

The Schuylkill was named by Dutch explorers in the early 1600s. Arendt Corssen of the Dutch West India Company sailed up the Delaware River and passed without noticing the mouth of the Schuylkill, which was covered with reeds. On his way back down the Delaware, the tide had changed and Corssen saw the mouth of the *Schuylkill* for what it was. He explored its navigable sections and gave it the name "hidden river."

As difficult as the Schuylkill was for Corssen to find, the name he gave the river has proved difficult for first-time visitors to pronounce and a continuing challenge for even lifelong Pennsylvanians to spell. There is a hard "C" sound at the beginning, not a soft "Sh": skoo-kill (although Philadelphians tend to pronounce it skook'll). *Schuylkill* is always a spelling bee champion breaker. Someone—certainly not Arendt Corssen—came up with a mnemonic to help kids remember how to spell it: Seven Cooties Hurry Up Your Leg—Kick It Lots, Lee!

★ ★

It's Not Weird, It's Mütter

Philadelphia

Whenever I told friends and acquaintances from Philadelphia that I was
working on a book called *Pennsylvania Curiosities,* almost immediately
would come the comment, "You gotta have the Mütter Museum in
there." Of course, the Mütter Museum is in here. If there were an
encyclopedia listing for "Curiosities, Pennsylvania," it would include a
little illustration of the Mütter Museum of the College of Physicians at
19 South Twenty-second Street, Philadelphia.

Where else could you see the cancerous tumor removed from the jaw
of President Grover Cleveland during a secret operation aboard a private
yacht in 1893? Where else could you find a body cast of the original Sia-
mese twins, Chang and Eng Bunker, who underwent an autopsy at the
College of Physicians after their death in 1874? Where else could you
find the "soap lady," a victim of yellow fever in the 1800s whose corpse
turned into a soaplike substance after being buried in alkaline soil?

What would become the Mütter Museum started with a collection of anatomical pathologies donated by Dr. Isaac Parrish in 1849.
It was expanded by the larger collection donated by Dr. Thomas Dent
Mütter in 1856, including bladder stones removed from Chief Justice
John Marshall and the skeleton of a woman whose rib cage had been
compressed by the habitual wearing of a tight corset. The collection
now includes a mind-boggling number of medical abnormalities and
antique medical instruments, including the first wooden stethoscope
invented in 1816, Florence Nightingale's sewing kit, and a full-scale
model of the first successful heart-lung machine designed by Philadelphia physician Dr. John H. Gibbon in 1953.

Although by laymen's standards, the Mütter Museum ranks high
on the "Ewwwww!" meter, it is a serious museum of medical history.
There is a display of 139 skulls from eastern and central Europe as well
as the skeleton of a man whose bones appear to have razor-sharp
edges, causing him to live and die in almost unimaginably excruciating
pain. And then there is the exhibit of the Mega Colon, a piece of large

★ ★

intestine that more closely resembles a giant caterpillar twenty-seven feet long and eight feet in circumference. It was removed from inside a man who failed to survive the operation.

The Mütter Museum's public-friendly profile was raised in recent decades through the tireless efforts and irreverent personality of museum director Gretchen Worden, who joined the museum staff as a curatorial assistant in 1975, and who rose through the ranks to become the public face (and saucy voice) of the formerly stodgy medical institution until her death in 2004. Gretchen would share with visiting journalists and prurient pals such off-exhibit items of interest as astounding abnormalities of male genitalia. Since her sudden death at the age of fifty-six after a long battle with Hodgkins disease, the museum has created a Gretchen Worden Room filled with some of her favorite anatomical grotesqueries floating in formaldehyde-filled jars. But not, you know, that one. For more information visit www.college ofphysicians.org/mutter-museum.

Now That's a City Hall!
Philadelphia

There is a famous tower in Copenhagen, Denmark, built in the early 1900s and decorated with a mosaic depicting "The Seven Wonders of the Modern World." Included among them is Philadelphia's City Hall, a modern wonder that celebrated its one-hundred-tenth birthday in 2011. City Hall stands at Philadelphia's ground zero, geographically, politically, and architecturally. It is literally the center of Center City, occupying four and a half acres where Broad Street would intersect Market Street. Like the middle of a compass, all Philadelphia directions—north, south, east, and west—use City Hall as their starting point.

Everything about City Hall is big. The thirty-seven-foot-tall bronze statue of William Penn on top of City Hall tower is the largest statue on a building in the world. The 548-foot-tall tower itself is the tallest "habitable" masonry structure in the world. At the time of its construction, it was the largest municipal building in the country, literally twice the size

★ ★

of the US Capitol. And the "time of its construction" was a period of almost forty years. Ground was broken in 1871 and the interior of the building wasn't finished until 1909, although the building was officially "presented" to the city in 1901 by the special Commission of the Erection of Public Buildings appointed by the state legislature.

You'll note that the name of the commission refers to Public "Buildings" not "Building." One of the first surprises citizens of Philadelphia experienced regarding City Hall was that it was one massive structure rather than four separate buildings occupying the intersection of Broad and Market. This led to City Hall being dubbed the "world's largest traffic obstruction" by countless millions of drivers, whether behind the wheel of a car or the reins of a horse and carriage in 1871.

Everything about City Hall is too much: 88 million bricks; enough marble, granite, and limestone to pave eighteen football fields; 250 individual pieces of statuary—the building simply overwhelms. When conceived, it was to be Philadelphia's statement about itself to the world, as overinflated as the building itself. Its architectural style, French Second Empire, had fallen out of style before the building was even completed. What was supposed to be a point of civic pride was seen as a civic embarrassment by many. In a nation falling in love with skyscrapers, City Hall was about as lean and mean looking as a wedding cake. Whereas New York's skyline reached for the stars, Philadelphia's squatted on its haunches. For eighty-five years no building in Philadelphia surpassed the top of City Hall tower (thirty-four stories) due to a charming "gentleman's agreement" known as the Billy Penn's Hat Rule.

Today there are several buildings in Center City taller than City Hall, its once dominant tower now a minor player in the city's skyline. Residual resentment toward City Hall as a symbol of Philadelphia stodginess has turned to affection. No one would dream of tearing down City Hall, as they proposed in the early 1950s. (It was discovered that it would cost more to demolish the structure than it did to construct it.) They just don't *build* buildings like City Hall anymore. In 1957 the American Institute of Architecture declared City Hall to be "perhaps the greatest single effort of late nineteenth-century architecture."

There are more than 240 sculptures adorning City Hall
including the thirty-seven-foot-tall bronze statue of
William Penn atop City Hall Tower. All the sculptures
are the work of one artist—Alexander Milne Calder.

★ ★

During the new millennium, City Hall got a face-lift that took eight years and cost $125 million, which is about $100 million more than the cost of building it.

Walking tours of City Hall are offered Monday through Friday at

Dixie Starts Here

Throughout American history there have been pairings of names that have become instantly recognized—Lewis and Clark, Woodward and Bernstein, Sears and Roebuck, Barnum and Bailey—but no two Pennsylvania names have had a greater impact on the way America sees itself than Mason and Dixon.

The story of what brought Charles Mason and Jeremiah Dixon to Pennsylvania in 1763 begins with a dispute almost a century earlier between William Penn and Lord Baltimore. In 1682, when Pennsylvania's "proprietor" William Penn arrived in his newly granted colony, the Calverts, the founding family of Maryland, had been settled for exactly fifty years. Both the Calverts and the Penns had been granted land by kings of England (both kings, as luck would have it, were named Charles). Charles I granted Lord Baltimore the province of Maryland in 1632. Charles I was separated from his crown, and subsequently his head, by Oliver Cromwell, and Charles II eventually assumed his father's throne in 1661. Maybe the records were lost along with the first Charles's head, but no sooner had the second Charles granted a charter to William Penn than the Calverts and Penns were yelping at each other over who owned what and where.

What would become the state of Delaware, for instance, was in dispute. Pennsylvania claimed "the lower three counties" as hers. Maryland said otherwise, and the people living in the three counties that compose the state of Delaware were already acting like an independent colony by the time two Englishmen, an astronomer and a surveyor by the names of Mason and Dixon, were sent over to clear up the mess.

12:30 p.m. Tours of the City Hall tower start every fifteen minutes from 9:30 a.m. to 4:30 p.m. Monday through Friday. The tour office is located in Room 121 of City Hall. Call (215) 686-2840 or visit www .phila.gov for ticket information and reservations.

The British courts had ruled that the east-west boundary line between Pennsylvania and Maryland should begin exactly fifteen miles due south of Philadelphia, which Mr. Mason and Mr. Dixon soon discovered placed them in New Jersey, of all places. But they persevered and four years later had completed the Mason-Dixon Line, which included an arc representing the Pennsylvania-Delaware border, as well as a north-south line representing the Delaware-Maryland border. But the Mason-Dixon Line that became famous through American history as the demarcation line between North and South, free and slave, Union and Confederate, was the east-west line separating Pennsylvania and Maryland.

The literal Mason-Dixon Line runs for 233 miles along 39° 43′ north latitude. It ends where Maryland meets West Virginia at the Pennsylvania border in Fayette County about five miles west of the Youghiogheny River Lake. The more symbolic Mason-Dixon Line between North and South was created by the Missouri Compromise in 1820. The line extended from Pennsylvania's southern boundary west to where the Ohio River empties into the Mississippi and farther west along 36° 30′ north latitude.

The Missouri Compromise separated America into free and slave states until the Civil War. By that time the South was known to all, friend and foe, as Dixie. In fact, Dixie takes its name not from Jeremiah Dixon but from the nickname for French currency used in the big river port in New Orleans. "Dix" was French for "ten-spot." Dixie was also the name of a popular black character in a minstrel show from 1850; Dixieland was where he lived.

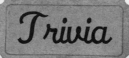

Why He's Called
the Founding "Father"

One of Philadelphia's best-known "inside" jokes has to do with
the statue of William Penn atop City Hall. The thirty-seven-foot-tall
bronze statue shows the Quaker-hatted Penn standing with his left
hand resting on a copy of Pennsylvania's Charter of Privileges spread
out on top of a tree trunk. His right hand is turned downward and
bent at the wrist slightly below his waist with his two-and-a-half-
foot-long fingers pointing outward in the direction of Shackamaxon,
the location on the Delaware River where Penn signed his famous
treaty with the Indians under a spreading elm tree.

As luck or circumstance would have it, Shackamaxon is northeast
of City Hall, which is the direction Penn is facing, which means that
Penn's face is never in direct sunlight, which further means his outstretched hand is seen only in silhouette shaded from the sun by
his body. When seen from the northwest, which happens to be the
straight line down the Benjamin Franklin Parkway from the Philadelphia Museum of Art, the outstretched fingers of William Penn's hand
seen in silhouette below his waist look more like his, well, let's put it
this way—no wonder he's called Pennsylvania's Founding "Father."
(See photo on page 71.)

The "dirty" angle of viewing William Penn has been the subject
of both civic embarrassment and mirth, not to mention the topic of
irreverent Philly T-shirt humor. It is the kind of detail proper Philadelphians pretend not to notice, although the desire to ignore the obvious can lead to ridiculous attempts to disguise it. For instance, in the
fall of 1972, the *Philadelphia Inquirer* published a business magazine
supplement featuring a prominent photo of William Penn atop City
Hall on its cover. What was not prominent, in fact, what was missing
altogether, was any sign of William Penn's offending hand, which
had been airbrushed out of the photo.

Since June 1976 this forty-five-foot-tall, ten-ton sculpture, *The Clothes-pin* by Claes Oldenburg, has stood in Center Square across the street from City Hall. It was installed during the Bicentennial celebration and many noticed that the shiny steel spring resembles a 7 and a 6. It didn't take long for Philadelphians begin to joke about its juxtaposition to City Hall. Why a sculpture of clothespin? "Because that's where we hang out our dirty laundry when one of our elected officials goes to jail on corruption charges." And since 1976 there have been dozens.

★ ★

The Liberty Bell: Cracks, Typos, Missing Chunks, and All
Philadelphia

I love the story of the Liberty Bell because, well, it's so totally American. It is a story of flaws overcome and scars worn proudly. It is a story of false starts and ingenious solutions. It is a story of misunderstandings and myths that make the simple truth all the more powerful.

For instance, the Liberty Bell never rang on July 4, 1776. And it was the Civil War, not the Revolutionary War, that brought the Liberty Bell to the attention of the world. And the famous "crack" most people recognize is actually a repair. And only a Pennsylvanian would probably notice or be chagrined by that fact that the word *Pennsylvania* is spelled wrong on the bell that countless millions have seen and touched.

First things first. The bell began life in 1751 when the Pennsylvania Assembly ordered a bell for the State House (now Independence Hall) in Philadelphia. The chairman of the assembly, Isaac Norris, ordered the bell from Whitechapel Foundry in London, specifying in his instructions: "Let the Bell be cast by the best Workmen & examined carefully before it is Shipped with the following words well shaped in large letters . . . By order of the Assembly of the Province of Pensylvania for the State House in the city of Phila 1752." (Note the spelling of Pennsylvania in Norris's instructions.)

The bell arrived in Philadelphia in September 1752. The first time it was tested, Norris wrote, "I had the Mortification to hear that it was cracked by a stroke of the clapper without any other violence as it was hung up to try the sound." To the rescue came John Pass and John Stow, two Philadelphia foundry craftsmen, who agreed to recast the 2,081-pound bell for a price of thirty-six British pounds, not to mention the immortality of having the names Pass and Stow forever emblazoned in large letters on the Liberty Bell.

Nobody had heard the sound of the original bell sent from England, so they had nothing to compare it to, but the community verdict on the Pass and Stow bell was a resounding "HATED it!" The assembly voted funds to purchase a new bell from London, but when it arrived

Anyone notice which word is misspelled on the Liberty Bell?

in 1754, everyone but Pass and Stow was disappointed to discover that it sounded no better than the Philadelphia recast. The new bell from England was placed in the State House cupola to ring the hours, and the Pass and Stow bell remained in the State House steeple to ring on special occasions. (In 1772 neighbors passed around a petition complaining that they were "incommoded and distressed" by the constant "ringing of the great Bell in the steeple" of the State House.)

The bell never rang on July 4, 1776, because the Declaration of Independence was at the printer's being reproduced. It summoned Philadelphians to the first public reading of the Declaration in the State House Courtyard on July 8, 1776. A year later the bell was removed from Philadelphia along with all the other bells in town to prevent the invading British troops from melting them down into cannonballs or Wilkinson sword blades.

After the Revolutionary War the bell returned to the State House, where it rang on special occasions such as the deaths of Presidents Washington, Adams, and Jefferson, and Supreme Court justice John Marshall. No one agrees on when the new crack first appeared, except that it was discovered before 1846 and that a repair job was attempted by drilling out the existing hairline crack so that the sides of the bell wouldn't rub together and cause a buzzing sound when rung. On February 14, 1846, while tolling for Washington's birthday, the buzz returned, along with the discovery of a new hairline crack. That was the end of the bell's ringing days, but only the beginning of its story.

Even before the crack became famous, the bell was adopted by the antislavery movement because of the Biblical inscription from Leviticus around the top of the bell: PROCLAIM LIBERTY THROUGHOUT ALL THE LAND AND UNTO ALL THE INHABITANTS THEREOF. To the abolitionists, the operative word in that passage was *all* as much as *Liberty*. The first use of the term Liberty Bell is dated 1839 in a poem about the bell in the antislavery publication *Liberator*.

The Civil War cemented the reputation of the Liberty Bell as a symbol for a fractured nation seeking to heal itself. In a way the crack in the bell was like America's broken heart over the 650,000 Americans who died, because everyone who died in the Civil War was an American. After being put on display during the 1876 Centennial Celebration in Philadelphia, the Liberty Bell toured the country several times. New Orleans, Chicago, Charleston, Boston, St. Louis, and San Francisco all hosted the bell during celebrations between 1885 and 1915. In those thirty years souvenir hunters had managed to chisel and chip away thirty pounds of metal from the bell's mouth (you can see for yourself). After that, the city of Philadelphia, which owns the bell, passed legislation forbidding the bell from ever leaving the city again. And it never has. (The Liberty Bell, enclosed in glass, can be seen daily from 9:00 a.m. to 5:00 p.m. at the new Liberty Bell Pavilion constructed in 2003 and located between

Chestnut and Market Streets on Sixth Street. Admission is free. Visit www.nps.gov/inde/liberty-bell-center.html for more details.)

Thinking about the Rodin Museum
Philadelphia

The Gates of Hell hangs in Philadelphia and *The Thinker* sits before it, pondering, perhaps, the choices one faces in life. These sculptures by the great French artist Auguste Rodin reside in a tiny but impressive museum on the Benjamin Franklin Parkway, Philadelphia's gateway boulevard modeled after the Champs-Élysées. The gardened gateway to the Rodin Museum itself is modeled after the facade of the Chateau d'Issy, which Rodin had moved to his studio in Meudon, France. Inside the museum are 125 sculptures completed by Rodin, the largest collection of his work outside Paris.

For this jewel box of a museum we have a movie-palace magnate to thank. Jules E. Mastbaum was a Philadelphia movie theater mogul back in the days when red carpets and velvet curtains and white-gloved ticket takers greeted arriving moviegoers, back in the days when movies were an event rather than a couple of hours to kill at the mall multiplex. You could fit a half dozen Rodin museums into one of Mastbaum's movie theaters back in the 1920s when Jules Mastbaum began collecting the works of the artist, who died at the age of seventy-seven in 1917. Among those works is *The Thinker,* perhaps the most famous statue in the world. Philadelphia's eight-hundred-pound bronze is one of seventeen casts made of the original. Mastbaum commissioned the museum housing Rodin's works to complement the massive Philadelphia Museum of Art a few blocks away. Among the masterpieces in the Rodin Museum are *The Burghers of Calais, Eternal Springtime,* and Rodin's epic bronze doors, *The Gates of Hell,* which the artist worked on for thirty-seven years. Ironically, and perhaps unknowingly, newlywed bridal parties frequently choose to have formal wedding day photos taken while posing in front of the ominous bronze doors of the *Gates of Hell.*

Get more information at www.rodinmuseum.org.

★ ★

They're Called Hoagies, Aren't They?
Philadelphia

Everyone knows that hoagies come from Philadelphia, right? But why? Why *hoagie?* And why have Philadelphia hoagies taken on a mystique of sorts that is absent from similar sandwiches in other cities? Elsewhere, these sandwiches are called heroes, subs, torpedoes, blimps, and—only in and around Norristown, Pennsylvania, for some reason— zeps. Certainly those names are more descriptive of the general shape of hoagies, long Italian rolls cut lengthwise and filled to overflowing with meats, cheeses, and veggies. They *do* resemble submarines, torpedoes, blimps, and zeppelins, not to mention that they require a heroic appetite to finish.

But for some reason the mythology of hoagies has spread throughout the land, especially in the last twenty years or so. You began to see and hear the word *hoagie* in places you never saw or heard it before—in *New Yorker* magazine cartoons and David Letterman monologues—key indications that hoagies have become hip. During a 2012 episode of *Late Night with Jimmy Fallon,* Suburban Philadelphia–raised Tina Fey, creator of *30 Rock,* offered to share a bite of the "Hoagie of Forgiveness" with Questlove, the leader of Fallon's house band, the Philadelphia-based Roots. Now hoagies are mainstream American junk food, like buffalo wings and Philadelphia cheesesteaks.

But the word *hoagie*—where did it come from? What follows is the more-or-less official version: During the First World War, Philadelphia's already booming shipbuilding industry went into overdrive. The shipyards provided ample work for skilled and unskilled Italian immigrants who arrived in Philadelphia in great numbers around the turn of the century. In 1890 there were 6,799 Italian-born citizens in Philadelphia; by 1920 there were 63,223, the vast majority of whom settled in South Philadelphia, not far from the city's largest private shipyard on Hog Island in the Delaware River.

The workmen at Hog Island were called Hoggies. An Italian Hoggie would typically carry his lunch in an oil-stained paper bag that contained an Italian roll sliced in half, slathered with olive oil on each side, and filled with cheese, tomatoes, lettuce, onions, peppers, and, if he was lucky, slices of salami. Imagine the aroma wafting around the workplace or a crowded streetcar from one of those sandwiches. Imagine someone saying, "I gotta get one of those sandwiches those Hoggies eat." So it doesn't take much imagination to see how the new sandwich sensation became known as a hoggie. How one of the *g*s became an *a* is anyone's guess. And how the "hah" sound morphed into the "ho" sound is a question for linguists to argue (although if it were up to marketing analysts the answer would be, "Don't you think *hoggie* sounds entirely too *piggy?*").

So Philadelphia, exclusively, enjoyed its hoagies by that name for the better part the century, always certain of the hoagie's superiority over the less enigmatically named subs, blimps, torpedoes, and heroes enjoyed by other cities. But sometime around 1990, the same way people in other cities started saying "Yo!" after all the Rocky movies, the word hoagie was embraced by people who wouldn't know Hog Island from Hoagy Carmichael.

One problem Philadelphians have with the success of hoagies as an export is with the rampant corruption of the "meaning" of the word hoagie. A hoagie can contain any number of meats, except chicken. A hoagie can be doctored to taste with any condiment, except mustard (for a long time, mayonnaise was the line, but that battle is long past). And a hoagie can be served cold from a refrigerator or, better, at room temperature. But never from an oven. A hoagie baked in an oven is called a grinder.

And a hoagie can never be what I found on an Internet website from Bedford, Indiana, under the heading "Hoagie Recipe": "In a large bowl mix together Velveeta, chipped ham, sliced eggs, diced onion, diced pickles, and chopped olives. In small bowl mix together mayonnaise and chili sauce. Add small bowl mixture to large bowl mixture and mix. Put mixture on buns of your choice and wrap each one in foil. Refrigerate until almost ready to serve. Heat in 450-degree oven for 15–20 minutes. Makes approximately 16 hoagies if you use hot dog buns."

★ ★

Whatever that is, it's not a hoagie. And whatever a hoagie is, it had to be invented in Philadelphia. Or Norristown—after all, zep is a great name for a hoagie.

The "Invention" of the Philly Cheesesteak
Philadelphia

Unlike the hoagie, the origin of Philadelphia's other five-star contribution to the American junk food pantheon, the cheesesteak (or for the lactose intolerant, the steak sandwich), is pretty much accepted

Home of the "Cheesesteak Nazi": Order the wrong way at Pat's King of Steaks and you're ordered to the end of the line. There's even a sign instructing newbies how to order correctly. Whatever you do, don't ask, "What's 'with'?"

Everybody in Philadelphia goes to Geno's—or Pat's across the street— for cheesesteaks at all hours, 24/7, except for Christmas and Easter.

as gospel. Like the fried baloney sandwich, the steak sandwich just sort of happened. But unlike fried baloney, the Philadelphia steak sandwich became a national gastronomic, not to mention marketing, phenomenon.

It was during the dark days of the Great Depression (don't all inspirational American success stories start out that way?) when Pasquale "Pat" Olivieri, the son of Italian immigrants who was born in South Philadelphia in 1907, was having a particularly bad day behind the counter of his hot dog stand at Ninth and Wharton Streets. No business, no prospects, and worst of all, Pat Olivieri was sick of eating hot dogs. So he splurged. "Get me some beefsteak," he said to his cousin, flipping him a dime to buy a chunk-a chunk-a burnin' love from the local butcher. Pat sliced the beefsteak into thin slices, tossed it into a skillet on top of some sizzling oil, and cooked himself a nice sandwich, which he was about to eat when—behold—a customer poked his head over the counter and asked, "What's that GREAT SMELL? I want whatever that is."

Pat Olivieri, hungry no doubt, was not a dope. He sold the sandwich out of his hand, the proverbial shirt off his back. And so a unique food industry was born. "Pat's King of Steaks" became a family dynasty that continues today. The original Pat's is still on the southwest corner of the triangle formed by Ninth Street, Wharton Street, and Passyunk Avenue, the "fertile crescent," if you will, of the cheesesteak culture. You can see a bronze plaque in the sidewalk outside the counter at Pat's, where Rocky Balboa stood dripping sauce on his shoes in the original *Rocky* movie.

Pat's became a twenty-four-hour-a-day operation, an all-night diner open to the elements, but customers didn't care. There was something about freezing one's buns off while waiting for a sizzling cheesesteak at three in the morning. People stood in line (still do, in fact) meekly waiting for the counterman to shout, "Next," at which time a customer had 2.7 seconds to give an order or be ordered to the end of the line. (And you thought the soup Nazi on *Seinfeld* was bad!) "Gimme a cheese with" means a cheesesteak with fried onions. "Two cheese without" means two cheesesteaks without fried onions. And woe be unto the person who asks the question, "What's with?" At that the counterman says, "Hey, fellas, we got one." All the kitchen crew put down their spatulas, crowd their faces into the two-by-two-and-a-half-foot window, and shout, "With onions! STOOPID!" You don't want to be standing at the front of the line when that happens.

Steak Wars: May the Cheese Be with You

In 1966 something unbelievable happened to Pat's cheesesteak kingdom. A rival steak sandwich shop opened on the southeast corner of Ninth and Passyunk, catty-corner to Pat's Steaks, calling itself Geno's. In the forty-some years since, the Great Steak Wars of Philadelphia have continued 24/7. The only days Geno's and Pat's are closed are Christmas and Easter. The war reached a peak in the mid-1980s when Geno's owner Joe Vento hung a banner across Ninth Street that said, "Geno's. The freshest meats, cheeses, and breads. Also clean!" You didn't have to read too deeply between the lines to understand who that last part was aimed at.

Throughout the Great Steak Wars, local politicians have wooed customers of each steak shop without declaring their personal preference. In one of the most brilliant diplomatic moves of his career, then-President Bill Clinton held a reelection rally in the middle of the intersection between the two steak shops in 1996. After the rally Clinton and Philadelphia's then-mayor, later-governor Ed Rendell walked to Pat's and ate a cheesesteak. When they finished they marched over to Geno's and ate a cheesesteak there. Then the president of the most powerful nation on earth told the assembled thousands that he couldn't choose which steak was better because they were both so good. That Clinton could charm the stripes off a zebra.

Such cheesesteak political correctness was abandoned in 2008 when, during the Pennsylvania Democratic presidential primary, Barack Obama and Hillary Clinton bypassed Geno's during their mandatory Philadelphia cheesesteak photo opportunity. Geno's owner Joe Vento, who died in 2011, had placed a sign in the window asking customers to order in English. Many took this as an anti-immigrant announcement. It even ended up under arbitration before the Pennsylvania Human Relation Commission. All the candidates abandoned Geno's after that. And to think all Joe Vento was trying to do was get people to pronounce "cheese with" the proper way in Philadelphia: "cheese wit."

★ ★

The Cowboy in the Rearview Mirror

Philadelphia

Frederic Remington was one of the most famous sculptors and illustrators in the late nineteenth and early twentieth centuries. It was Remington, on assignment to Cuba to illustrate Spanish atrocities and Cuban rebels before the outbreak of the Spanish-American War, who cabled the complaint to newspaper magnate William Randolph Hearst that there were no atrocities, and there was no war. "You provide the

The Cowboy, **overlooking Kelly Drive in Philadelphia, is Frederic Remington's only life-size sculpture.**

★ ★

pictures," Hearst cabled back. "I'll provide the war." Which he duti-
fully did.

Remington was most famous for his artwork depicting the American West. His illustrations and sculptures of the drama of western
landscapes and native inhabitants, and his sculptures of ranch hands
and sodbusters, are classic American art icons. But the only life-size
statue Remington ever completed stands on an outcropping of rock
along Kelly Drive in Fairmount Park. The bronze, called simply *The
Cowboy,* shows a rider pulling hard on the reins of his horse on the
edge of a precipice. The horse's tail stands straight out behind as an
indication of fast motion or, perhaps, a stiff headwind.

Remington himself chose the exact site for the sculpture to stand,
overlooking a slight bend in the road immediately below. When Remington chose the site, however, the river drives were cinder-covered
horse-and-buggy thoroughfares where the fastest traffic traveled at
ten miles an hour. Now the speed limit is forty miles per hour and
Kelly Drive is a busy and heavily traveled commuter route. Because
there is no place to pull over on Kelly Drive to admire the statue, most
motorists only see it as a blur flashing past on their way to and from
work.

Rock and Roll Ringing Rocks

Upper Black Eddy

Pennsylvania has a number of fields where boulders were deposited
by retreating glaciers during the last ice age. Perhaps the most famous
is Boulder Field in Hickory Run State Park in Carbon County, where
boulders as round as cantaloupes and as big as Volkswagens are piled
on top of one another in an eerie landscape surrounded by trees. But
there's only one field where you can play rock and roll on the rolling
rocks.

Ringing Rocks Park near Upper Black Eddy in Bucks County has
been a place of mystery since the original inhabitants noticed that
the boulders strewn about the field rang like bells when struck with a

★ ★

Bring a ball-peen hammer if you want to hear the bell-like tones of the boulders at Bucks County's Ringing Rocks Park.

tomahawk. The same effect can be produced with a ball-peen hammer these days, and more than one musical group has traveled to the Ringing Rocks in an attempt to create the ultimate rock music. The first rock concert in the field was conducted by Dr. J. J. Ott, who led a group of musicians playing more traditional instruments in a performance for the Buckwampum Society of Bucks County in 1890. Dr. Ott played lead boulder in the concert. A witness at the time reported, "The clear bell-like tone he was playing could be heard above the horns."

Over the years the theories as to why the Ringing Rocks ring have ranged from Native American spirits to UFOs to glaciers. One thing we know is that the Ringing Rocks are not a glacial deposit. They were the result of erosion, perhaps from an ancient riverbed. Within the past thirty-five years, the mystery of what makes these boulders ring has been explained by geologists as the result of molten magma cooling, placing the unique deposits of hard dark diabase minerals within under enormous stress. The effect of this stress was like tightening a guitar string. The rocks in the center of the field away from trees and under direct sunlight ring better than the rocks along the perimeter. Some people believe that the Ringing Rocks are the result of some bizarre magnetic energy field, which causes compasses to spin wildly and camera film negatives to be cloudy when developed. Scientific tests have revealed no unusual energy emissions from the area, which of course hasn't stopped anyone from claiming that weird things keep happening there. Back in 1987, during the so-called Harmonic Convergence, a group of New Age believers gathered around the Ringing Rocks to chant "Om." The rocks did not chant back. (Call 215-757-0571. The park is located two miles west of Upper Black Eddy.)

King of the Oldies
Upper Darby

"I'm having a bad day," says Val Schively. "I'm usually more manic than this." It's hard to imagine Schively on a good day because on a bad day the man *Rolling Stone* magazine once dubbed the "emperor of oldies" is as manic as, say, Benny Krass in those famous ten-second—"You wuz robbed!"—TV commercials. The key difference between Benny Krass's Store of the Stars on South Street and Val Schively's "oldies capital of the world" at 40 Garrett Road in Upper Darby is that Krass actually wanted customers. Schively's R&B Records store is about as welcoming as an outlaw biker bar. If it had a doormat it would say, SCRAM. Instead there is a big red and white traffic sign on the front door that reads, DO NOT ENTER with the smaller words UNLESS

★ ★

YOU KNOW WHAT YOU WANT barely visible in the middle. Above that is
another sign. NEW RULES, it reads. 5 MINUTES AND YOU'RE GONE! Peek-
ing out between the two signs is a bug-eyed crustacean on a piece of
driftwood bearing the words, THE CRAB IS IN.

The "crab" of course is Val Schively. "You walk in here with an attitude and you're going to meet Godzilla," Schively warns. I wouldn't
describe him as "bug-eyed," exactly, but when he tells a personal story
his unblinking blue eyes tend to bulge and glisten like Rodney Danger-
field's while his arms and hands move in all directions simultaneously,
one second looking like a symphony conductor, the next like a flight
deck crewman landing a jet on an aircraft carrier. And this is Schively
on a bad day, mind you. In the more than fifty years that he has been
earning a living by selling vintage records, the sixty-eight-year-old
Philadelphia music industry icon has had many more good days than
bad. "I'm blessed to be doing something I love," he says. "Most people hate their jobs. I love mine." Customers, on the other hand . . .
not so much. In 1977 Schively told a writer from *Rolling Stone,* "For
some reason record collecting attracts a bunch of weirdos." Thirty-four
years later he has softened his language if not his opinion. "Record
collectors are basically . . . off center," Schively says. Another word for
"off center" is "eccentric" and Val Shively could be the poster boy for
Eccentrics Anonymous. As he speaks he is standing in a narrow aisle
carpeted with cat fur, crud, cardboard scraps, and record sleeves on
the second floor of his shop. On either side of him are 45 rpm records
stacked on sixteen shelves from floor to ceiling. This is the messiest of
the three similarly stacked floors of his business, which doesn't look
like a business so much as a reality show intervention waiting to happen. "I'm a hoarder," he says. "I live in clutter. I save everything. I
have every check I've ever written. And if I die tomorrow my wife will
have everything in the trash by the weekend."

Shively is known internationally as the guy who has the rare vinyl
recording no one else has. And he probably does. Somewhere. He'll let
you look for it but don't ask him where. He's got Chuck Dabagian for

When Val Schively is having a bad day, you don't want to walk into his oldies record store with an attitude.

that task and many others. Chuck is Guy Friday to Schivley's Robinson Caruso on this island of oldies, his sole employee for thirty-five years ever since he began hanging out at the store as a teenager. "Chuck is the only guy who knows where everything is," Schively says, describing that skill as "job security." Knowing where "everything" is in the seemingly random chaos of this landfill disguised as a record store is Einsteinian in its simplicity: $e=mc^2$ equals "Ask Chuck." Ninety-five percent of R&B Records business is mail order and the few walk-in customers are either accidents, oldies pilgrims, or decades-long faithful

Val Schively talks with his hands. One minute he is a symphony conductor, the next he's waving like a crewman on the flight deck of an aircraft carrier.

★ ★

like Denny Thomson from Douglasville, who started hanging out at Val Schively's record store in 1972, talking, playing pinball, and listening to music. In those days the typical hours of the store were an eccentric 3:00 p.m. until 4:00 a.m. On this weekday afternoon Thomson has stopped in and the old stories flow. "It's not like I changed his life," Schively says. And Thomson replies quietly, "Yes, you did."

Val Schively's passion, his raison d'etre as a collector and a fan, is doo wop. He prefers to call the genre "male vocal harmonies" of the 1950s and 1960s. He plays me one of his favorites, Johnny Carbone and the Five Discs singing "Never Let You Go" on an old-fashioned lunchbox-sized 45 rpm record player. It's awesome. But Val Schively's passion is older than an eight-track tape in an iPod world. He knows it's coming to an end, knows he's a dinosaur after the comet struck, knows he is extinct yet still walking. "When I go, this goes," he says, gesturing to the more than four million vinyl 45s stacked above, below, and around him. But not just yet. Not today. For now, even on a bad day, Val Schively is the last king of the Doo Wah Diddies.

To see Val in action check out www.youtube.com/watch?v= qMkgZyWs3Ww.

When the Rebels Took York
York

York, Pennsylvania, holds the distinction of being the only capital of the United States ever to fall to Confederate troops during the Civil War. Of course, York wasn't the capital of the United States at the time, nor had it been for almost one hundred years. But York was technically the capital of the United States in 1777, after Congress had fled Philadelphia when British troops occupied the city during the Revolutionary War. It was in York that the Articles of Confederation, America's first constitution, were adopted by Congress.

On June 26, 1863, Confederate general Jubal Early and nine thousand troops marched into York and occupied the town without a battle. The Stars and Stripes were hauled down from the flagpole in

the town square and replaced with the Confederate battle flag. York was the largest northern city ever to fall to Robert E. Lee's invading Army of the Potomac. The Confederate occupation of York lasted four days. As the historical display in the York tourist center notes, on June 30, 1863, "Like many future visitors, Jubal Early and men traveled on to Gettysburg."

The House That Hoffman Built
York

Bob Hoffman was a man's man and proud of it. Only a man's man would have the confidence to have a nearly nude larger-than-life-size bronze statue of himself cast and placed along a busy highway outside his place of business. You can see Bob Hoffman in bronze next to Interstate 83 outside York. The statue stands in front of the Weightlifting Hall of Fame next to the York Barbell Company, which Hoffman founded. Hoffman was already an old man when he posed for the statue, but he still looked strong enough to lift an Oldsmobile.

Inside the Weightlifting Hall of Fame are artifacts from the era known as a "Strongmanism," when weight lifting was the stuff of carnivals and vaudeville acts. There's the 220-pound dumbbell used by nineteenth-century strongman Louis Cyr, who lifted it easily over his head with one hand. Then there's the gaudy belt presented by the *National Police Gazette* to Warren Lincoln Travis for being the World's Strongest Man in 1906. There are photos showing feats (and feets) of strength, such as a strong man on his back supporting a bench holding sixteen men on the bottom of his feet.

The Bob Hoffman Story (1898–1985) is told in another room, showing young Hoffman after he returned to York following World War I. He founded the York Oil Burner Company, the precursor to York Barbell Company. Hoffman organized a weight lifting club among his employees that soon developed into a national weight lifting organization. The first weight lifting championships in America were held in York, which soon became known as Muscletown, USA. Hoffman

Mural of Bob Hoffman, muscleman extraordinaire and York, Pennsylvania, entrepreneur.

turned his attention to full-time physical fitness in 1932 when he purchased *Strength and Health* magazine (there's a photo of four men lifting Hoffman and another man in an automobile in front of the publishing company offices). By the time he died at the age of eighty-seven, Hoffman was recognized as the Father of World Weight Lifting and the company he founded as "the strongest name in fitness."

Alongside the Weightlifting Hall of Fame is the Bodybuilding Hall of Fame, which is not about how much you can lift as much as how muscular you can become. Big difference. The heroes, of course, in

★ ★

the Bodybuilding Hall of Fame are the original Mr. America, Steve Reeves, star of many badly dubbed Hercules movies in the 1950s and 1960s, and Mr. Universe, Arnold Schwarzenegger, who, as the caption next to his photo noted, "has had several movie roles since his retirement from competition." There's a photo of Schwarzenegger on the cover of a 1970 bodybuilding magazine where he is identified as "Arnold Strong, movie and TV star." Who knew he'd become governor of California? For more information visit www.visitpa.com/york-barbell-hall-fame.

The Harley Factory Tour: No Ties Required
York

You're not allowed to bring a camera with you when you take the guided tour of the Harley-Davidson Final Assembly Plant off Route 30 in York. It may have something to do with industrial secrets, but most likely it's a safety measure. The last thing they need at the Harley assembly plant is some wide-eyed biker enthusiast with a camera stepping in front of a forklift speeding around the 650,000-square-foot plant. And let me tell you, this tour is for real.

The first thing you have to do is turn over your camera to the tour guide, who locks it up for safekeeping. In exchange you'll receive a pair of plastic safety glasses and a radio receiver with an earpiece. The need for this soon becomes apparent because this is a working factory and working factories are loud. (I said, WORKING FACTORIES ARE LOUD!) Carl was the tour guide for my group of about twenty people, some of whom had come from as far away as Germany to see the inside of an American motorcycle factory. Carl is a retired schoolteacher, and as he led us onto the factory floor from the visitor center, we could hear his heavy breathing in our earpieces. Just when members of the tour were beginning to make amused eye contact about what we were hearing, Carl announced into his headset, "If you hear me breathing it's because I have asthma. If you don't hear me breathing, call 911."

★ ★

As I said, this is a working factory, and the first thing Carl tells us is to stay inside the yellow lines painted on the floor so that we don't wander into the path of forklifts and carts moving heavy equipment from one end of the factory to the other. "That motorcycle you see there," says Carl, pointing to a finished product coming off the end of the assembly line, "was ordered by a customer more than a year ago." Harley's success in recent years has been a combination of a first-rate product meeting incredible customer loyalty and patience. Harley owners are a breed unto themselves. Not only are they willing to wait more than a year for the Harley of their choice, but they seem to rejoice in the process. Despite that the Harley Davidson Company has retooled the assembly process to meet demand. The new assembly facility now turns out a completed motorcycle every eighty-nine seconds. "You see anyone wearing a tie here?" Carl asks, as the tour group pauses in front of the testing area, where the finished product is taken off the assembly line and run through the gears up to seventy miles per hour on a stationary treadmill. "You can't tell the bosses from the workers because everyone's a worker and everyone's a boss." The uniform of the day is T-shirts and blue jeans, with an impressive number of employees preferring well-worn Harley-Davidson T-shirts.

The tour itself takes the better part of an hour, and by the end of it, you are bound to be a new member of the Harley cult, even if you ride a rice burner. Tours are free and begin hourly. Afterward you return to the visitor center where you're invited to sit on a new Harley model and dream. Harley-Davidson factory tours are Monday through Friday. For more information, tour hours, and highly suggested reservations, call (877) 883-1450 (toll free) or (717) 852-6590 prior to your visit for up-to-date tour information or visit factorytour.com/tours/harley-davidson-motor-company.cfm.

Pennsylvania: The Land of Sheetz and Wawa and Turkey Hill

Like ancient Gaul was famously described by Julius Caesar, Pennsylvania is divided into three parts: Sheetz, Wawa, and Turkey Hill. These are the names of the Pennsylvania dairies that operate twenty-four-hour convenience stores familiar to anyone who travels by automobile across the state. There are hundreds and hundreds of them. Combined, the three companies generate revenues of more than $10 billion. For the lactose intolerant, that's a lot of moolah.

What distinguishes each of the ubiquitous convenience store franchises, especially among first timers, is, well, their names. Sheetz? Seriously? That was the best name you could come up with? Wawa? You're kidding, right? Who named Wawa—a one-year-old? And what kind of name is Turkey Hill for an ice cream store?

Pennsylvanians barely notice what many out-of-state visitors find at first puzzling and hilarious. Not unlike the names of certain Pennsylvania towns, such as Intercourse and Grime Lick. Sheetz is a family name of an Altoona-based business empire that started with five dairy farms. Wawa was the name of a dairy in Delaware County that took its name from the Native American (Lenni Lenape) word for "geese." The Indians tried to imitate the sound of geese—"wawa" (and when you think of it, the English word for the sound geese make flying overhead, "honk honk," would make Indians laugh). Turkey Hill, headquartered in Conestoga, was the name of the dairy.

Clearly none of these family-owned dairy businesses submitted the company name to focus groups for approval before they got into the convenience store business during the 1960s. When I was growing up, Wawa was the name of a popular brand of milk with the advertising slogan, "Mama, I want Wawa!" Now people around Philadelphia are more likely to say, "Meet'cha at the Wawa for coffee" than associate the name with milk. Each year Wawa stores sell close to 200 million cups of coffee served in cardboard cups decorated with geese.

To be honest, I didn't even discover Sheetz and (not so much) Turkey Hill until I started driving around the state while researching the first edition of *Pennsylvania Curiosities* back when Bill Clinton was president. At the time it seemed to me like Sheetz was a western Pennsylvania Wawa with gas pumps. I remember seeing a tanker truck unloading fuel at a Sheetz store off Route 219 near Johnstown. On the side of the tanker was a Sheetz logo and a photo of what looked like a burrito. And above that were the words, "Follow this truck for gas."

In the beginning I said that Pennsylvania was divided into three parts. This is true but not accurate. There are lots of Turkey Hill Minit Markets but they are not as obvious, nor do they define the state geographically or as dramatically as the Great Divide between Sheetz Pennsylvania and Wawa Pennsylvania. The east-west frontier separating the two highway coffee-stop empires starts where the Susquehanna River crosses the Mason-Dixon Line into Maryland and runs northeast to the New York–New Jersey–Pennsylvania borders. Everything to the left (the west) is Sheetz Pennsylvania. To the right (east) is Wawa Pennsylvania, a much smaller geographic area but home to half the population of the state.

In the coffee war between the state, Pennsylvania is half and half.

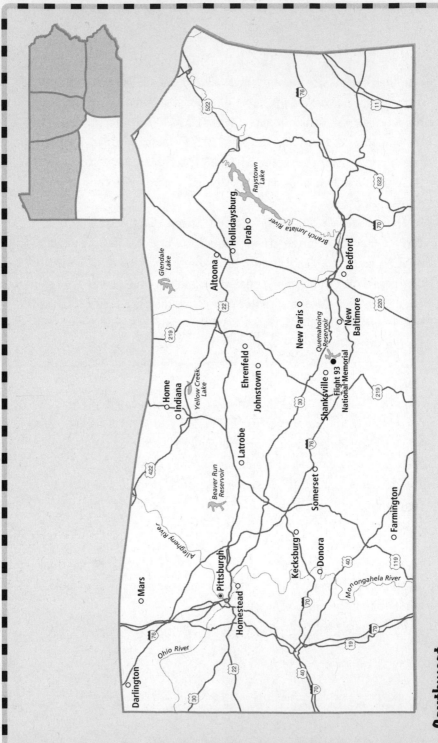

Southwest

2

Southwest

While the hip *East Coast girls of Philadelphia were wearing velvet and lace in 1776, Pittsburgh girls, what few there were, dressed in buckskin or whatever was the female fashion on the frontier. Southwestern Pennsylvania was where East met West, civilization met wilderness, European met Iroquois, transportation technology met unpassable mountains. And it has the battle scars to show it. The Pittsburgh skyline surrounds the original site of Fort Pitt; Altoona has a railroad curve named after it where the battle to cross the Allegheny Mountains was won by the steam engine and Irish laborers; the city of Johnstown shows evidence of its three losing battles against flood water; and the tiny village of Shanksville bears witness to the current war on terrorism.*

The Southwest is defined by the Mason-Dixon Line along its lower counties. Its weirdest border feature is to the west with what was originally a pinky finger of Virginia (now West Virginia) that extends between Ohio and Pennsylvania as far north as New York City. That finger, or panhandle, is defined by the southern shore of the Ohio River, which starts in Pittsburgh and flows north to Monaca. There it turns to the southwest to the border of Ohio and West Virginia and then dramatically southeast, creating this narrow peninsula of West Virginia, which a famously wordy legislator from neighboring Greene County once indelicately described as being "thrust toward Pennsylvania like a pig's genitalia." It was in Southwestern Pennsylvania where George Washington surrendered for the only time in his military career in a battle that launched the French

★ ★

and Indian War. Mr. Rogers' neighborhood is located here. Andy Warhol grew up here, as did Arnold Palmer and Josh Gibson. Looking for
a Smog Museum? You can find it in Donora. There's a flying saucer
in Mars and an acorn-shaped UFO in Kecksburg. Hollidaysburg is the
home of the Slinky. And Home is a real place with a strange story. It's
all here in Southwestern Pennsylvania.

This 3-D billboard in Somerset County two miles west of the entrance
to the Flight 93 National Memorial has confused eastbound motorists
on the Lincoln Highway (Route 30) since it was erected during the tenth
anniversary year of the terrorist attacks in America on the day known
simply as 9/11. What appears to be a blessing to the forty passengers
and crew members who fought back and died while preventing the
hijacked airliner from reaching its intended target in Washington, DC, is
actually an anti-abortion political message.

★ ★

The Curve That Made a City

Altoona

Altoona has been famous for more than 150 years for one thing, a
bend in the railroad tracks called the Horseshoe Curve. In fact, the
only reason there is a city called Altoona (Cherokee for "highlands of
great worth") is that the Pennsylvania Railroad decided to cross the
Allegheny Mountains in 1850. Up until that time, a trip from Philadelphia to Pittsburgh took three days, in an ingenious but almost
comically complicated series of transfers from train to boat to train to
boat. You'd start out by train in Philadelphia and travel to Columbia in

**A curve so famous they named a beer after it
(the Horseshoe Curve in Altoona).**

★ ★

Lancaster County, where you'd board a mule-pulled canal boat up the Susquehanna River. After negotiating a series of eighteen locks, you'd arrive in Hollidaysburg in Blair County, where you would board the Allegheny Portage Railroad, which carried the entire canal boat over the mountains to Johnstown in Cambria County. There, an inclined railroad deposited the canal boats and passengers into the Conemaugh River for the final leg of the journey through sixty-six canal locks to Pittsburgh.

There had to be a better way. The problem was that the mountains were too steep for a train to climb and too wide to tunnel through. It took a Pennsylvania Railroad engineer by the name of J. Edgar Thomson to come up with the idea of building a curve into a V-shaped wedge carved out of the mountain in the middle of the nowhere that was to become Altoona.

Construction started in 1851 and was accomplished by several hundred Irish immigrants using gunpowder, pickaxes, and pack animals. The massive earth-moving project was literally done by hand. The 220-degree curve is 2,374 feet long. The distance between the tracks on either side of the U shape of the curve is 1,800 feet. The tracks rise 91 feet per mile, and the west side of the curve is 122 feet higher than the east side. Without the curve the grade over the mountains would have been six to eight degrees, which would have worn out engines and brakes. With the curve the grade over the mountains is a manageable 1.8 percent. When it opened in 1854, the Horseshoe Curve was considered an engineering marvel. Virtually all train traffic, both passenger and freight, heading to Philadelphia from the west still uses the two remaining tracks through the curve.

The Horseshoe Curve National Historical Landmark is located 5 miles west of Altoona up a winding stretch of road past the Kittanning Reservoir. On the ride up the mountain, Molly and I saw a black bear standing in the middle of the road—it was exciting. He was as scared of us as Molly was of him. The irony of the curve built for trains and named after a horse's footwear is that it is best seen from an airplane.

There is no grand vista available from the opposite slope of the mountain. You can't see the curve from street level, and when you do take the short incline ride from the Horseshoe Curve Visitors Center to the track bed ninety feet above, you can't see the curve from there either. Standing there at the bottom of the U in the curve, all you can see are railroad tracks that bend in the distance in either direction until they are obscured by trees. If you're lucky, a train might pass, but the sight looks remarkably like a train passing. The only difference is the screech of the train wheel flanges holding on to the curve as the train rounds the bend and disappears into the trees. Maybe the dead of winter is the best time to visit the Horseshoe Curve. All that pesky Pennsylvania foliage doesn't spoil the view.

Why Altoona?

Altoona

If one picture speaks a thousand words, then the expression on my daughter Molly's face speaks two: Not again! It was hard for my then ten-year-old to travel for hours across the state, rarely taking her eyes off her Game Boy to look at the mountains, and finally arrive at our destination only to discover that it's not an amusement park but a *museum*. A museum about *trains,* no less. (A little-boy museum, if ever there was one.)

The Altoona Railroaders Memorial Museum is much more than a collection of antique locomotives. It is a stirring tribute to a way of life. Altoona started as a working village carved out of a wilderness by necessity and the accident of geography. It became a city, one of the largest in the state, and was one of Pennsylvania's proud industrial workshops until its inevitable decline after World War II. *Railroaders* is the key word in the name of this museum. It's about the people who worked for the Pennsylvania Railroad; it's about life in a railroad town when locomotives ruled the rails. "A dirty city was a good city because it meant people were working," says Sally Price, a railroad employee featured in one of the exhibits. "We always considered it gold dust,

Like most people in the 1920s, Babe Ruth
traveled to Altoona by train.

not coal dust. That's what made Altoona run." What made Altoona
run was what made Altoona filthy in its heyday, when hundreds of
smoke-belching locomotives passed through town on the sixty-four
eastbound tracks and seventy-two westbound tracks that dominated
the middle of town where the 218 acres of the Pennsylvania Railroad
repair shops were located.

Today the museum stands where the great locomotives were once
serviced. On the second floor you'll see a life-size figure of a woman
crossing the Twelfth Street bridge as the trains pass underneath,

causing the kind of updraft made famous by Marilyn Monroe standing over a subway vent in *The Seven Year Itch*. The figure must have been that of a city girl, because the caption information notes that country girls held down their skirts in the updraft, while city girls held on to their hats. Another item of interest is a classy-looking metal device about the size of an eyeglasses screwdriver. It has a wire loop at the end that was used to remove burning cinders from a person's eyes. (Railroaders Memorial Museum, 1300 Ninth Avenue, Altoona; 817-946-0834. Open 9:00 a.m. to 5:00 p.m. Monday through Sunday April through October; closed Monday November through March. Admission charged. www.railroadcity.com. *Note:* This site has listings of all the Altoona sites mentioned in this book.)

Grand View, No Ship
Bedford County

In its heyday during the 1930s, the Ship Hotel near the summit of the Allegheny Mountains on the Lincoln Highway in Bedford County was a tourist attraction capable of attracting star-caliber guests. Over the hotel's lifespan Henry Ford, Thomas Edison, Calvin Coolidge, Will Rogers, J. P. Morgan, John Barrymore, and Joan Crawford all stayed there. They came for the view, as did other tourists, and they came for the novelty of wining and dining and sleeping in a guest cabin in a wooden ship more than two thousand feet above sea level. The SS Grandview Hotel started life as a private castle but was modified to look like a ship perched on a mountainside, and after its dedication in May 1932, it did a thriving business even during the Depression. Even though you couldn't find a more dramatic view anywhere else in the state of Pennsylvania, the tourist business for the "Ship Hotel" was scuttled by the opening of the Pennsylvania Turnpike. (The turnpike siphoned off most of the east-west traffic.)

Located on a south-facing bend in the road on Route 30 near the 2,464-foot summit of Pennsylvania's largest mountain range, the SS Grandview Hotel offered a grand view of "three states and seven

★ ★

An artist's rendering of the Ship Hotel was on display at an antiques store not far from where the hotel actually stood.

counties," as the hotel signs advertised. The view is indeed stunning, but you can't see the counties for the trees. The heavily forested panorama spread out below is punctuated by an occasional farm and lake, but the view does not include those helpful black lines and dashes to indicate where one state or county ends and another begins. The SS Grandview was once the most prominent landmark on the Pennsylvania section of the Lincoln Highway. Today, all that's left worth seeing of the SS Grandview is the view itself, since an early-morning fire destroyed the wooden structure on October 28, 2001. As of this

★ ★

writing, all that remains on the site are the blackened trees and the concrete foundation rubble of the former hotel, which had been closed to the public for more than two decades before the fire. But you can see photos at http://brianbutko.wordpress.com/2007/12/02/film-of-ss-grand-view-ship-hotel-1972.

Ironically, without the ship in the way, the grand view is more accessible to travelers. You can still pull over into the modest parking area that served the hotel and take a gander at a vista that the hotel advertised as encompassing up to sixty-three miles on a clear day. The three states visible within that view are Pennsylvania (well, DUH-uh!), Maryland, and West Virginia. The seven counties are Bedford and Somerset, Pennsylvania; Allegheny and Washington, Maryland; and Mineral, Hampshire, and Morgan Counties in West Virginia. But believe me, they all look like trees.

Nudist Volleyball Super Bowl
Darlington

They've been playing nudist volleyball in Beaver County (you can stop laughing now) since the White Thorn Lodge opened in rural Darlington in 1962. Since 1971 the fame of White Thorn's annual week-after-Labor-Day-weekend buck-nekkid volleyball competition had spread throughout nudist circles so that it achieved the status of the official nudist Volleyball Super Bowl. The forty-third annual competition will be held in 2014, but this naked Super Bowl XLIII isn't X-rated. It's a family affair that attracts up to fifteen hundred nude volleyball enthusiasts each year.

Teams play in a round-robin tournament that lasts the better part of two days on the lodge's eleven volleyball courts. Not all the competitors are practicing nudists. "You can tell the ones who aren't," said White Thorn president Lawrence Hettinger. "We call them 'cottontails'," a reference to the tan lines so conspicuous among nonnudists. Basically it's good volleyball played in the woods near the Pennsylvania-Ohio border. In 2009 *ESPN*, the magazine, assembled a team of serious and newbie

★ ★

volleyballers to test the mettle (skin?) of the competition. Former-pro beach volleyball player Michelle Rauter of Vancouver, who played against men's teams for the *ESPN* side, found the quality of competition to be surprisingly competent only with more, you know, balls in play. The *ESPN* team won only one match. *ESPN* writer Eddie Matz, who played and wrote about the experience, described his teammates after the experience as, "We've gone from strangers who barely know each other to friends who know each other barely."

Still, there are some seeming incongruities at a nudist Volleyball Super Bowl. Souvenir T-shirts, for instance. And if you're looking to identify your favorite team by their uniforms, forget it. It's all skins all the time. One nice touch is the nude barbecue grills over at Walt's Wonderful World of Burgers, where Walt Lippert serves up hamburgers while wearing nothing but an apron to protect himself from grease splatter. "We may be nudists," said Walt, "but we're not stupid." They have another saying out there at White Thorn: "When you're around a bunch of naked people and you're the only one wearing clothes, you feel like an idiot." The nudist Volleyball Super Bowl attracts competitors from as far away as Florida, California, and Canada, and the competition is broken down by skill levels. There are men's, women's, and coed divisions. Up to ninety teams participate and, although clothing is optional, it is frowned upon. For more information visit www.whitethornlodge.org/public/superbowl.html.

How Donora, Pennsylvania, Changed the World
Donora

I was just a kid the first time I heard the name Donora, Pennsylvania. It was mentioned on a popular network TV cop drama—some 1960s equivalent to all the CSI forensic investigative shows these days—and it involved a life-threatening air-pollution emergency in Los Angeles that no one was taking seriously until this one guy in a lab coat raises his finger and says, "Donora!" like he was shouting, "Eureka!" "Come again?" says one of the investigators. "Donora, Pennsylvania, a small steel town near Pittsburgh on a river between two mountains. One day about twenty years ago, there was an air-temperature inversion [this was the first time I had ever heard that term either, which thankfully the guy in the lab coat explained]. That's when cool air clamps down on top of warm air like a lid on a pot. The smoke from the steel mills couldn't escape, trapped between the mountains. Twenty people died in a single day. It was the deadliest air-pollution catastrophe in United States history."

And it remains so to this day. What happened in Donora, Pennsylvania, on Halloween weekend in 1948 scared the bejabbers out of environmental scientists who recognized it for what it was, as a film would document—"an inconvenient truth" that many in post–World War II industrial America would first ignore and then deny. In July 1950 the scholarly journal *California Medicine* reported the findings (note the "allegedly") of a five-month investigation by the US Health Service into the Donora massacre. "Twenty persons allegedly died as a result of pollutants in the atmosphere and some several hundred more were affected," the journal reported, noting that the Public Health Bulletin No. 306 was an "exceedingly attractive publication about the size of *Fortune* (magazine)." Fortunes, of course, were at stake if US Steel and the Donora Zinc Works had been found liable for the deaths caused by countless millions of cubic feet of untreated sulfur dioxide, fluoride, and other pollutants pumped into the air around Donora year-round—let alone continuously during the emergency of October 30–31, 1948. Well, America wasn't ready to deal with that. Not quite yet.

What you have to understand is that smoke meant life to the Mon Valley mill towns of Western Pennsylvania, to Monessen and Monongahela and Clairton and McKeesport and Braddock and Homestead. When the furnaces shut down, the home hearths suffered. "That's not coal dust; that's gold dust," mill workers would say of the grime that built up so thick each day they could write their names on the hoods of their cars—cars they couldn't have afforded without it. But even by the stoic standards of Mon Valley life, Halloween weekend that year

Continued on page 114

The Mother of All Highways

"Most baby boomers, and even more of their children, have never heard of the Lincoln Highway," a history of America's first transcontinental automobile roadway, published by the Lincoln Highway Association. Being a baby boomer, I took this personally. Whaddaya mean "never heard of the Lincoln Highway"?! Everyone knows about the Lincoln Highway, right? Certainly every Pennsylvanian should have heard of it, considering that eighty-four communities, from Oxford Valley in Bucks County on the east to Smith's Ferry in Beaver County to the west, are part of the Pennsylvania route of the original Lincoln Highway that linked New York with San Francisco.

Then I realized that I'm a little biased, considering that I grew up less than a mile away from the Lincoln Highway, which is called Lancaster Avenue from the Philadelphia area westward to the Lancaster area, where it becomes Philadelphia Pike. By whatever name it is known locally (in Greensburg, Westmoreland County, it's called Pittsburgh Street), the Route 30 portion of the Lincoln Highway meanders for 320 miles across the southern tier of Pennsylvania through some of the most spectacular scenery in the state.

The plan for a transcontinental automobile route was adopted in 1912. It was scheduled for completion in 1915, in time for the Panama-Pacific Exposition hosted in San Francisco. The chief advocate for what he called the Coast-to-Coast Highway was Carl Fisher, owner of the Indianapolis Motor Speedway, who proposed that the roadway be built with private funds. It wasn't until Henry Joy, president of the Packard Motor Car Company, came up with the idea of naming the highway for Abraham Lincoln that funds began pouring in. Pennsylvania is pivotal in the cross-country route that starts at Times Square in New York City and heads south through New Jersey and into Pennsylvania along Route 1. In Philadelphia, the Lincoln Highway makes its big west turn toward the Pacific coast on Route 30, and the route number doesn't change until it becomes Interstate 80 in Granger, Wyoming. "We're thirteen years older and a thousand miles longer than Route 66, but for some

A few miles west of the Flight 93 Memorial is this mural on a barn celebrating the Lincoln Highway Heritage Corridor and America's first transcontinental highway.

reason fewer people seem to know about the Lincoln Highway," says Olga Herbert. "I guess we needed a popular TV show named after it." Herbert is the executive director of the Lincoln Highway Heritage Corridor, a state-sponsored organization that is part of the Pennsylvania Heritage Parks Program. The corridor embraces two hundred miles of the Lincoln Highway, through mostly rural and mountainous sections of Pennsylvania, from the York County line on the east to the Allegheny County line on the west. In coming years the Lincoln Highway Heritage Corridor, which was created in 1995, will try to promote more public awareness of the highway's history and its attractions.

Already the corridor is marked by 152 distinctive signs that resemble the three thousand concrete markers that were placed virtually every mile along the original coast-to-coast Lincoln Highway. The new signs have a big blue *L* with a Lincoln penny above it.

The most recent development of national interest along the Lincoln Highway was the opening of the still-uncompleted permanent Flight 93 National Memorial in 2011. Its entrance is on the south side of the Lincoln Highway midway between the county seats of Bedford and Somerset. The new access will undoubtedly bring more visitors to the site in Stonycreek Township rather than the emergency entrance to the Temporary Memorial site off Lambertsville Road leading to Shanksville.

★ ★

Continued from page 111

was different. In her 2002 book about the "killer smog" of 1948, *When Smoke Ran like Water,* Donora native and Carnegie Mellon University professor and epidemiologist Dr. Devra Lee Davis described the scene that day through interviews. Like a Stephen King horror movie, an eerie yellow fog rolled into town. At three in the afternoon, car headlights could barely penetrate the curtain of moist smoke. The annual Halloween parade took place on Main Street that Friday afternoon and costumed children disappeared from their parents' sight within a matter of yards. At football practice the day before the big game against Monongahela High School, Donora High coach Jimmy Russell had to yell "Kick!" to let his players know the ball was in the air.

On Saturday fans could hardly see the action. It was like the famous "Fog Bowl" NFL playoff game between the Philadelphia Eagles and the Chicago Bears when an impenetrable fog rolled into Soldier Field off Lake Michigan, obscuring that game to a national TV audience. With Monongahela leading in midgame, from the public-address loudspeakers came a call to Donora's star tight end, Stanley Sawa, telling him to "Go home! Go home now!" With helmet in hand, he ran down Fifth Street to his house to find his father dead. By ten o'clock that morning, nine Donorans had died. By ten o'clock the next morning, eighteen were dead. The local funeral home had run out of caskets by the time the Donora Zinc Works agreed to "dead fire" the furnaces Sunday morning. By that time one-third of the population in a town of thirteen thousand was seriously ill. Had not heavy rains fallen Sunday afternoon, November 1, and wiped most of the poison from the air, the death toll would have been much higher.

It was Walter Winchell who broke the news of the Donora disaster to "Mr. and Mrs. America and all the ships at sea." The syndicated radio newsman reported on Halloween night, "The small, hardworking steel town of Donora, Pennsylvania, is in mourning tonight as they recover from a catastrophe. People dropped dead from a killer fog that sickened much of the town. Folks are investigating what has hit the

★ ★

area." Today we know that what hit the area was the proverbial piper seeking his pay. The bill on decades of heedless pollution pumped into the atmosphere came due in a deadly and personal way for the citizens of Donora. Their unknowing sacrifice was like a fire bell in the night for the forces of clean air, clean water, and responsible industry. It took years but the movement took hold. In 1965 Pennsylvania passed its first clean-water legislation and, a year later, clean-air legislation. In 1970 an "Environmental Bill of Rights" was adopted. It ain't perfect, but it's so much better than many who suffered can imagine. In 2008, on the sixtieth anniversary of the killer fog, the Donora Smog Museum opened in a storefront building at 595 McKean Avenue. Its proud T-shirt slogan with smokestacks rising behind it reads, "Clean air started here." To find out more about the museum visit www.visit pa.com/donora-smog-museum.

Great Names Etched in Granite
Donora

One afternoon in June when my daughter, Molly, and I drove across the Monongahela River bridge that connects Westmoreland County with Washington County, the first thing we noticed was a big sign announcing our destination: DONORA. the home of champions. hub of the industrial mid mon valley. That's quite a mouthful. A couple of hundred yards away, I saw something else that made my jaw drop. It was the Donora War Memorial honoring the men and women who had fought, and many who had died, for their country in the uniform of the US military from this western Pennsylvania town with a population of about 5,500. There are 4,900 names etched in the black granite panels, a breathtaking number from such a small town. There are forty-one names from the Civil War and sixty names from Desert Storm, which was the most recent war when the memorial was planned, but by the time it was dedicated in November 2003, America was at war again. There are panels ready to add the names of Donorans who have served in Afghanistan and Iraq.

★ ★

The Donora War Memorial includes the names of local residents who fought in every US conflict from the Civil War until Desert Storm.

Stan Musial is one of the names on the Donora War Memorial. Yes, that Stan Musial. Stan the Man was born Stanislaw Franciszek Musial on November 21, 1920, the son of Polish and Czech immigrants who lived in a house on Sixth Street in Donora. He won the National League MVP award in 1943 after batting .357 in a pennant-winning season for the St. Louis Cardinals. After being drafted into the navy, Musial served on a repair ship at Pearl Harbor before returning to the Cardinals in 1946 and winning the MVP again with a .365 average while leading St. Louis to a World Series victory over Ted Williams's Boston Red Sox. Musial, whose other nickname was the Donora Greyhound, was a pitcher in high school. One of his teammates was Ken

★ ★

Griffey Sr.'s father. Both of the famous baseball Ken Griffeys were
born in Donora—the senior on April 10, 1950, and the junior on
November 21, 1969 (Stan the Man's birthday). Both became all-stars
for the Cincinnati Reds, and at the end of his career, Ken Griffey Sr.
signed with the Seattle Mariners, which had just signed his rookie
son. On August 29, 1990, Ken Griffey Sr. and Ken Griffey Jr. became
the first father and son to play together on the same team in Major
League Baseball when the Mariners took on the Kansas City Royals.
Two weeks later the Griffeys became the first father and son to hit
back-to-back home runs in the same game. It only gets better: In St.
Louis on Sunday, June 20, 2004, Father's Day, with his father in Busch
Stadium watching, Ken Griffey Jr. hit his 500th home run, a hit that
tied him with Ken Griffey Sr.'s career total of 2,143 hits.

First in War: George Washington and Fort Necessity
Farmington

We all know the story, perhaps apocryphal, about young George
Washington cutting down a cherry tree and then, when questioned
about it, beginning his confession with the words, "Father I cannot
tell a lie . . ." Fewer of us know about another youthful indiscretion by
the Father of Our Country, who if confronted with the evidence would
have to fess up: "I cannot tell a lie. . . . I started a world war."

The facts are these: In May of 1754, George Washington, twenty-
two and newly commissioned as a lieutenant colonel in the Virginia
militia, led a party of forty frontiersmen into the heavily forested wilderness of what is now Fayette County, Pennsylvania, to meet an advancing group of French soldiers moving southeast from Fort Duquesne at
the Forks of the Ohio River, what is now downtown Pittsburgh. Earlier
Washington had been sent by the governor of Virginia to tell the
French forces to leave the land then claimed by Virginia. The French
told young George to take a hike. He returned that spring with armed
men and Native American allies led by Seneca chief Tanacharison,
also known as Half King. Washington's men came upon the French

★ ★

encampment at dawn. The French, not expecting an attack, had not posted sentries, and Washington's men quickly surrounded them.

Then came that ever-popular anonymous trigger finger and historical description, "a shot was fired." Could have been a French finger, could have been a Virginia finger, could have been an Indian finger, but the French still rising from sleep caught the worst of it. Thirteen were killed and twenty-one captured. The first shots had been fired in what would become the French and Indian War in North America and the larger global conflict between England and France called the Seven Years' War that did not end until 1763. But the domino effect doesn't end there. The huge cost of the Seven Years' War led England to levy higher taxes on her American colonies, leading inexorably to the Revolutionary War and the Declaration of Independence. And all because of an itchy trigger finger.

The controversy surrounding the skirmish near Uniontown in what became Jumonville Glen was the eighteenth-century equivalent of the Gulf of Tonkin incident, which led to the massive American military buildup in Vietnam. Besides the issue of who shot first and why, there was the question of how the French commander, Ensign Joseph Coulon de Jumonville, died—whether he was killed in battle or executed by a blow from Seneca chief Half King's war club after the surrender. The few French soldiers who escaped returned to Fort Duquesne, and Washington knew a French retaliation "by considerable forces" would be swift. And he was right. No sooner had word of the sneak attack reached the French garrison than a force of six hundred French soldiers and one hundred Indian allies were on the march under the command of Ensign Jumonville's brother, Captain Louis Coulon de Villiers.

Washington withdrew his men to a position in the Great Meadows eight miles away where he built a circular wooden stockade and low defensive earthworks at a site he dubbed Fort Necessity. Whatever the French word for "payback" is, it happened on a miserable rainy day five weeks later. Superior French forces taking shelter behind trees surrounded the vulnerable fort on marshy ground in the middle of the

**Today the site resembles a wooden Stonehenge
in a Western Pennsylvania meadow.**

meadow. Washington's three hundred Virginians bolstered by one hundred regular British army troops from South Carolina were running out of dry powder, and more than one hundred were dead or wounded. It could have been a massacre. Instead at 8:00 p.m. the French commander called a truce and offered generous terms for the surrender of Washington's command. His troops would not be taken as prisoners of war. They would be allowed to withdraw to Virginia with their weapons. A little after midnight, Washington signed the document in which he took responsibility for the "assassination" (Washington later said he thought the words meant "death of") of Ensign Jumonville, a document that the French used for considerable propaganda value. And on July 4, 1754, George Washington surrendered his command to hostile

forces for the first and only time in his long military career. The French burned Fort Necessity to the ground and returned to Fort Duquesne to await the return of George Washington under the ill-fated expedition by British general Edward Braddock the following year.

Today Fort Necessity National Battlefield is only one of two battle-grounds from the French and Indian War to be operated by the National Park Service. It is open sunrise to sunset year-round, and visitors can see the Great Meadows and the circular wooden stockade, which resembles a colonial Stonehenge in this setting. The battlefield is located eleven miles east of Uniontown on Route 40, the Old National Road. The visitors' center (Fort Necessity/National Road Interpretive and Education Center, 724-329-5811) is open from 9:00 a.m. to 5:00 p.m. year-round except for national holidays. An entrance fee of five dollars is charged for individuals fifteen and older. Visit www.nps.gov/fone for the most complete information.

Everyone Knows It's Slinky
Hollidaysburg

Who knew? Certainly not Richard James, who invented it. And not his wife, Betty, who named it. And not even the first customers, who bought out the entire inventory during a Christmas shopper demonstration at Gimbel's Department Store in Philadelphia in 1945. Who knew that a simple spring in a box would become one of the most recognizable toys in the world, an American icon made in Pennsylvania called the Slinky? Who knew that the Slinky would become part of the Smithsonian Institution's permanent Americana exhibit? Who knew that the US Postal Service would honor the Slinky with its own postage stamp in 1999? Who knew that "happier than a Slinky on an escalator" would become a TV commercial catch-phrase in 2012? Who knew it would take a world war to inspire an invention that has lasted longer than the Third Reich?

Everyone knows the Slinky jingle. At least 90 percent of the American adults polled in 1995 knew the jingle, probably because they

★ ★

owned a Slinky as a child or because they had bought one for their own children. Today the sales of Slinky Toys by James Industries in Hollidaysburg in Blair County have equaled the population of the United States—surpassing 300 million. That's a lot of shhhhillNGG shhhiillNG-Ging down the stairs.

It all started during World War II at the Philadelphia Naval Shipyard. In 1943 a young Penn State graduate named Richard James was working as a naval engineer, trying to develop a system to stabilize sensitive monitoring equipment aboard ships in pitching seas. James was experimenting with springs of various sizes when, as the story goes, he noticed one spring fall off a stack of books, uncoiling itself and then righting itself on the book below, before continuing its journey to the next level. "Radar-shmadar," James may or may not have muttered to himself, but in any language it was "Eureka."

For the next couple of years, when he wasn't working to bring the Axis powers to their knees, James worked on his postwar plans to bring millions of kids to their knees to play with his toy without a name. Betty James scoured the dictionary looking for a word that fit the toy. She chose "slinky" because it meant "stealthy, sleek, and sinuous"—not to mention it started with a sibilant.

Slinky it was, a name as simple and delightful as the toy. In 1946 Richard James borrowed five hundred dollars to pay a local machine shop to press wire into a coil, eighty feet of wire per coil. He badgered Gimbel's buyers into allowing him to demonstrate his toy to Christmas shoppers, using a portable set of stairs. In ninety minutes, his entire stock of four hundred Slinkies was sold at one dollar a Slinky. And so it began.

The Slinky story isn't entirely a happy one, although it has remained a family one. In 1960 Richard James abandoned his wife and six children to pursue what his children describe as a "missionary cult" in Bolivia. He nearly bankrupted James Industries in the process with his contributions to the cult. Betty James packed up her children and moved back to her family and hometown roots in Hollidaysburg,

★ ★

where Slinkies have been manufactured ever since, using the same equipment designed by Richard James. In 2001 Betty James was inducted into the Toy Manufacturers of America Hall of Fame, the same year the Slinky was declared the official state toy by the Pennsylvania legislature. Betty James died at the age of ninety in 2008. Her son Thomas now runs the company.

I had to ask about something that has bothered me ever since I followed my first Slinky down the stairs. "What do you call it when the coils of a Slinky get tangled together?" I asked. "Is there a technical name for that?" "Yes," replied Thomas James. "It's called broken."

The Terrible Truth about Home, Pennsylvania
Home

Unless you live in Indiana County, you've probably never heard of Home, Pennsylvania, except as the title and location of what is almost universally considered to be the most grisly, brutal, and disturbing episode of the *X Files* ever aired on network TV. It was the second program to air in the fourth season of the *X Files* in 1996. The episode begins with the word *Home,* which dissolves and is replaced by the word *Pennsylvania.* Agents Mulder and Scully are dispatched to investigate the discovery of a corpse of a terribly malformed infant. They discover a Mayberry-type town complete with a sheriff named Andy and a deputy named Barney, both of whom are horribly murdered by a pair of mutant brothers who live in a farmhouse without electricity, with a third brother who is actually their father. As Mulder and Scully close in on the family's terrible secret, they discover the limbless torso of the mother still alive under a bed on a rolling dolly. She was still breeding children from this incestuous trio of sons. The mother tells Scully, "I can tell you don't have no children. Maybe one day you'll learn the pride . . . the love . . . when you know that your boy would do *anything* for his mother." The show ends with two of the sons shot dead by the FBI agents while the other brother/father carries his mother to the trunk of his car, places her

★ ★

tenderly inside, and then drives off presumably to find a place to continue breeding their own children.

Creepy doesn't begin to describe the episode called "Home." Fox refused to air it again on regular TV, but it still appears on cable TV reruns and on DVD, where it has gained a cultlike status among *X Files* aficionados. Although it was shot in rural British Columbia in Canada, residents of Indiana County are not exactly thrilled by the notoriety surrounding Home, Pennsylvania, an unincorporated town with a population of about 180. Whenever he's asked about the *X Files* episode, Home resident Mike Miller, a blues musician, says, "I don't know. I was playing a gig the night they shot that" and walks away. Not only is Miller from Home, he is an albino—which is not a bad thing for a bluesman. In college he says he looked like "the illegitimate spawn of Johnny Winter" with shoulder-length white-blonde hair. Miller described his first day in English class at nearby Indiana State University in 1991 when the instructor asked the class to introduce themselves and where they live. "My name is Mike Miller, I'm from Home, and I play in a blues band." Classmates rolled their eyes in disbelief, and the guy behind him said, "Yeah, right, [obscenity]. I'm from Home too." Miller had to show his driver's license to satisfy the doubters. "This happens to everyone from Home," Miller said. "The exact same thing happened to my dad during his first day in college right down to the "Yeah, right, [obscenity]. I'm from Home too."

All this confusion could have been avoided if the new post office for the area hadn't been established inside Hugh Cannon's house in 1834. It was called the "Home" post office because Cannon sorted the mail on a table inside his home. In 1838 a surveyor named Meek Kelly (great-great-grandfather of movie star Jimmy Stewart) was asked to lay out a village by one of Indiana County's first lawyers, Daniel Stannard. Early maps show the village name as Stannardsville or Kellyburg, but the name Home stuck. Besides, how scary could an *X Files* episode called Kellyburg be?

Why Home? Why Not? Why Ask? Because Who Else Will?

Molly and I were still more than two hundred miles from where we live when we arrived at Home. Actually, we passed through Home doing forty miles an hour on the Buffalo-Pittsburgh Highway, also known as Route 119, one of the lovelier north-south Pennsylvania roadways to take if you want to see what the state really looks like. We were in a hurry to get from Indiana to Punxsutawney before Jimmy Stewart could text message the groundhog and tell Phil to make like a shadow. We were cruising with the wipers on intermittent in a slight drizzle when, on a green bend in the road that revealed wider green fields beyond, out of the corner of my eye, I saw one of those blue Pennsylvania town markers with yellow letters that said VILLAGE OF HOME with more writing underneath. There wasn't much of a town to see: no traffic light or business district, just a fork in the road where Route 85 splits off Route 119 and a little past that a roadside restaurant called, what else, Home Made.

Should I turn around to investigate? This is the problem with traveling with teenagers. They barely tolerate the cool stuff on the itinerary, let alone a "change of plans." Before I could even say, "Let's go back and check out that neat sign," I could hear my own inner father saying, "Ix-nay on the U-urn-tay if you want to avoid an ulk-say by Olly-may." The newspaper comic strip *Zits* described the attitude I was facing in a three-panel-strip in November 2007. Two fifteen-year-olds, a boy and a girl, are talking over lunch. "My new philosophy is to live in the moment," the boy says. "Unless the moment, you know, sucks." In the last panel the boy says, "Then I live in some other moment." And the girl says, "Works for me." And so we motored on toward Punxsutawney, where every day is exactly the same and where there is never a sucky moment. A father can dream, can't he?

But what about Home? When I was researching the second edition of *Pennsylvania Curiosities*, I discovered the Schuylkill County community of Hometown, Pennsylvania, another Home town I had never heard of. Hometown had a story, so why wouldn't Home? But both places offer that precious Abbott and Costello "Who's on First?" possibility. Here's a Pennsylvania state trooper questioning a guy: "Where do you live?" Home. "I know that, but what's the name your neighbors call the place where you live?" Home. "Does your town have a name?" Sure it does. "And that name would be . . . ?" A second guy walks up and tells the first guy not to answer the question. The trooper says, "And why is that?" Because he's from Home and that answer will drive you crazy. "Really, and where might you be from?" Hometown.

If that's stretching a joke, then tell me why people still think a third baseman named "I don't know" is funny.

★ ★

"It's a Wonderful Life" Town

Indiana

Indiana, Pennsylvania, is the perfect name for a mythical all-American hometown. In a town called Indiana, Pennsylvania, you can almost imagine a young Jimmy Stewart walking streets with names like Elm, Maple, and Church, past the library and the courthouse, on his way to his father's hardware store where he'd sweep up after school. You can imagine a photo of Jimmy posing with his proud parents as he leaves home for the first time to attend Princeton University, and later a photo of Jimmy in uniform during World War II, in which he flew twenty-five missions as a bomber pilot. What happens next you don't need to imagine because you've probably seen it on television at least a dozen times, especially around Christmas. You see Jimmy Stewart just back from the war and in despair, standing on a bridge about to hurl himself into the rushing water below. His family would be better off if he was dead, he mutters to himself, if he had never lived at all. And the rest, as they say, is *It's a Wonderful Life.*

In 1946, despite his medals for valor overseas, despite his Academy Award for Best Actor in 1940, Jimmy Stewart was just another out-of-work actor in Hollywood. "Frankly," he wrote about that time, "I was just a little bit scared." Like his Oscar-winning character in *The Philadelphia Story,* the returning GI from western Pennsylvania had seen "hearthfires and holocausts." When director Frank Capra approached him that year to play a role Capra had a hard time explaining, Stewart said, "Frank, if you want to do a picture about a guy who jumps off a bridge and an angel named Clarence who hasn't won his wings yet coming down to save him, well, I'm your man!"

More than seventy years later, *It's a Wonderful Life* is still a classic and Jimmy Stewart (1908–1997) is still an American icon, especially in his hometown, which resembles the fictional Bedford Falls of the movie. Shortly before his death, Stewart wrote a magazine article describing *It's a Wonderful Life* as his favorite movie role. "From the beginning there was something special about the film," he wrote

Jimmy Stewart as classy as ever.

of the elaborate stage set depicting Bedford Falls' main street, with seventy-five buildings and twenty full-grown oak trees. "As I walked down that shady street the morning we started work, it reminded me of my hometown, Indiana, Pennsylvania. I almost expected to hear the bells of the Presbyterian church, where Mother played the organ and Dad sang in the choir."

On May 20, 2008, Indiana celebrated their son's 100th birthday with a week of events entitled, "100 Years of America's Hometown Hero." These included a community church service, a historic walking tour, a picnic, live music, an Air Force flyover, and a formal dinner.

At the Jimmy Stewart Museum, visitors can see movie posters, photos, and other Stewart memorabilia. There are film clips of famous Jimmy Stewart movies, and every Saturday afternoon a full-length movie starring Stewart is screened in the intimate museum theater. A bronze statue of Indiana's favorite son, which Jimmy Stewart unveiled during his seventy-fifth birthday celebration in 1983, stands on the lawn of the Indiana County Courthouse at Eighth and Philadelphia Streets. Across the street a sundial marks the former location of J. M. Stewart and Sons Hardware, where his father, Alex, displayed his son's Academy Award statuette in the front window. One block west is a plaque on a stone placed on top of steps leading to a house that no longer stands. The plaque reads: "ON THIS SITE WAS THE BIRTHPLACE OF JAMES M. STEWART." It could just as easily have read, ON THIS SITE WAS THE BIRTHPLACE OF A WONDERFUL LIFE.

The Jimmy Stewart Museum is located on Indiana's main street, at 835 Philadelphia Street, on the third floor of the Indiana Free Library. It is open 10:00 a.m. to 5:00 p.m. Monday through Saturday, and noon to 5:00 p.m. Sunday. Tell 'em Clark sent you. Call (800) 83-JIMMY or (724) 349-6112 or visit www.jimmy.org.

★ ★

Floodtown, USA
Johnstown

The last survivor of the original Johnstown Flood died in 1997 at the age of 108. His name was Frank Shomo and he died in his sleep, just as certainly as he would have died as a sleeping infant more than a century earlier when the wall of water arrived at his house twenty miles downstream and a county away from Johnstown, Pennsylvania. His father saved him, and Frank Shomo never tired of telling the story he was too young to remember, but which would become the defining story of his life.

Talk about defining stories. Who among us can hear the name Johnstown without immediately adding the word *flood?* What Chicago is to *fire* and what San Francisco is to *earthquake,* Johnstown is to floods. Not once. Not twice. But three times. All during Frank Shomo's lifetime.

The original Johnstown Flood in 1889 killed twice as many people as the Chicago Fire of 1871 and the San Francisco Earthquake of 1906 *combined!* The official number of dead is listed at 2,209, placing it second in mortality among natural disasters in US history, behind the horrific hurricane in Galveston, Texas, in 1900 that claimed upward of 6,000 lives (Hurricane Katrina by comparison killed 1,833 people). At Johnstown ninety-nine entire families perished together, including 346 children. Because of that, the bodies of 750 of the dead were never identified. Bodies were later found as far away as Cincinnati. The cruel irony of the Johnstown tragedy was that nearly as many people died from fire as from water. After twenty-four hours of torrential rainfall, the dam broke on the earthen reservoir on the South Branch of the Conemaugh River. It happened a little after three o'clock in the afternoon on May 31, 1889. The dike collapsed and a wall of water seventy-five feet high and a half-mile wide swept through town, breaking gas mains as it carried away buildings, igniting floating debris trapped beneath bridges, creating an inferno atop the deluge.

★ ★

It was the biggest story in America since the Civil War. A newspaper reporter from New York wired back a story from Johnstown that began, "God stood on a mountaintop . . ." to which his editor wired back, "Forget flood. Interview God." In Philadelphia, soon-to-be internationally famous reporter Richard Harding Davis wrote dispatches from Johnstown describing the discovery of a prisoner found drowned in his locked cell in the local pokey. A catcher's mask lying in the mud, wrote Harding Davis, looked like it had been "hastily flung off to catch a foul ball." By the 1920s Johnstown was known for one thing only. In movie theaters around the country a message on the screen at intermission would read, "Don't Spit on the Floor—Remember the Johnstown Flood."

The infant Frank Shomo was a man in his late forties when the second great flood struck Johnstown on St. Patrick's Day in 1936, killing twenty-five. It had been a cold winter, piling up fourteen feet of snow that didn't begin to melt until a storm accompanied by fifty-degree weather struck in mid-March. The river swelled to seventeen feet above normal.

Then there was the bizarre event of July 20, 1977, when what was supposed to be a passing storm system hovered over Johnstown like a bad check waiting to be cashed. In nine hours the stalled storm dropped almost a foot of rain. Three dams broke. Eighty-five people died. Frank Shomo, then a mere eighty-seven, had to be physically evacuated, protesting all the while that he'd seen worse than this before.

Even as government disaster crews were rushing to Johnstown after the deadly 1977 flood, local entrepreneurs had put a smile on the face of catastrophe. Street-corner hucksters were selling souvenir T-shirts bearing the message "Floods–3, Johnstown–0."

The Johnstown Flood National Memorial is located at the base of what remains of the dam that burst that deadly day in 1889. For more information on the museum visit www.jaha.org/FloodMuseum/history.html.

Where the Heck Is Kecksburg?

Kecksburg

As the crow flies, the village of Kecksburg is located a mere fifty-seven miles southeast of Mars. So is it any wonder that a UFO landed in the woods near this Westmoreland County farm-country hamlet nearly five decades ago? Obviously a returning Martian aircraft lost its way home to Butler County and made an unscheduled stop before disappearing again. At least that's one theory that has not been advanced as an explanation for what happened over the skies of eastern Ohio and western Pennsylvania in the twilight hours of December 9, 1965. Thousands of people claimed to have seen a flaming object streaking southeastward over Pittsburgh. Witnesses said the object made three sudden and deliberate changes in direction before dropping beneath the tree line two miles north of the Pennsylvania Turnpike, where hundreds of late-afternoon motorists watched it descend. "Unidentified Flying Object Falls Near Kecksburg. Army Ropes Off Area," declared the front page of the *Tribune-Review,* the daily newspaper in nearby Greensburg, in the next day's edition. Later editions on December 10, 1965, reported, "Searchers Fail to Find Object." Witnesses reported seeing armed military troops and vehicles sweeping the wooded area where the object had fallen or landed. Volunteer firefighters from Kecksburg and other neighboring towns, responding to a report of an airplane crash, were blocked by state police from approaching the site. Curiosity seekers were waved away at gunpoint by soldiers and threatened with arrest. Before the authorities arrived, one witness, a machinist named Jim Romansky, got close enough to the crash and/or landing site to see a partially buried object. He described it as metallic, bronze-colored, and acorn-shaped, large enough for a man to stand inside. Romansky said the outside of the object appeared to be a single piece of metal without rivets or seams. On the bottom, around what would be the fat part of the acorn, he saw strange markings resembling Egyptian hieroglyphs. (Cue eerie music: Oooo-OOOO-Weeeee-Oooooo . . .)

Later that night another witness watching from the window of his house saw a military-drab-painted flatbed truck with no cargo drive toward the scene. The same truck drove back along the same road with *something* about the size of a Volkswagon Beetle in the cargo bed covered with a tarpaulin. The truck disappeared into the night and so did any official acknowledgment that something had fallen from the sky near Kecksburg. Despite the extraordinary number of eye witnesses (including news media) to a large military presence in the area, the only nonclassified record released by the US government of the events of December 9, 1965, was discovered years later in the files of the Air Force's Project Blue Book. After a report of the coordinates of the impact site of a skyborne object from a radar station in Oakdale, Pennsylvania, "a three-man team has been dispatched to Acme" (a nearby town used as the post office address for many in the Kecksburg area) "to investigate an object that started a fire." The search team found nothing, according to the file.

So what the heck happened in Kecksburg almost fifty years ago? And why have the unanswered questions and the government's refusal to declassify information from that period, during the height of the Cold War, continued to this day? It's not like the story has gone unnoticed all these years. Local talk radio and "UFO-ologists" have kept the story alive in public memory. In 1990 the Kecksburg Unidentified Flying Object Incident was featured on the syndicated TV show *Unsolved Mysteries,* complete with a fabricated prop depicting a seven-foot-tall acorn-shaped bronze object with strange writing around its base. That wire-and-plaster prop is currently on display on a twelve-foot-tall wooden tower behind the Kecksburg Volunteer Fire Company on Water Street just off Route 982. The only other permanent reminder that something strange happened in Kecksburg is a street sign identifying Township Route No. 493 leading toward the UFO landing site as Meteor Road. Of course, no meteor was ever discovered near there, either.

National interest in the Kecksburg incident was raised more recently when in October 2003 Bryant Gumbel hosted a two-hour special on

An acorn-shaped UFO "prop" used in the television show
Unsolved Mysteries sits atop a twelve-foot-high platform
outside the Kecksburg Volunteer Fire Company.

the Sci-Fi channel called *The New Roswell: Kecksburg Exposed*. The
special featured a town hall meeting with about fifty residents of the
community, some of whom witnessed the events described and others who think it's all a bunch of hooey. It is clear from the TV special,
and from the people I spoke to in Kecksburg two days after it aired,
that the community is still divided over the truth of what, if anything, occurred. "I was a teenager when that was supposed to have

happened," said a fifty-year-old resident, "and if something fell out of the sky, I would have known about it." As for the town meeting televised two nights earlier, he said, "I've lived here all my life and I didn't recognize half the people and half the names in that town meeting— and this is a small community. Everybody knows everybody."

Clearly, however, enough happened on December 9, 1965, that everyday citizens stand by their story and a growing list of sophisticated professionals have added their weight to petitions and lawsuits seeking declassification of government documents pertaining to the Kecksburg incident. President Clinton's former chief of staff, John Podesta, joined the Sci-Fi channel and others in Freedom of Information lawsuits seeking release of pertinent information from NASA, the Department of Defense, and the US Army and Air Force.

After more than four decades, the US government is finally acknowledging its failures to release information pertaining to what happened in the skies over Western Pennsylvania that night. In October 2007 a spokesman for NASA admitted that two boxes of documents from 1965 dealing with the Kecksburg incident were missing. In a ruling following a Freedom of Information lawsuit filed in 2003, federal judge Emmet Sullivan ordered NASA to go back and find the missing records and turn them over to the court. "NASA has been stonewalling and now it's required to do the search it didn't do in the first place," said New York journalist Leslie Kean, who filed the Freedom of Information lawsuit. "It's a victory for patriotic people who didn't like being told that they were making things up." The judge commented, "I can sense the plaintiff's frustration because I'm frustrated." But none of it made a difference. In 2009 the investigative journalist announced that that the government had failed to "find" anything in its files to illuminate the events of that night in December 1965 or afterward.

If the unidentified object was Soviet in origin, why would it still be classified? (Stan Gordon, a Greensburg investigator, verified with the Russian space agency that KOS 96, a failed Soviet probe of the planet

Venus, reentered the atmosphere over Canada the same day at 3:18 a.m., more than thirteen hours before the Kecksburg sighting.) If it was indeed extraterrestrial in origin, well, Pennsylvania's Roswell is as mysterious and intriguing as what happened in 1947 in what we in the Keystone State should start calling "New Mexico's Kecksburg." More recently, however, an older nemesis than the Soviet Union has drawn attention as the possible origin for the flaming skies over western Pennsylvania that night. When in doubt, blame Hitler. As recently as 2011 there have been reports on the Discovery Channel, the History Channel, and cable Science Channel suggesting a connection with between the Kecksburg mystery and Nazi experiments in what is called "Die Glocke" a time-traveling chamber known as the "Nazi bell" that allowed a high-ranking member of the Third Reich to escape capture at the end of World War II. The last Nazi sighting in Kecksburg was during a rerun of a *Seinfeld* episode. There was soup involved.

Wanna See the Glass-Lined Tanks of Old Latrobe?
Take Exit 14 off the NJ Twp
   Latrobe

Latrobe, Pennsylvania, a city of 8,900 residents on the western edge of the Allegheny Mountains, is famous for being the birthplace of Arnold Palmer (1929), the banana split (1904), and Rolling Rock beer (1939). Arnie's Army, the name given to the legions of fans who followed Palmer from hole to hole during his glory years on the PGA tour, had nothing on the loyalty shown over the decades by Rolling Rock enthusiasts who treated the brew as a Pennsylvania icon and the city of Latrobe as its shrine. Rolling Rock wasn't just another Tom, Dick, or Bud of a brew marketed by the giant national beer companies in St. Louis or Milwaukee. No, Rolling Rock was a triumph of mom-and-pop retailing and word-of-mouth marketing. During the famous wedding scene in the Academy Award–winning movie *The Deer Hunter,* Robert De Niro's character, Mike, urges Linda (Meryl Streep) to drink a Rolling Rock because "it's the best beer out there." Now *THAT'S* effective

All that remains of the old Rolling Rock Brewery
is the grimy ghost image of the Rolling Rock
label left after the sign was removed.

product placement. Rolling Rock was distinctive from other beers,
from the color of its bottle (green) to the nickname for its seven-ounce
bottle (pony) to the label on the bottle (painted on the glass rather
than printed on paper) to the mysterious "33" on the back of the
bottle (Thirty-three letters in the ingredients? Thirty-three words on

the label? The year 1933, in which Prohibition ended?), and most of all to the pledge etched on the back of the bottle and committed to memory by all loyal Rock drinkers: "Rolling Rock—From the glass-lined tanks of Old Latrobe, we tender this premium beer for your enjoyment as a tribute to your good taste. It comes from the mountain springs to you." Ah, Rolling Rock. It was like drinking from a waterfall.

And then, the unthinkable. In the year 2006 the Latrobe Brewing Company, this western Pennsylvania institution, this wholesome symbol of hometown pride and small-town fame, was sold to Anheuser-Busch. On July 31, 2006, the Latrobe brewery on the Loyalhanna Creek in a residential neighborhood on the north side of the railroad tracks was shut down. And the beer that made Pennsylvania famous was now brewed in the industrial meadowlands of North Jersey—in Newark, "For Crying Out Loud," New Jersey. Rolling Rock beer had become just another national brand name, its uniqueness trampled like a pony beneath the huge furry hooves of Clydesdales. And the mountain springwater promised on the label now came straight from the Passaic River. Since Anheuser-Busch can do anything it wants to, the Rolling Rock bottle looks exactly the same as it did when it was brewed in "Old Latrobe" and the "we tender this premium beer" pledge appears word for word on the back of the bottle with a remarkable prefix: "To honor the tradition of this great brand, we quote from the original pledge of quality."

When Molly and I visited Latrobe in the summer of 2007, the brewery was shuttered and all signs of the six-plus decades of Rolling Rock history were gone from the building except for a grimy ghost image of the horse on the Rolling Rock label created by the elements of wind and rain and dirt from a large sign once bolted to the side of the building. Today the old Rolling Rock brewery is the home of the Boston Beer Company, which makes Samuel Adams.

Penn State: Love Me Like a Rock

Rolling Rock has enjoyed astounding popularity among Pennsylvania college students over the years. Its legend was cemented among generations of Penn State students and alumni at the famous Rathskeller bar at the corner of Pugh Street and College Avenue in downtown State College, where for years the standard order for an individual was "a coupla Rocks" because they were the seven-ounce ponies rather than the twelve-ounce long-necked "horses."

In what may have been the first documented case of supersizing, in the fall of 1972 during a crowded Penn State home-game football weekend, a customer weary of continually returning to the bar to order "a coupla Rocks" asked if he could buy a case instead. Like Archimedes in his bathtub, Rathskeller owner Dean Smith uttered something that sounded like "Eureka!" And so began the Skeller tradition of selling twenty-four-bottle cases of Rolling Rock beer consumed on-site. Four pals chip in, six ponies per pal, no problem, no mess, and the empties end up back in the case on the table. Brilliant!

Supersizing led to stupendous sizing. In 1983 new owner John O'Connell decided to celebrate the Rathskeller's fiftieth birthday since the end of Prohibition in nineteen—that number again—thirty-three. The then-existing *Guinness Book of Records* world record for "most cases of beer sold by a bar in a single day" was two hundred cases by a thirsty tavern in Germany. On November 9, 1983, Skeller sudsers out-cased the German record holders by a mere 703 cases. By closing time the Penn State champions of the world had polished off 903 cases of Rock. Do the math. That's a case per customer on a day when 903 people stopped by to have a beer, or two, or twenty-four. "Case Day," as the annual event became known, peaked in 1996 when a decade-plus-long record 1,053 cases were sold in a single day. Sometimes too much of a good thing becomes, well, a thousand cases of beer consumed by college students in a single day. The Rathskeller, now called the All-American Rathskeller, no longer sells Rock by the case.

★ ★

A Town Called Mars
Mars

Life in Mars is pretty much the same as life in any other small town in western Pennsylvania. The only difference is that visitors passing through other towns aren't apt to greet locals with "Nanu nanu" or "Take me to your leader." Last fall (2012), the Fightin' Planets of the Mars Area High School football team finished a stellar 9-1 season, but native Martians took it in stride. According to Lester Kennedy, who wrote about life in Mars for the town's centennial booklet published in 1973, "Mars is situated 55 miles southwest of Venus (Pa.); 1,875 miles northeast of Mercury (Nev.), and 925 miles north of Jupiter (Fla.). It is approximately 35 million miles, at point of closest approach, from the planet Mars." More prosaically, Mars is eighteen miles north of Pittsburgh and twelve miles southwest of Butler. Except for its uncommon name, Mars is typical of thousands of small towns strewn across the length and breadth of America.

My wife Sara and I never would have discovered life in Mars if we hadn't been looking for a place to stay in or around Pittsburgh on the night before the Steelers were to play the Philadelphia Eagles at Heinz Field in October 2012. We searched and searched for any vacancies. We had no idea that an entire city, an entire western side of a state from Washington on the south to Beaver Falls and New Castle on the north could have all its hotels, motels, and no-tell rooms booked up because of a football game. Now we do and we advise you to plan accordingly if ever you decide to pop into Pittsburgh and spend the night on the day before a big game without making a reservation ahead of time. Our unplanned visit to Mars—where there was no room at the spaceport, either—in search of lodging turned out to be not even halfway to where we eventually found a vacancy in a Bates Motel equivalent off a lonely stretch of highway just outside Youngstown, Ohio—three counties and more than fifty miles away from downtown Pittsburgh. Sheesh!

Mars (population 1,713) is a borough not quite a half-mile square in the southern part of Butler County. Its claims to fame are its name

★ ★

Welcome to Mars, Pennsylvania, Home of the Fightin' Planets.

and an aluminum flying saucer modeled after Warner Brothers cartoon character Marvin the Martian's. The saucer usually sits in the town square on Grand Avenue, although it's small enough for teenage pranksters to move it around town from time to time. There's a blue Pennsylvania town marker in downtown Mars that is inaccurate on two counts. It says, MARS, named after the star of Mars. Founded 1876. Upon last sighting Mars was a planet, not a star, the fourth rock from the sun. And Mars dates its incorporation as a community to the opening of the Mars post office in 1873 in the home of one Samuel Parks. The origin of the name Mars is also disputed. The minority opinion is that Mrs. Parks was a student of astronomy and suggested the name. The majority opinion is that Mars was chosen to honor the political patron responsible for Mr. Parks's winning the post office contract, the Honorable Samuel Marshall. For a brief period in 1877, the town was on the verge of being named Overbrook, because of the opening of a B&O Railroad station bearing that name, but because there was already an Overbrook post office in Philadelphia (also named after a Pennsylvania Railroad train station), the name Mars stuck.

Today, Martians tend to live more comfortably with their alien identities than the citizens of, say, Roswell, New Mexico.

Step On Up to the "Church on the Turnpike"
New Baltimore

The Pennsylvania Turnpike has 512 miles, five tunnels, fifty-five interchanges, twenty-two service plazas, and one Catholic church. In fact, the Pennsylvania Turnpike may be the only limited-access toll road in the country that has steps leading from the shoulder of the highway up an embankment and into a church. You can see the steps on either side of the turnpike at mile marker 129 in New Baltimore between the Bedford and Somerset exits.

So what's up with that? The "Church on the Turnpike," as St. John the Baptist Catholic Church has become known to countless travelers over the years, was founded by German immigrants in 1824. The church building itself, which stands about one hundred yards off the south side of the turnpike, was built in 1890. It resembles a miniature European cathedral and was built by hand by artisans from the parish. In 1937 when the right-of-way for the Pennsylvania Turnpike was being surveyed, the route chosen for the new highway cut right through the cemetery of St. John's eighty-acre plot in Somerset County. A deal was struck between the Turnpike Commission and the Trustees of St. John's. The existing graves would be excavated and moved in exchange for access in perpetuity for travelers on the turnpike who wanted to stop at the church. Concrete steps with metal railings were built up the sides of the embankments on both east- and westbound lanes (the latter steps lead up to the Findley Street overpass).

The deal was struck in good faith and has never been rescinded. The church is frequently visited by travelers pulling over to the shoulder when they see the large lighted cross of St. John's beckoning from the side of the turnpike. The church's message sign with its schedule of masses is turned toward the highway, and according to St. John's pastor, Father Mark Begley, most "off-turnpike" Mass-goers prefer to attend the 6:00

What, No Galaxy, Pennsylvania?

There's an Atlas in Northumberland County, which is as good a place as any to start a tour of the world and the near solar system, courtesy of Pennsylvania towns with names like Moon, Mars, and Venus. A traveler crossing the state might scratch his or her head and check the road map: "I didn't know Dallas was in Pennsylvania. And Houston. And Austin. Not to mention Denver, Brooklyn, Milwaukee, Sacramento, Richmond, and Buffalo!"

There's a Frisco, Pennsylvania, but no San Francisco. There's a Bangor and a Salem and a Reno and a Knoxville, but they aren't followed by Maine, Massachusetts, Nevada, or Tennessee. Entire states have a Pennsylvania after their names. There's a California, a Virginia, an Idaho, an Iowa, an Indiana, and even an Oklahoma, which is appropriate because the most famous Oklahoman is buried in the Pennsylvania town that bears his name, Jim Thorpe. There's both a Yukon and an Alaska, Pennsylvania.

Americans of Irish descent can visit Dublin, Belfast, Ulster, Munster, Donegal, Sligo, Waterford, and Derry without ever leaving Pennsylvania. There's even an Irishtown and a Paddytown. German Americans will feel right at home in Germany, Berlin, East Berlin, Hamburg, Nuremburg, and not one but two Germantowns,

Saturday evening mass or the 10:30 Sunday morning mass. "I get a lot of people who come off the turnpike during the day looking for someone to hear their confession," said Father Begley. "They've been traveling and maybe they've done some things they wish they hadn't done, and they want to confess in a place where they're not known and they'll never be seen again."

a Germanville, and a Germania. Homesick Scots can go to either Glasgow or Scotland, with maybe a side trip to Brogue. Italians can tour Milan, Rome, Verona, and Florence, not to mention Little Italy neighborhoods in cities across the state. There's a Frenchville and a Paris too, and if Gallic pride can handle a visit, Pennsylvania also has its own Waterloo.

There's an English Center, Pennsylvania, as well as London, Oxford, Cambridge, Lancaster, York, and Nottingham. Pennsylvania has its Gibraltar and its Corsica and Malta too. There's a Poland and a Warsaw. There's a Moscow and a St. Petersburg. There's a Dalmatia and a Bohemia and a Macedonia and a Moravia. There's Athens and Sparta and even Troy. South of the border but still in the state are Mexico, Lima, and Santiago. To the north (but not that far north) are Finland, Sweden, Ottawa, Halifax, and Newfoundland, Pennsylvania.

The Middle East is well represented in this Middle Atlantic state. There's Egypt and Luxor and Jericho and Palestine and Hebron and Galilee and Bethlehem and Nazareth and Jewtown. There's Bagdad and Tripoli and Crete. Unlike their Middle Eastern namesakes, these communities aren't likely to go to war with each other. But if they did, they could always work out a peace agreement at Geneva, Pennsylvania.

They call St. John's Catholic Church in New Baltimore the "Church on the Turnpike" for good reason. Travelers on the Pennsylvania Turnpike can stop for Sunday services without taking an exit. There's parking and stairs leading to St. John's on both east- and westbound sides of the turnpike.

Truckers like the lighted cross outside St. John's because it is a land-mark midway between the Bedford and Somerset exits. A few years ago, the lights on the cross were broken, and Father Begley said that he received phone calls from passing truckers offering to help pay for new lights for their nighttime beacon. The parish paid for the new lights without the truckers' contributions.

In Search of Gravity Hill

New Paris

I was on the verge of summoning Leonard Nimoy to help me solve the mystery of Gravity Hill. The mystery wasn't what happens at Grav-ity Hill (water flows uphill, cars on a downhill slope roll backward) or even why that happens (scientifically speaking, there is no explanation, although optical illusion is the most cited reason), but rather *where* Gravity Hill is in Pennsylvania.

Gravity Hill was one of the first "curiosities" I was urged to find by callers to a Philadelphia radio talk show I was hosting. "It's some-where in Bucks County," I was told, "up near Yardley." Other callers disagreed. "No, it's near New Hope," said another. "No, it's definitely in Warrington." People knew exactly where it was but they couldn't tell me how to get there. I started calling police stations in the area, figuring that if there was a Gravity Hill in the neighborhood, the cops would know about it. Some did; some didn't. But it was always in the next town over.

I began asking people I'd meet in my travels around the state. "Yeah, there's one of them in Lancaster County," said Larry Homan, a chainsaw sculptor. "Water flows uphill. It's a road in the middle of a cornfield." I never gave up on finding Gravity Hill, wherever it was, but I was beginning to think it was a rural myth. Then, as luck would have it, I came across a brochure for the Bedford County Visitor Bureau touting "Gravity Hill, New Paris, Pa." When I told Dennis Tice, direc-tor of the Bedford County Visitor Bureau, how long I'd been looking for Gravity Hill in Bucks County, he deadpanned, "Yeah, we bought it from them and moved it up here." Directions to Gravity Hill are available on the Bedford County Visitor Bureau website (www.gravityhill .com), but be forewarned, it's not easy to find.

Molly and I were lucky: We found it pretty much on our first try. The directions say to take Route 30 (the Lincoln Highway) to Schellsburg in Bedford County. At the only traffic light in town, make the turn onto Route 96 north toward New Paris (formerly Mudtown) and travel for about four miles. You want to turn left onto Bethel Hollow Road (State Route 4016), which is just before a small bridge that is not a bridge so much as a roadway over a culvert. We had to make a U-turn here, once we realized that was the bridge. There's only one way to turn onto Beth Hollow Road, so turn there and follow it for 6/10 of a mile to a fork in the road, and bear left. Stay on this road for another mile and a half until you come to a stop sign. Bear right and travel several hundred yards until you see the letters *GH* spray-painted on the road. (You were expecting, maybe, a neon sign saying WELCOME TO GRAVITY HILL?) Proceed past the first *GH* about ¹⁄₁₀ of a mile and stop your car. Put it in neutral. And start screaming as you begin to roll up what looks like a downhill slope.

Molly and I found Gravity Hill at about three o'clock on a Thursday afternoon. There was already a minivan with a Virginia license plate, filled with children, stopped in the middle of the road, testing the phenomenon. It's a little creepy being there, actually, because you are in the middle of a rural road with no one nearby. When I got out of the car to take pictures, the Virginia van pulled away, perhaps out of nervousness. I gave Molly the video camera to record our experience, which ended up with both of us yelling at each other because she insisted on shooting in the opposite direction of what I wanted. At one point when we were videotaping the experience, a car pulled up from the other direction and slowed down next to us. I rolled down my window and told the woman driving that "this is the place." She smiled and said, "I know; I grew up around here. When we were teenagers we used to come up here to see if water really would flow uphill." She

★ ★

Is this uphill or downhill? Can you tell from the photo?

gave me a mischievous look and added in a whisper, "But we used to do it by peeing." "Eeeeewwwwwww," said Molly, after the lady drove away. Fortunately, we had come prepared with a bottle of Poland Spring water. Molly manned the camera as I poured the water, which on video is very clearly shown flowing in some direction. You will have to take our word for it that it was uphill.

There are actually two Gravity Hills a short distance from each other. The second one is marked by a telephone pole with the number

69 on it. To me, this Gravity Hill just a few hundred yards down the hill was more powerful than the first. I could actually feel it in my stomach. It felt like a rubber band wanting to pull me back from the direction I was going. Molly didn't feel the rubber band sensation in her stomach, but she was freaked out by how fast our car started rolling backward uphill in neutral on what looked like a downhill slope. "Ohmygod, ohmygod," she kept saying, as I added "Ohmygod, ohmygod," while trying to keep the car on the road as it raced backward. It was truly weird.

Gravity Hill is by no means unique to Pennsylvania. In fact, the phenomenon has become fairly well commercialized in other states. They go by different names: Spook Hill in Lake Wells, Florida; Mystery Spot in Santa Cruz, California; the Oregon Vortex in Gold Hill, Oregon; and Gravity Hill in Mooreville, Indiana, to name a few.

There Ain't No Zombies like Pittsburgh Zombies
Pittsburgh

Life as we knew it ended forty-five years ago in a hillside cemetery outside Evans City, Pennsylvania, where Pittsburgh commercial filmmaker George Romero shot the opening scenes to his classic low-budget horror thriller *Night of the Living Dead.* From the moment Johnny (Russell Streiner) teases his sister Barbra (Judith O'Dea), "They're coming to get you, Barbra. See, there's one of them coming now," while visiting the grave of their father, the reanimated bodies of the undead have been roaming Western Pennsylvania (and the rest of the world) in their insatiable hunger for living human flesh. Romero's 1968 zombie pic spawned more than a dozen sequels, prequels, rip-offs, remakes, and homage spoof comedies, such as 2004's *Shaun of the Dead,* where British slackers battle the undead with vinyl record albums and cricket bats, and *Night of the Living Bread,* an eight-minute short where mutant slices of white bread, muffins, and communion wafers come to life and attack people who ward them off with weapons of mass bread destruction like electric toasters. But zombies really became

✦ ★ ✦ ★ ✦ ★ ✦ ★ ✦ ★ ✦ ★ ✦ ★ ✦ ★ ✦ ★ ✦ ★ ✦ ★ ✦ ★ ✦ ★ ✦ ★ ✦

mainstream with the success of the cable TV series *The Walking Dead,* which takes place in Atlanta, which happens to be the home of the Center for Disease Control, which happened to issue guidelines in 2012 (just to get people's attention) of what to do in the case of a "zombie apocalypse." I think there was duct tape involved.

For his own part Romero, a New York native who attended Carnegie Mellon University in 1960, stayed true to his Pittsburgh filmmaking roots. He cast local actors in every role in the original black and white version most of us saw in drive-in movie theaters back in the day (you don't know what a drive-in is? Let me put it this way—pre-zombie, post popcorn). The first zombie seen in *Night of the Living Dead* is William Hinzman from the nearby Allegheny County borough of Coropolis (also birthplace of *Batman* actor Michael Keaton). Hinzman's long angular visage has become the gold standard of undead countenances and has served him well in a motion picture acting career in which he has played deceased flesh eaters as recently as the 2005 comedy classic, *The Drunken Dead Guy,* where Hinzman appears in the role of "the experienced zombie." In Romero's first well-received sequel, 1978's *Dawn of the Dead,* he returned to the Pittsburgh area— specifically the recently opened indoor mall in suburban Monroeville. (Spoiler Alert: This is why Seth Rogen was wearing a T-shirt that said "Monroeville Zombies" in the 2008 movie *Zack and Miri Make a Porno* about two wacky kids from Monroeville.) *Dawn of the Dead* starts in a TV station in the city of Philadelphia, then under siege by long dead but still-voting residents of South Philly, later ending on the roof of a zombie-infested mall off Route 22 just east of Pittsburgh.

Day of the Dead, Romero's 1985 sequel, was filmed in the Lawrence County borough of Wampum, Pennsylvania, and his third-quel, *Land of the Dead,* brings it all back home to Pennsylvania, even though it was filmed in Toronto. In this version, Pittsburgh is the last city on earth and not a bad city at that, considering, you know, that they're surrounded by zombies. Romero tells a story of Pittsburgh as a triangular island with rivers on two sides for protection and a

★ ★

zombie-zapping electrical fence guarding the land access from the east. Essentially this was the same geographic advantage that caused the French and English to go to war over Fort Duquesne/Fort Pitt. Downtown Pittsburgh was a well-defendable point of land. Unfortunately, the postapocalyptic leaders of humanity's last viable outpost were no more enlightened than Pennsylvania politicians have been since the days of robber baron industrialists.

Land of the Dead ends with the zombies taking over Pittsburgh and eating the fat cats in Fiddler's Green. And the unlikely hero, or at least the living dead-man-walking with the most dignity, is a zombie in a gas station mechanic's overalls named Big Daddy. In life Big Daddy is actor Eugene Clark, and he was a college football player drafted by the Pittsburgh Steelers, until the siren call of Hollywood cast him into zombiehood.

I won't give away the ending, but I'll tell you it involves the Monongahela River on the south and the Allegheny River on the north.

The Three Rivers Ferry
Pittsburgh

Thousands of people in Pittsburgh take a boat to get to Steelers football games. It's the best way to beat the traffic on game day. For five dollars you can get a round-trip ticket on the ferry-size water taxis that shuttle back and forth across the Monongahela River from South Side to the stadium complex on the north side of the Allegheny River opposite downtown Pittsburgh.

During research for the first edition of *Pennsylvania Curiosities* I took the football ferry packed with Steelers fans to one of the last home games to be played at Three Rivers Stadium in 2000. It was a rainy Sunday in October and the opposition, the then-winless Cincinnati Bengals, was as dreary as the weather. But the fans were upbeat, even the Bengals fans, one of whom carried a sign that said, I'LL GO ANYWHERE FOR THE BENGALS' FIRST WIN. Three Rivers Stadium was

The mighty Pittsburgh native and Pirate shortstop Honus Wagner's statue is among the great Pirates players honored with statues outside PNC Park.

★ ★

flanked by the construction sites of the two new stadiums being built to accommodate the Steelers and the Pirates. On the ferry ride across the river, I asked a fan what the new Pirates stadium would be called. "They're going to call it PNC Park," he said. "That's because they have windows in the men's rooms." It took me a minute, but I got it. But in 2012 I found that concept to be a reality nearby. Former Steelers running back Jerome Bettis opened a sports bar across the street from both the outdoor sports stadiums (stadia?), Heinz Field and PNC Park, on the north side of the Allegheny River. At the Jerome Bettis "36" Grille there are windows (one-way mirrors, actually) over the urinals in the men's room so you can keep your eye on the action. I suppose putting a TV in the men's room could have served the same purpose, but, hey.

Three Rivers was a saucer-shaped concrete bowl of the same age, style, and fate of Veterans Stadium in Philadelphia. Each city has replaced its single multipurpose stadium with separate baseball and football stadium a short distance from each other. The Steelers' new home, Heinz Field, opened on October 7, 2001, with the Steelers' home opener against, who else, the Cincinnati Bengals. Pittsburgh's Three Rivers area has always been associated with the city's professional sports. Two Pennsylvania historical markers were placed outside Three Rivers Stadium to commemorate America's first professional football game and the first World Series.

The first professional football game was played on November 12, 1892, in nearby Recreation Park between the Allegheny Athletic Association and the Pittsburgh Athletic Association. Allegheny won, with the winning touchdown being scored by William "Pudge" Heffelfinger, who was paid five hundred dollars to play. He was the first football player ever to be paid outright, and professional football dates its origin to that game. The first World Series was played at Exposition Park, on the site of Three Rivers Stadium, in October 1903 between the National League Pittsburgh Pirates and the American League champion Boston Pilgrims (later to be called the Red Sox). Games four through seven of the best-of-nine-game series were played on the site, featuring Hall of Famers Honus Wagner for Pittsburgh and Cy Young for Boston. The Pilgrims won the first World Series five games to three.

Finding Pittsburgh's Vatican
Pittsburgh

You can't get to Troy Hill by accident. You have to know where you're going or else you won't find it. And you get the feeling that the residents of this hillside Pittsburgh neighborhood overlooking the Allegheny River and the Strip District like it that way. It took Molly and me at least three tries to find Troy Hill, even though it is hiding in plain sight—much like St. Anthony's Chapel at 1704 Harpster Street, where there are more first class relics of Catholic saints than anywhere in the world outside of the Vatican. A first class relic is a bone fragment from the remains of a person elevated to sainthood. And there are thousands of saintly bones on display in ornate reliquaries at St. Anthony's Chapel, which is only slightly harder to find that Troy Hill itself.

This century-old chapel is only open to the public from 1:00 until 4:00 p.m. on Tuesday, Thursday, Saturday, and Sunday. Molly and I arrived at one o'clock on the last Thursday in June only to be informed that Sister Margaret, the nun who gives the guided tour of St. Anthony's Chapel, was on a trip home to Ireland. Talk about timing. We were allowed to explore the hushed chapel by ourselves among a handful of worshipers saying the rosary or kneeling in private prayer. It is a gorgeous church, reminiscent of a vastly larger European cathedral tucked away on a small street in a north-side Pittsburgh residential neighborhood. Here stacked almost floor to ceiling behind the main altar are physical remains of more than four thousand saints placed inside reliquaries, which are boxes that resemble cathedrals themselves. The side aisles of the chapel are lined with large niches containing life-sized hand-carved wooden figures depicting the fourteen Stations of the Cross (and guarded by an alarm system).

Please do not touch.

   How this remarkable sanctuary of saintly remains came to Troy Hill
is the story of one priest and one parish. But mostly one priest. Father
Suitbert G. Mollinger, a Belgian priest from a wealthy family, became
pastor of the Most Holy Name of Jesus Parish in 1875. The parish rec-
tory adjoins the chapel and Holy Name of Jesus Church is across the
street. In the 1880s during a time of much political and cultural unrest

★ ★

in Germany and Italy, Father Mollinger made several trips to Europe and acquired thousands of relics from Catholic churches, hundreds of which included original certificates of authentication dating back to 1714. From a twenty-first century perspective, some of the holy relics gathered by Father Mollinger require a leap of faith. For instance there is one reliquary shaped like a monstrance (an ornate vessel used to display the Blessed Sacrament or communion wafer), which is said to contain a sliver of wood from the True Cross (on which Christ was crucified) as well as relics from Saint John the Baptist, Mary Magdalene, Saint Lawrence, Saint Dionysius, Saint Blase, Saint Stephen (the first martyr), Saint Anthony of Padua (for whom the chapel is named), and a shred of the Sacred Winding Sheet (sometimes called the Sacred Shroud of Turin). Other relics include a sliver from the table at the Last Supper and a piece of the veil worn by Mary, mother of Jesus. A pretty impressive collection even for nonbelievers to behold.

When parishioners of the Most Holy Name of Jesus failed to raise money to build a separate chapel for the relics, Father Mollinger financed the construction himself with his inheritance from his wealthy family in Belgium. The enlarged chapel was dedicated in 1892, the same year Father Mollinger died. In his later years the priest became famous as a healer himself, and on display in the chapel were the crutches of hundreds of the faithful who claimed to have been cured by Father Mollinger's hands (some of those crutches can be seen at the St. Anthony Chapel Gift Shop across the street). Upon his death, and because he left no will, Mollinger's family members descended on the chapel and virtually looted it of anything that could be carried away—crystal chandeliers, candelabras, and a black onyx altar among them. Subsequently the chapel and what remained of its contents were sold to the Most Holy Name of Jesus Parish for thirty thousand dollars. St. Anthony's Chapel is only opened to the public twelve hours a week, so perhaps it's best to call first (412-323-9504), if only to make sure Sister Margaret isn't off gallivanting in Ireland.

Oh, that Kind of Strip, Stoopid!

Pittsburgh's "Strip District" isn't what it sounds like. I remember on a visit to Pittsburgh when I was researching the first edition of *Pennsylvania Curiosities*, I asked locals where the nightlife area was. I was told Carson Street on the Southside (of the Monongahela River) and "the Strip District." I made some Philadelphia assumptions, I'm afraid. Years ago there was an area called "the strip" along Locust Street in Center City Philadelphia where a man could find female companionship for an agreed upon price. And there were no shortage of nightclubs and bars featuring

The Leaf and Bean coffee shop and cigar store is the funkiest, friendliest place to hang out in the Strip District. Hippies must use the back door.

athletic women exercising on vertical poles that seemed to cause their clothing to fall off one garment at a time.

I didn't quiz my Pittsburgh informants about the exact nature of the "Strip District" because, well, I'm not that kind of guy. And besides, I was traveling with my daughter Molly. But my east-state presumptions about what "Strip District" means were proven ridiculous and false during a visit to Pittsburgh while researching the third edition of *Pennsylvania Curiosities* in 2008. And wouldn't you know, it was Molly who made the discovery.

Molly, who was in fifth grade the first time she accompanied me on my Pennsylvania explorations, was now a high school graduate when we wandered into the Strip District on our way to Troy Hill. "Let's get some coffee," she suggested, so I turned left off Liberty at 22nd. In front of us was a funky open-garage door of a coffee shop and cigar store called the Leaf and Bean. (Is this heaven? No, it's Pittsburgh!)

If the Big Lebowski was a real person and a Yinzer, he would abide in the Leaf and Bean. It is laid back, it is powerfully positive, and it doesn't take itself too seriously. Among the many handwritten announcements scribbled on the white paint on the sides of the front doors are, "Restrooms are for the well behaved." And "Be nice or be gone." There's a printed sign in the window over the doors that says, HIPPIES USE BACK DOOR NO EXCEPTIONS (with a big arrow pointing to the right). I walked around to the right. There is no back door. Molly declared it to be the best cup of coffee she ever had.

That's when I discovered The Strip, which gets its name from the narrow strip of flat land it occupies on the southeast side of the Allegheny River and Grant's Hill. The Strip is located above Downtown on Penn Avenue, from Eleventh to Thirty-third. But most of the action is concentrated between, say, Fourteenth and Twenty-second. It's the kind of street that invents itself every day, from the established businesses to the street vendors hawking vegetables, T-shirts, and jewelry. It reminds me—to make another Philadelphia comparison—of what would happen if hip and happening South Street merged with the old world, open-air Ninth Street Italian Market.

Continued on page 159

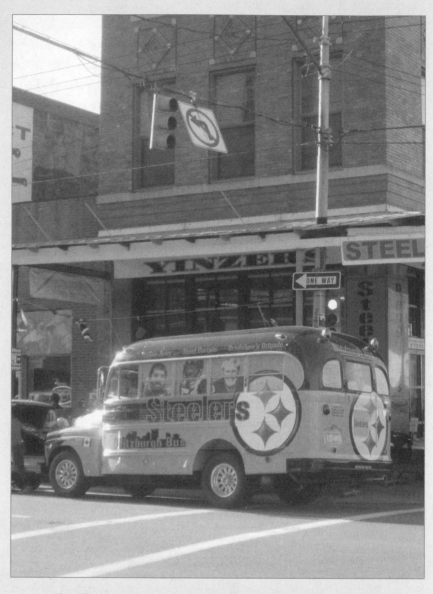

The Blitzburgh Bus parked in front of Yinzers on Penn Street in the Strip District is painted yellow and black, the same colors worn by players on all of Pittsburgh's professional sports teams.

Continued from page 157

My second visit to The Strip started at the Leaf and Bean again, on an even better day. A glorious Saturday afternoon in October, which happened to be the day before my Philadelphia Eagles were to play the Pittsburgh Steelers at Heinz Field. This time my traveling companion was my wife (imagine that!) and we settled in for a cup-pa-joe at the coolest little seegar-smokin', live music, open garage door corner in Pittsburgh.

On the corner of Twenty-second and Penn Avenue a half block away, a shiny gold and black bus with big block letters spelling STEELERS on the side and BLITZBURGH BUS beneath that was parked in front of a store selling Pittsburgh professional sports teams' athletic gear. The name of the store was Yinzers (which, if it were in Philadelphia selling home team gear, would be called Youse Guys) but in Pittsburgh fans have fewer color choices to confuse them among their preferred sport loyalties. All the pro sports teams in Pittsburgh—Steelers, Pirates, and Penguins—wear the same colors. Black and gold. The bridges are painted the same colors, for crying out loud. (And there are a million bridges or tunnels in and around Pennsylvania's second city. . . . Well, maybe not a million. But at least fifty-seven.)

Black and gold, gold and black goes with anything. Pittsburgh looks good in those colors. That must be why I counted at least five other stores along the strip selling Steelers gear in your face at the door. It was like pumpkins at Halloween. And these were stores, not tent vendors. Throw street vendors in and there were at least eight businesses actively pushing T-shirts, jerseys, caps, and stuff involving one team in a five-block strip. How does that oversaturation work unless there are a zillion Steelers fans? Evidently there are. In 2011 *USA Today* reported that the Steelers ranked No. 1 in sales of NFL team-related gear. The most popular individual player jersey by sales is Steelers safety Troy Polamalu.

Primanti Bros.: Home of the Pittsburgh Sandwich

The birth of the Pittsburgh sandwich mirrors the creation of the Philadelphia cheesesteak. Both were invented in the same year, 1933, during the Great Depression. Both were created by brothers running sandwich shops that catered to late night/early morning truckers making pickups or deliveries of meat and produce in busy food market areas—the Olivieri Brothers along the Ninth Street Italian Market in South Philadelphia and the Primanti Brothers on Eighteenth Street in Pittsburgh's Strip District. Both are located similar distances from Downtown Pittsburgh and Center City Philadelphia respectively. And both of them were open 24/7, making them meccas for hungry revelers in the wee hours after the 2:00 a.m. closing time of bars across Pennsylvania. Both still attract long lines of customers at three in the morning.

Like the Philadelphia cheesesteak, the Pittsburgh sandwich was invented by accident (or was it necessity?). You can read more about the cheesesteak elsewhere (see pages 84–85) but the story told about the invention of the Pittsburgh sandwich is that brother Joe Primanti was the first to serve a sandwich featuring grilled meat, coleslaw, sliced tomato, and french fries all slopped together between two slices of Italian bread and served wrapped in waxy deli paper without a plate or utensils. This was a no-nonsense *man's sangwich* that could be eaten with one hand by busy truckers while driving to the next pickup or delivery.

Eighty years after the creation of the first Pittsburgh sandwich, the original Primanti Bros. restaurant has been joined by sixteen others in the Pittsburgh area and three more Primanti Bros. in Florida. I must admit I felt like a timid newbie looking at the menu and

	$6.29
	$5.49
PITTS-BURGER" CHEESE STEAK (#2 BEST-SELLER)	$5.49
DELUXE DOUBLE EGG & CHEESE	$5.99
CHEESE COMBO (swiss, american & provolone)	$6.29
JUMBO BALONEY AND CHEESE	$6.39
HOT or SWEET SAUSAGE & CHEESE "made fresh daily"	$6.49
GENOA SALAMI & CHEESE	$6.49
HAM & CHEESE	
CAPICOLA & CHEESE	
KIELBASA & CHEESE	$6.39
BACON & CHEESE	$6.39
TUNA FISH & CHEESE	$6.39
Imported SARDINE & CHEESE	
TURKEY BREAST & CHEESE	$6.39
HAM OR BACON, EGG & CHEESE	$6.69
ROAST BEEF & CHEESE	$6.69
KNOCKWURST & CHEESE	$6.69
PASTRAMI & CHEESE	$6.39
CORNED BEEF & CHEESE	

"Almost Famous" HOT CHILI, BREAD
"Delicious" VEGETABLE SOUP, BREA
"Fresh" PRIMANTI FRIES, side order
CHEESE FRIES
CHILI FRIES
SMALLMAN ST. FRIES, chili, cheese, b
Whole KOSHER DILL PICKLE
COLE SLAW, "sweet & sour"
Italian BREAD & BUTTER
LARGE POP
BOTTLED WATER
FRUIT JUICES
ICED TEA

There's nothing fancy about the original Primanti Brothers sandwich shop. No plates, no glasses, no knives and forks. Every sandwich is served on paper.

wondering about the correct way to order a Pittsburgh sandwich at 9:30 a.m. on a Sunday morning at the original Primanti's on the Strip. At Pat's Steaks in Philadelphia, if you mess up or choke when giving your order, you can get sent to the end of the line. It's like something out of a *Seinfeld* episode, except they're cheesesteak Nazis. And I had been told that Primanti's servers have a similar reputation for . . . let's call it "gruff efficiency."

As I looked over the menu on the wall (where a large pop, what we call a large soda east of the Alleghenies, costs the same as a bottled water, $1.79), I didn't want to order the Pittsburgh equivalent

of an Egg McMuffin from the breakfast menu. I wanted that manly Pittsburgh sangwich no matter what time of day it was. I told the woman taking our order behind the stainless steel counter, "I'm looking for that sandwich that has the french fries and . . ." Before I could finish she said, "All of them." I looked at the menu again. Sardine and cheese? Pastrami and cheese? Jumbo "baloney" and cheese? Tuna fish and cheese? Kielbasa and cheese? "All of them come with. . ." I began to ask. "All of them," she answered with that token gruff efficiency.

So I ordered the "Pitts-Burger (with a circled TM after it) Cheese Steak," which the menu advised was the "#2 Best Seller." Hmmm, sounds a bit derivative, I thought. My wife ordered a nice bacon, egg, and cheese breakfast sandwich. Our orders soon arrived, wrapped in white deli paper. Still no plates or utensils. Nothing to wash. Same as it ever was. Napkins came from a typical upright shiny metal diner napkin dispenser. Walls, tables, chairs, and floor—everything could be washed with a high pressure hose, and possibly is.

Every Pittsburgh sandwich served at Primanti Brothers comes with the works—french fries, sliced tomato, and vinegary coleslaw—whether you want it or not.

The Pittsburgh sandwich was plenty manly. The half-inch-thick slices of Italian bread were fresh and soft with a crunchy crust, the handful of french fries inside stuck out from every angle; the meat was more burger than beefsteak; there may have been cheese but

I couldn't taste it. In fact, the dominant flavor of the sandwich was from the coleslaw, which was vinegary, almost like sauerkraut. I was expecting a sweeter, white creamy mayonnaise-based coleslaw. The Primanti coleslaw is described as being "Italian dressing–based," which I now know means "vinegary." It was an unpleasant surprise, like tasting salt when you expected sugar. If it's an acquired taste, I didn't acquire it the first time.

Meanwhile, Sara had discovered that when the lady behind the counter said, "All of them," she meant it. My wife had ordered bacon, egg, and cheese on bread without the works. But when it arrived her sandwich was as thick as mine and stuffed with

The number two best selling Pittsburgh Sandwich at Primanti Brothers is a "cheesesteak." Hmmmm.

the same signature toppings of french fries and coleslaw. Neither of us finished our first Pittsburgh sandwich. Maybe it was too early in the morning. Or maybe it was like Mexican food, a taste most people love that I've never discovered.

★ ★

An Unlikely Pittsburgh Native

Pittsburgh

Pop artist Andy Warhol's celebrated fifteen minutes of fame take up an entire seven floors of an industrial building in downtown Pittsburgh just a few blocks away from the house where he grew up. It's hard to say which is more unlikely, that a character like Warhol is a product of Pittsburgh, or that a city like Pittsburgh would be home to the Andy Warhol Museum if he weren't a hometown boy. The facts are that Warhol lived in Pittsburgh until leaving for New York to continue the art career he had begun while studying painting and design at the Carnegie Institute of Technology.

The "unlikely" Andy Warhol Museum in Pittsburgh.

★ ★

Andy Warhol was an odd chap, to say the least, and his oddness and his talent are on display at a museum devoted to his work on Sandusky Street not far from Pittsburgh's new stadiums. He was a mama's boy, Warhol was, and his mother joined him in New York following his father's death three years after he left Pittsburgh in 1949. Julia Warhola and her husband, Andrej, had immigrated to Pittsburgh from the Carpathian Mountain area of what is now Slovakia. Among the personal items on display in the Andy Warhol Museum are postcards the son sent his mother from his travels around the world. "Hi, Im alright im in Rome now its real nice here. Bye," he wrote in 1956. Other postcards with virtually the same unemotional and ungrammatical message were sent to his mother from other countries.

The answer to that is found in the five hundred works of art that are on display, making the Andy Warhol Museum the most comprehensive lone-artist museum in the country. The pop art Campbell's soup can paintings are there, as well as the stylized portraits of Marilyn Monroe, Elvis, and Natalie Wood. The story of Warhol's life in the New York art and music and movie-making and magazine-publishing scene is told in various exhibits on different floors. His talent is undeniable.

The Andy Warhol Museum, at 117 Sandusky Street, is open Tuesday through Sunday. Call (412) 237-8300, or visit www.warhol.org.

Mister Rogers: Children's Icon or "Mud Monster"?
Pittsburgh

The real Mister Rogers' Neighborhood was in the Oakland section of Pittsburgh where the iconic children's TV host and creator produced his daily show aired nationally on PBS from the Oakland studios of WQED, Pittsburgh's public television station, from 1968 until 2001. He was born Fred McFeely Rogers (yep, that's where Mr. McFeely, the mailman and frequent visitor to Mr. Rogers' TV home, got his name—from Rogers maternal grandfather, Fred McFeely) in Latrobe, Pennsylvania, in 1928.

By the time of his death in 2003 at age seventy-four, Rogers had entertained and educated three generations of children and parents

Hardly a "mud monster," but many in Pittsburgh find the statue in honor of children's TV show *Mr. Rogers Neighborhood* creator Fred Rogers to be less than cuddly.

with his soothing voice and gentle humor. His signature opening never changed. The show began with Mr. Rogers walking in the front door of his house and singing the song "It's a Beautiful Day in the Neighborhood" as he hung up his coat, donned a cardigan sweater, and then took off his shoes before slipping on a pair of sneakers. The daily ritual always ended with the words, "Please won't you be my neighbor."

And it is that familiar television moment that is celebrated in the Fred Rogers Memorial Statue on the North Shore near the stadium complex hosting both stadiums for the football Steelers and baseball Pirates. As gentle as Fred Rogers' legacy is, the statue has come under withering criticism since its unveiling ceremony in November 2009, during which a speaker described the eleven-foot-tall bronze statue of a seated Mr. Rogers tying his sneakers as "daring, difficult, and just dazzling."

To many Pittsburghers the $3 million statue by sculptor Robert Berks is called "lumpy Mr. Rogers." After the statue debuted, comedian Jimmy Kimmel panned it on his network TV show, saying the memorial sculpture "made the nicest man in the world look like a mud monster." In more measured criticism, the head of the nearby Warhol Museum said, "More than anything else, it doesn't look beckoning and warm. The statue doesn't resemble him at all." It certainly didn't look beckoning and warm on the cold and cloudy day I photographed it. Not quite a mud monster, but I wouldn't want to live in its neighborhood.

The Black Babe Ruth
Pittsburgh

If Josh Gibson had been the same race as Babe Ruth, Forbes Field in Pittsburgh might have been called "The House That Gibson Built." But Josh Gibson was a black man playing baseball in the 1930s, the same era as the Babe, which meant that he couldn't play on the same team with white major leaguers. Instead, he played his entire baseball career for two of the greatest teams in Negro League history, the Pittsburgh Crawfords and the Homestead Grays.

Continued on page 171

167

Steely McBeam Meet Joe Magarac

When the Pittsburgh Steelers decided to create a costumed mascot for the team's seventy-fifth anniversary year, which happened to follow a Super Bowl Championship season in 2006, more than seventy thousand names were entered in a name-the-new-mascot contest. The winning name selected, Steely McBeam, fits the costumed mascot character—a rugged, square-jawed, hard-hatted steel worker dressed in black overalls and a yellow flannel shirt—like a pair of work gloves. What a great name, Steely McBeam.

There's a certain honest directness in holding a contest to invent a name for an imaginary character that is supposed to represent the values of a city and its working people. No one in Pittsburgh would call Steely McBeam anything other than a marketing tool, but the more I read about the origin of the mythical steelworker Joe Magarac, the more I suspect the greasy hand of manipulation by big business rather than the authentic and spontaneous result of tall tales told by Slavic immigrants who found work in steel mills along the Monongahela River.

Joe Magarac (pronounced *mah-gah-rats*), which means *donkey* or *jackass* in Croatian, was supposed to be to Pittsburgh steelworkers what Paul Bunyan was to North Woods lumberjacks, what Pecos Bill was to cowboys, or what John Henry was to steel-driving railroad men. He was a mythic hero who liked nothing better than to work in steel mills twenty-four hours a day, seven days a week, where he happily did the work of twenty-nine men. (Why twenty-nine men? Why not a hundred?) Joe was either a giant seven feet tall or a GIANT "as tall as a smokestack." He could cup a cauldron full of molten metal in his bare hands and squeeze out perfectly formed steel rails. He not only made steel, he was made of steel. Although he was born in Pittsburgh, he was also born inside a mountain in Minnesota's Mesabi iron range.

This fifteen-foot-tall statue of folklore (fakelore?) steel worker Joe Magarac stood for years inside a nearby amusement park. Now it stands it at the front gates of a steel plant in North Braddock.

The first published reference to Joe Magarac, man of steel, appeared in *Scribner's Magazine* in November 1931, seven years before the first *Superman* comic book. The author of the story headlined "The Saga of Joe Magarac: Steelman" was Owen Francis, who claimed to be a former steel worker who had heard stories about

the mythical giant from Slavic immigrants working the furnaces around Pittsburgh. In those stories Joe Magarac frequently saved steelworkers' lives with tremendous feats of strength and selfless bravery. Despite working 24/7 making steel, he would somehow wander past weight-lifting contests by steelworkers, where nobody recognized him (despite his being somewhere between seven feet and a smokestack tall) and would easily best some blowhard from Johnstown who had claimed he was so strong that he could pick himself up by his own belt and hold himself out at arm's length with one hand.

As the story went, mighty Joe Magarac died by his own hand. He hurled himself into a ladle of molten metal in order to make the steel stronger. Some believe that he is alive and waiting to come back once a closed steel mill opens again. What a depressing, nihilistic, and inhuman story that is! Object lesson? Work hard, die young, leave nothing behind. Oh, and most of all, be happy while doing it. The lesson of a fool.

Despite folklore researchers' attempts to verify the story, they could find no evidence of an oral tradition by Slavic immigrant steelworkers of telling Joe Magarac tall tales. They'd never heard of the guy. This did not stop the fakelore of Joe Magarac from being promoted by monied interests such as US Steel. Over the decades there have been dozens of statues, murals (such as the epic one at Carnegie Library), paintings, and other public representations commissioned of Joe Magarac as a heroic symbol of the selfless steel-making man. For years, one of those monuments, a fifteen-foot-tall statue of Joe Magarac bending steel above his head, was an attraction at Kennywood Park, the popular amusement park on the south side of the Monongahela River in West Mifflin.

In 2009 the statue was donated to US Steel. It now stands behind the gates of the Edgar Thomson Steel Works along a sad and barren stretch of the main thoroughfare through the once-bustling town of North Braddock located just a few miles downriver from Pittsburgh's gorgeous Golden Triangle. Say it ain't so, Joe.

Continued from page 167

Homestead is a steel town just a few miles downriver from Pittsburgh; the Negro League Grays played their home games at Forbes Field in Pittsburgh when the Pirates were out of town. The Grays signed a strapping eighteen-year-old from the North Side named Josh Gibson in July 1930. In that year's Negro League World Series between the Grays and the New York Lincoln Yankees, Gibson hit a home run over the 457-foot wall in left center field at Forbes Field, a feat that would not be repeated until thirty years later, when Mickey Mantle did it during the 1960 World Series. The following week the Negro League World Series shifted to New York, and Gibson became the only player ever to hit a ball out of Yankee Stadium—a shot measured at an impossible 600 feet.

Catcher Josh Gibson was nicknamed the Black Bomber during a sixteen-year career in which he hit 800 home runs while batting over .300. When Gibson jumped over to the rival Pittsburgh Crawfords in 1932, he joined a team with five future Hall of Famers all playing at the same time, something not even the 1927 Yankees can claim. Besides Gibson, future Hall of Famers playing for the Crawfords included his battery mate Satchel Paige, Oscar Charleston, Judy Johnson, and "Cool Papa" Bell.

Gibson returned to the Grays in 1936 and finished his career in 1946, winning the Negro League batting title for the ninth time in his final year. The following year, Josh Gibson had a stroke caused by a brain tumor and died in his Strauss Street home on Pittsburgh's North Side. When Boston Red Sox slugger Ted Williams was inducted into the Baseball Hall of Fame in 1966, he said, "I hope that some day Satchel Paige and Josh Gibson will be voted into the Hall of Fame as symbols of the great Negro players who are not here only because they weren't given a chance." That day came in 1972. Josh Gibson was inducted into Major League Baseball's Hall of Fame despite never having played for a National or American League team.

Today in Pittsburgh, Josh Gibson's career is marked with a Pennsylvania historical marker at 2217 Bedford Avenue, where his baseball career started at Ammons Field.

★ ★

A View with a Pew
Pittsburgh

Pittsburgh is the only city in America where a visitor standing on the sidewalk admiring the skyscrapers can get a stiff neck from looking down. That's because the best view of the spectacular Pittsburgh skyline is from aptly named Grandview Avenue in Mount Washington,

Dominick and Eugene Meet Birdy

Two of my favorite movies of all time are set and shot in Philadelphia and Pittsburgh. The Philadelphia movie is *Birdy*. The Pittsburgh movie is *Dominick and Eugene*. They are enough to do a state proud.

I live in West Philadelphia, not far from where they filmed the opening sandlot baseball scenes in *Birdy*, which is a movie about unlikely friends who become brothers. I recognize by intuition the hilly Pittsburgh neighborhood streets traveled by the trash truck in *Dominick and Eugene*, which is about unlikely brothers who become friends and more.

Birdy stars Matthew Modine as the title character who raises pigeons and wants to fly like a bird, and Nicolas Cage as his friend Al, who raises girls' heartbeats and wants to know what Birdy knows about life and aerodynamics that he doesn't. It's hilarious and sad and wonderful and more Philadelphia than most movies ever touch. They've even got the William Penn statue joke in there. "Hey, Birdy, remember when we'd get those old ladies to look up at City Hall tower?" asks Al as the camera shows the Founding Father in all his unintentional randiness (see pages 71–74). Birdy and Al go off to war

the hilltop neighborhood directly across the Monongahela River from downtown Pittsburgh and the famous Golden Triangle. Even on a cloudy day, the view is impressive; but on a sunny day or a clear night, the view of the sparkling river city hundreds of feet below is breathtaking. So impressive is the vista that in May 2003 *USA Weekend* magazine ranked the "Nighttime view from Mt. Washington, Pittsburgh"

(in the movie it's Vietnam, in the book it's World War II, in reality it doesn't matter), where Al loses half his face and Birdy loses half his mind, the remaining half being that of a bird. His better half.

Dominick and Eugene stars Tom Hulce and Ray Liotta as the title characters, the former being a beloved but obviously brain-injured municipal trash-truck loader, the latter being his brilliant and loving but obviously stressed-out medical student twin brother. Jamie Lee Curtis is thrown in as a love interest, but it's really a story about brothers coming to grips with losing each other's company after all these years. One shiver-me-timbers moment of dialogue comes after Dominick's dog has been killed by a car. The trusting and innocent and inconsolable Dominick is praying before the altar of his parish church. After he rises from his knees to leave, a well-meaning parish priest tries to console him with hollow words about a doggie heaven. The now furious Pittsburgh trash man turns tail and stalks halfway up the aisle. Then he turns, glaring first at the priest and then at the crucified figure of Christ above the altar. "If I was God," he says, "I wouldn't let that happen to my boy."

I don't want to give away the ending to either movie (they're on DVD, people!), but I will tell you the final word of dialogue in *Birdy*: "What?"

number two on its top-ten list of America's Most Beautiful Places. Pittsburgh's skyline outranked views of number four Hawaii, number five San Francisco, number eight Key West, and number ten Savannah, Georgia. Not too shabby.

You can't actually get a stiff neck from looking down on downtown from the 1,200-feet-above-sea-level elevation of Mount Washington, but you can be eyeball to eyeball with someone staring back at you from an office window on the fifty-fifth floor of the sixty-four-story US Steel Tower, Pittsburgh's tallest building. Architecturally, to me the standout building in the Pittsburgh skyline is its third tallest, the awe-some glass-turreted Pittsburgh Plate Glass building. It is simply stun-ning, appearing both modern and medieval, like a castle or a keep built from dark glass. Nearby is Fifth Avenue Place, which looks like a power drill in midtransformation to becoming a spaceship. From Grandview Avenue that building's top mast looks like a drill bit being clenched by its four pyramid-shaped spires meeting in the center.

Looming in the distance from the hills northeast of downtown is a very important-looking building with a very important-sounding name—the Cathedral of Learning. It was built, as you might expect with a name like that, as a statement about the importance of educa-tion. It is ground zero at Pitt, the defining landmark on the spacious University of Pittsburgh campus. It was conceived in the best of times and completed during the worst of times, between 1926 and 1937. During the depths of the Great Depression, Pittsburgh schoolchildren were encouraged to "buy a brick" for a dime to finish construction. When completed, the Cathedral of Learning, at 535 feet, was not only the tallest building in Pittsburgh, but it was a Billy Penn's hat-width away from being the tallest building in Pennsylvania. (Philadelphia City Hall, with its thirty-seven-foot-tall bronze statue of William Penn on top, is thirteen feet taller.) Gothic is the only way to describe the Cathedral. It looks like it belongs in the dark skyline of the Gotham City depicted in the *Batman* movies. The Cathedral of Learning has 2,529 windows. (Take THAT, Pittsburgh Plate Glass Building!)

"Keeping spiritual watch over Pittsburgh."

The grand view from Grandview Avenue continues. Look to your left past the bridges, to where the Monongahela meets the Allegheny to form a new river called the Ohio. On the far side are the two new professional sports stadiums—one for baseball, one for football—built with taxpayer money. They replaced storied Three Rivers Stadium, home of both the football Steelers and the baseball Pirates during their glorious championship seasons. So panoramic is the view from up there, you are tempted to tell the person next to you, "Hey, I can see your house from up here."

Is it any wonder that they built a church with the best view of all? From the sidewalks and skyscrapers of downtown, the impressive view to the south is dominated by a mountain and defined by the church on top. St. Mary of the Mount Catholic Church at 403 Grandview Avenue is a Pittsburgh landmark, as impressively conceived architecturally as any of the Golden Triangle skyscrapers. From an office-tower window, the panoramic view of the Pittsburgh skyline enjoyed by churchgoers is blocked by other buildings. But every skyscraper has a clear view of St. Mary of the Mount.

A neighborhood church built with neighborhood funds, St. Mary of the Mount has the best perch in the big city. Dedicated on December 19, 1897, the vaulted Gothic church faces downtown Pittsburgh with an enormous spire-shaped window above its front doors. From this mountaintop vantage with the sunlight streaming through this stained-glass window, what other Biblical theme could have been more appropriate to illustrate than the Ascension? The people who live on the steep streets of Mount Washington are proud of their church, proud of their grade school (founded 1909), and proud of St. Mary of the Mount High School, which graduated its first class of seniors in 1918, and which boasts of having the oldest active alumni association in America. Well into its second century, St. Mary of the Mount has joined the twenty-first century by creating a website (www.smomp .org) bearing the church's self-described mission: "Keeping spiritual watch over Pittsburgh."

Great View, If You're So Inclined
Pittsburgh

Compact downtown Pittsburgh offers a dramatic skyline when seen from any angle, but perhaps the best and most dramatic view is from the top of Mt. Washington, the Pittsburgh neighborhood that looks down on the skyscrapers rising on the north side of the Monongahela River from its perch on a ridge on the south side. Looking up at the steep slope of Mt. Washington from the opposite shore, the expression "You can't get there from here" leaps to mind. A mountain goat might be able to. But you can too, if you're so inclined. And Pittsburghers have been so inclined for 130 years and counting.

The Duquesne Incline consists of two bus-size wooden structures that resemble Victorian-style private train cars from the late 1800s. The difference is that these cars travel vertically rather than horizontally. You might say that the Pittsburgh inclines were America's first urban

From Grandview Avenue you can see the skyscrapers of Downtown Pittsburgh on the north bank of the Monongahela River not far from where the Mon meets the Allegheny to form the Ohio River.

⋆ ⋆

elevated railways, but actually they were more like America's first mass-transit elevators. The four-hundred-foot ride on a thirty-degree angle to the top of Mt. Washington takes two and a half minutes; the two cars heading in opposite directions pass each other midslope. Large windows—front, back, and side—offer spectacular views not to be missed by anyone untroubled by vertigo. A round-trip ride costs a dollar.

From the top of Mt. Washington, the city of Pittsburgh lays itself open like a huge oyster with a breathtaking pearl gleaming in the middle. To the west of the Allegheny River are the new Pirates and

This round viewing platform juts out from Mt. Washington off Grandview Avenue and offers a breathtaking view of Pittsburgh's Golden Triangle.

★ ★

Steelers stadiums. In the middle is a glowing fountain, the centerpiece of Point State Park, where the Monongahela River meets the Allegheny to form the mighty Ohio River. To the west is downtown Pittsburgh, with its impressive skyscrapers, home to more national corporate head-quarters than its cross-state big brother and rival, Philadelphia. You can take it all in from the observation deck at the top of the Duquesne Incline. There's also a museum in the waiting room, telling the story of Pittsburgh's triumphs and travails.

At one time there were fifteen inclines serving the city and its work-ing-class neighborhoods in the hills surrounding the riverside mills and factories. But after private automobiles became commonplace in the wake of World War II, one by one the inclines shut down. Only two inclines serve the city today. The Monongahela Incline, Pittsburgh's first, was built in 1870 and is still in operation about a mile west of the Duquesne Incline, which was built in 1877. In 1962 the Duquesne Incline, then operated by the city-owned transit company, was shut down because it was unprofitable. A year later the community ral-lied and took over the operation of the cable car system under the Society for the Preservation of the Duquesne Heights Incline. Today it is operated by friendly and enthusiastic volunteers who recognize first-time travelers and ask how they liked their ride after the return trip. Seventy-five percent of the Duquesne Incline's riders these days are tourists rather than commuters.

There is one bit of Pittsburgh tradition that lives on among those with certain romantic inclinations. The Duquesne Incline is still a popu-lar place for young Pittsburgh gentlemen to ask the ladies they love for their hand in marriage. Who could turn down a young man with the world at his feet? The hard part—getting an empty car in which to pop the question—is a lot easier if you have the right password to let the incline operator know a proposal is in the offing. "If you ask the right question, you can get a car that's empty except for the two of you," said David Miller, president of the Duquesne Incline preservation society. "The right question is, 'Fred Smith still work here?'" And don't

★ ★

ask unless you mean it. On a beautiful Saturday in October 2012 I saw a wedding party posing for photos at the top of the Duquesne Incline, so obviously Fred Smith is still working in Pittsburgh.

Top of the Duquesne Incline where a wedding party poses.

Hail to the Chiefs, Pennsylvania

There's a President, Pennsylvania, not too far from Polk, in Venango County. On your way from President to Polk on Route 62, you have to go through the town of Franklin. You can bypass Franklin on your way from President to Clinton in Fayette County, but you'll come perilously close to the nearby town of Breakneck, which somehow seems appropriate. You can't get from President to Bush or Gore because those towns don't exist, which also seems appropriate.

The President–Clinton trip is one of the President-to-president road trips in Pennsylvania. You can travel from President to Truman in Cameron County and President to Harding in Luzerne County. Of course, you could also resign yourself to drive from President to Nixon in Susquehanna County.

Early American presidents are much better represented. There's the President–Washington trip, followed by President–Adams, President–Jefferson, and President–Madison. Those are the first four presidents in order, and I suppose you could make it five if you added a few hundred miles on the President–Adams trip to include Quincy, located—interestingly—in Franklin County. (The man was *everywhere*!) The President–Monroe trip would be next, followed by President–Jackson way up in Susquehanna County. There is no Van Buren and no Harrison. But the Presidential journeys pick up with President–Tyler, President–Polk, and President–Taylor.

Due to Pennsylvanians' good taste, there is no President–Fillmore trip. Nor is there President–Pierce. Nor, amazingly, President–Buchanan. (James Buchanan was the only Pennsylvanian to be elected president, which makes Pennsylvania sort of the Phillies of presidential politics: one winner in all those years.) President–Lincoln can be driven in an afternoon; so can President–Grant even if you add the side trip to Ulysses in Potter County.

The Day the Passengers Said No

Somerset County

They died in a puff of smoke. Literally. One brief billowing black cloud against the bluest of skies was the only visible evidence that something awful and monumental had just happened in Pennsylvania's Laurel Highlands that terrible Tuesday morning in September twelve years ago.

A photograph of that modest puff of smoke hovering like a malevolent cartoon storm cloud over a peaceful landscape of red barns and green pastures was taken minutes after the crash of Flight 93 by a neighbor living a mile and a half away. That photo appears in one of the interpretive exhibit panels at the uncompleted Flight 93 National Memorial located between Bedford and Somerset.

The official entrance is off Route 30, where the road is still called the Lincoln Highway, and this entrance is miles away from the crude crushed-stone access road I had used to visit the temporary Flight 93 Memorial several times over the years. The new entrance makes clear what the old one could not. It allows a visitor to feel the terrible isolation of this anonymous place made sacred by the courage of Flight 93's passengers and crew. As bleak as the landscape of this spent strip mine was at the temporary memorial site, the new entrance road takes a deliberate route over three miles of serpentine curves to reveal the natural beauty that surrounds that man-made desolation. We do live in a beautiful state, you and I.

Even on a bad day in mid-October, even on a cold, windy, umbrella day like the Saturday morning when my wife and I made our pilgrimage, the Flight 93 Memorial site is emotionally devastating to witness, its starkness amid the surrounding loveliness, its intentional solemnity leading inevitably to the question: What would we have done? If we were among those passengers plucked by fate to decide how they would die, where would we have been—on our feet or in our seats?

The larger consequences of that decision are expressed graphically on the Flight 93 foldout brochure. On the front side is an artist's rendering of the memorial's white marble wall displaying the names of the forty passengers and crewmembers. On the back side is a photograph of the United States Capitol building, the terrorists' probable target, a mere twenty minutes flight time away. I was expecting to be deeply moved by the Flight 93 Memorial experience, but I was not prepared to be blown away by the series of random interactions with people intimately connected to the events of 9/11. The night before our visit, Sara and I went to dinner at the Pine Grill in Somerset, recommended by the desk clerk at the motel we stayed in, who raved, "The food tastes like food."

On the wall inside the front door of the Pine Grill is a framed copy of the September 12, 2001, local newspaper, *The Daily American*, with the front page headlines, "America Under Seige" and "Terror Touches Somerset County." Beyond that was a line of twelve customers waiting for tables. Sara noticed a couple of open seats at the bar, so we took them and were able to order dinner.

Sitting to my left was a young man named Jake Hayman and his father, Bob. We talked football for a little bit—the Eagles were playing the Steelers that Sunday—but I eventually got around to the crash of Flight 93. "Where were you that day?" I asked Bob Hayman."I was there," he said.

Hayman, who is a volunteer firefighter in Somerset (population 6,200), was at work as a safety supervisor at the Snyder potato chip factory in nearby Berlin. He and others were gathered around a TV set watching the news from New York and the Twin Towers attacks when the call came for him to report to the crash site near Shanksville. "There was *nothing*." Hayman said, meaning the debris he expected to find at the scene of a plane crash. "Hard to believe that there was an entire airplane that fit into a hole that small. There was this smoking crater and this awful smell." The smell was due to the thousands of gallons of aviation fuel on a fully loaded jet plane bound for San Francisco from New York that impacted the earth nose first and upside down at a speed of over 560 miles per hour.

Visitors to the Flight 93 Memorial can see the impact site of the doomed aircraft about 100 yards from here through rough-hewn 4x4 wooden rails made from nearby trees left standing after 9/11.

As we spoke, a woman who had been seated across the bar walked up to the two of us and said, "I heard you talking about Flight 93. My mother was on that plane. She was the oldest passenger to die." Try to imagine that moment. I didn't know what to say or how to react. I introduced myself and Bob Hayman, telling her, "This man was one of the first responders that day." She immediately hugged him like family.

What are the odds of meeting two strangers so quickly with a personal story like this? My wife explained, "This is a small town." But the woman, Betsy Kemmerer, comes from an even smaller town in the Poconos—Effort (population 2,200)—more than two hundred miles away. On September 11, 2001, she was living in Mt. Olive Township in North Jersey just down the street from her mother's apartment. That morning Betsy Kemmerer drove her mother, Hilda Marcin, then seventy-nine, to Newark International Airport for a flight to San Francisco to stay with her other daughter in Danville, California. "Mom hated the East Coast winters," she said.

The next morning I saw the name Hilda Marcin etched in white marble among the forty names on individual panels that make up the memorial wall pointing like an arrow to the crash site that is marked by a boulder in the distance. At the end of the wall was a rough-hewn wooden fence cut from the trunks of trees near the impact crater. Visitors could peer between the timbers at the boulder about one hundred yards away.

Nearby stood a gray-haired volunteer guide in a green National Park Service jacket. In his left hand he held an umbrella; in his right he held a plastic model of the Boeing 757 aircraft that was Flight 93. He demonstrated how the hijacker pilot rocked the aircraft back and forth, gaining altitude, then diving suddenly to drive the heroic members of the passenger revolt away from the cockpit door. Finally, as passengers breached the door, the terrorist pilot rolled the plane into a suicidal dive that ended the murderous journey of the only hijacked aircraft that didn't reach its target that day.

The guide, too, offered his personal story. He said he lives locally and works for a government agency he would not name "until after I retire." He arrived at the crash scene on the morning of September 12 with a canvass team tasked with reporting anything they found. He described the crash site as dangerous with unstable footing and sharp shards sticking up everywhere. "And I'm not the most athletic guy in the world," he said.

A few steps into the search field he stumbled and fell to his hands and knees. At first grateful he was not injured, he then noticed a

★ ★

shredded tree trunk at eye level a few feet away. Embedded in the bark was a credit card. He called over an FBI agent to collect and tag the possible evidence. "Not until I read the official report on the Flight 93 investigation did I realize that I had found the credit card used by the hijackers to buy the tickets on that flight," he said. "That ended up being the beginning of the money trail connecting the terrorists."

How do you thank a hero you've never met? Every day hundreds of visitors leave messages of gratitude to the martyred passengers and crew of Flight 93 at the unfinished national memorial honoring the forty who died on Pennsylvania soil on September 11, 2001.

Unbelievable, I thought. No one would believe that such a remark-able sequence of random encounters could have happened in real life. And yet, what could be more unbelievable than what we all saw with our own eyes that day?

And on that raw, bleak, windswept October morning, in a place where any reasonable person would rather not be in such conditions, I counted ten cars in the parking lot with out-of-state license plates, including those from Michigan, California, Idaho, and Nebraska. If you build it, they will come. Then, on our way back to Route 30 on that haunting winding road from oblivion, as if summoned on cue by the heavenly powers of Hollywood, or perhaps Iowa, we saw a seemingly endless stream of headlights from at least thirty different cars arriv-ing slowly and reverently to this proud Pennsylvania field of shattered American dreams.

America's County, USA
Somerset County

There are sixty-seven counties in Pennsylvania, sixty-eight if you count America's County. "America's County" is the name registered with the US Patent and Trademark Office by the Chamber of Commerce of the former Somerset County in the Laurel Highlands of western Penn-sylvania. The Chamber of Commerce announced the name change in July 2003, the first anniversary of the rescue of nine miners from the flooded Quecreek Mine.

Some chutzpah, you might say. What makes Somerset County any more "America's County" than Adams County, where the Battle of Gettysburg was fought? Or Chester County, where an ill-clad Con-tinental Army suffered the winter of 1777 at Valley Forge? Or Phila-delphia County, the state's only city-county, where the Declaration of Independence and the US Constitution were born?

Somerset County is merely one of several southern Pennsylvania border counties hard on the Mason-Dixon Line where north met south, east met west, and history was made. Is Somerset more American than

★ ★

neighboring Fayette County, site of Fort Necessity National Battlefield, where in 1754 British troops under the command of a twenty-two-year-old Virginia militia colonel named George Washington fought and lost the first battle of the French and Indian War? Pennsylvania is one big America's County. What makes Somerset so special?

Three words: *That was then.* During the first decade of the twenty-first century, Somerset County has had compelling reasons to justify its prideful slogan. Somerset County's previous claim to fame had been the Somerset exit on the Pennsylvania Turnpike. But then, in the span of less than a year, this thinly populated, rural, and largely unnoticed county was visited by two events that riveted the attention of America and much of the world: the first was a tragedy, the second a triumph, and each symbolizing something important, something essential about everyday heroes in America.

In July 2002, television viewers around the country shed tears of relief when then Pennsylvania governor Mark Schweicker appeared on TV after a three-day drama that no one had seriously expected would end happily at the Quecreek Coal Mine. "All nine are alive," the governor announced. Ten months earlier and exactly eight miles away, the passengers of United Airlines Flight 93 had died in a fiery crash upon impact into an inactive strip mine owned by the same coal company that owns Quecreek.

Eight miles and ten months separated these events. People in Somerset were still reeling from the heartbreak of September 11, after sudden death dropped out of the sky and into their backyard, when the next summer they learned that nine of their own were trapped hundreds of feet underground in a mine shaft: nine local residents, in all likelihood doomed. Such loss they'd suffered before. They were familiar with miners who never returned from work. But after September 11, somehow it didn't seem fair. Was it an accident of geography—or because of it—that sleepy Somerset County had been singled out?

And then a miracle. Working without reliable maps and little more than a hunch, rescuers drilled frantically and struck the air pocket where the miners had sought refuge. Elation turned to despair when the drill bit broke on the larger man-size rescue shaft being drilled. Below ground by the fading light of their miner's lamps, nine men wrote final words of love to their families, then placed them in plastic bags buttoned inside their pockets. And then they bid farewell to each other and tethered themselves together with rope so that if their bodies were swept away by the rising water, at least they would be found—if they were ever found—together. And then . . . the second drill bit arrived! The frenzy among rescuers aboveground grew even as the men below grew quieter and quieter. And finally, late on a Saturday night, national news interrupted TV programs all around America. "All nine alive."

I'll admit, I cried like a baby. I sniffled in front of my family, and then I excused myself to the bathroom where I let it all out. I cried from happiness and cried from shame because I had written the miners off for dead in my heart. And then they were alive again. It was a miracle, wasn't it? But how? Why? A year later during the first-anniversary ceremonies at the site of the Quecreek rescue shaft, a former state official gave voice to a common feeling. Planes don't crash in Somerset County, but coal miners do die. "It was like the angels of Flight 93 were watching over this place," said David Hess, the state secretary of environmental protection during the rescue. "It was almost like they said, 'Not these men. Not here. Not again.'"

America's County, Pennsylvania. I don't know what I expected to find when I drove from Philadelphia to Somerset County, 225 miles due west on the Lincoln Highway. What I wasn't expecting were windmills. Six of them. Huge, white, modern windmills just south of Route 31 on a hilltop the same distance away from Quecreek as the Flight 93 impact site. Since the year 2000, I learned, America's County has built fourteen windmills generating enough electricity to power 2,500 homes for a year. I'd never seen a windmill at work before. They look like little boys flailing their arms at bullies. Whoosh, whoosh, whoosh, touching nothing but air. But still they turn because they have to. What is a windmill without wind? What is a hero without courage?

Home of the Original Bird Condo

During our travels through western Pennsylvania, my daughter, Molly, and I saw several ornate and well-constructed multi-

dwelling birdhouses, but nothing to compare to this aerial Taj Mahal on Main Street in Somerset, a living and currently occupied memorial to J. Warren Jacobs, the original builder of the famous Purple Martin House. Jacobs (1868–1947) was a carpenter and amateur ornithologist who designed the first of these bird condos for purple martins, acrobatic *swallows* that eat insects plucked out of the air and even drink on the fly by skimming over ponds, lakes, or rivers with an open beak (now I get it . . . swallows!). There's an annual Purple Martin Festival at the end of June in the Mason-Dixon Historical Park near Mt. Morris in Greene County (the southwestern-most county in Pennsylvania), home of the Jacobs Birdhouse Company in Waynesburg, Warren Jacobs's hometown where he built the first such structure in 1912.

A Memorial to a Very Happy Ending
Somerset County

It is almost impossible to overstate the nature of the miracle that took place deep beneath the earth of Bill and Lori Arnold's dairy farm about six miles north of Somerset, Pennsylvania. During three days in late July in 2002, the Arnolds' farm became the rescue site for the Quecreek miners, the nine who emerged alive and whole against all odds. That event changed the Arnolds' lives as much as any of the families touched by angels that day. Since then, while working full-time as dairy farmers, the Arnolds created the nonprofit Quecreek Mine Rescue Foundation to operate a museum and memorial on the site of the rescue on their property just one hundred yards off Route 985.

The memorial is marked by rusting hulks of rescue equipment, including a large cylindrical airlock designed with the help of the navy that was never actually used. Also at the site you can see the actual rescue shaft where the miners emerged, as well as the six-inch airshaft drilled within the first hours to provide the miners with breathable air. Inside the barnlike education center/museum is the actual rescue capsule, the bright yellow tubular metal cage that was lowered hundreds of feet and returned with living miners. The most striking feature at the center of the memorial site is a seven-foot bronze statue of a coal miner, apparently on his lunch break, reading a book. So much dignity and expressiveness can be found in this statue of a middle-aged miner reading by the beam of the light on his hard hat, a thick book cradled in hard, veined hands, his pickax resting on a rock next to his knee, his right arm resting on his metal lunch pail as comfortably and naturally as if he were sitting in an easy chair. If you climb up and look over his shoulder, you can see the words of the page the miner is reading: "They who work the mines and they who read great books are but one."

The proud miner statue brings poignancy and humanity to what is otherwise a display of industrial equipment. The Arnolds have plans to add thirty-one bronze figures around the site to capture the moment of the rescue.

Now more than ten years later, Pennsylvania understands more fully the extraordinary good fortune that visited this site in July 2002. The 2006 incident at Sago Mine in West Virginia, the 2007 incident at Crandall Mine in Utah, and the twenty-nine miners who died in the Upper Big Branch, WV, mine disaster in 2010, showed America just how devastating these catastrophes can be.

The Quecreek Mine Rescue Site is open seven days a week, year-round during daylight hours. Programs at the education center/ museum take place Tuesday through Saturday, 11:00 a.m. until 5:00 p.m., from April 1 until November 1. Call ahead for information at (814) 445-4876, and check out their website at www.quecreek.org for directions and the most current update.

"They who work the mines and they who read great books are but one."

3

Northeast

NEPA, as Northeast *Pennsylvania is sometimes called, mostly by peo-*
ple who don't live there, is coal country. Hard coal country. Anthracite.
Unfortunately, the coal industry hasn't been hot in Pennsylvania since
corruption and greed led to the Knox Mine Disaster in 1959. As tragic
as the final chapters of the coal industry have been, the capital city
of NEPA, Scranton, has achieved an almost cult status among fans of
the NBC hit comedy TV show The Office, *about the travails of a paper*
company in a paperless society. And then, of course, there is the vice
president of the United States who grew up in Scranton, and never fails
to remind people of that. Especially during skits on Saturday Night Live.
Some of the best and worst stories in Pennsylvania history unfolded in
these irresistible mine-scarred valleys, stories of Indian massacres, immi-
grant Irish worker insurrections, towns on fire fifty years and counting.
And home to the best and funniest people you'd ever want to meet.

Northeast Pennsylvania extends from the New York border on the
north and east through the Endless Mountains to the still wild Delaware
River, which continues as the border with New York southward until
Port Jervis, where New Jersey meets New York. Pennsylvania never actu-
ally touches New Jersey except by bridge, which residents of both states
seem to like. On the Delaware the Northeast ends its most east point at
the appropriately named city of Easton, home of Crayola crayons, which
are pronounced "crowns" by many on both sides of the river.

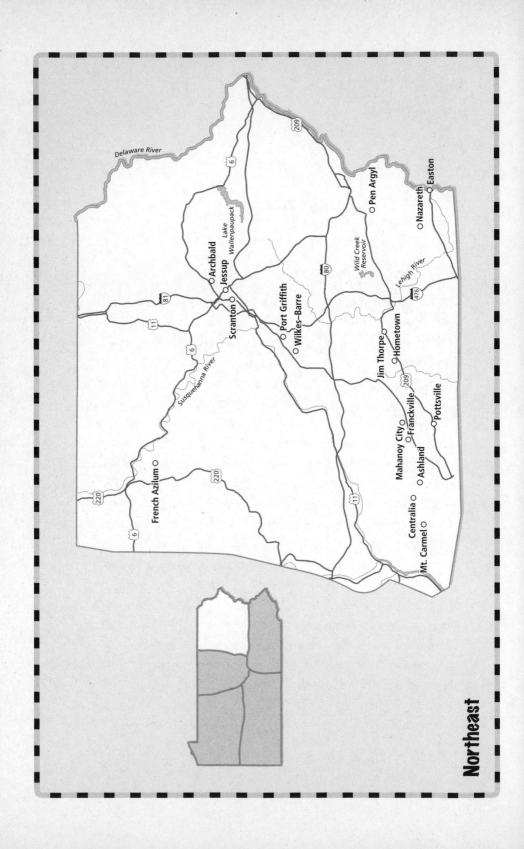

Northeast

Befitting coal country, the largest pothole in the world can be found in Archbald. Perhaps the strangest story about a town in the Northeast is that of French Azilum in Bradford County, which was founded in 1793 as a refuge for French royalty seeking to escape the reign of terror during the French Revolution. The largest building in the settlement was reserved for the queen, Marie Antoinette, who never lived to see, or enjoy a dessert, in Pennsylvania. And a story like that could only be topped by what happens in Jessup every Memorial Day Weekend. You have no idea.

The Northeast Extension of the Pennsylvania Turnpike leads motorists to Scranton, not the North Pole. But you wouldn't know it by this CAUTION: DEER CROSSING sign featuring a leaping deer with a bright red nose. The Rudolph sign is the work of a prankster who applied a plastic red nose to several such signs on the turnpike.

The World's Largest Pothole

Archbald

Pennsylvania has an official state bird (the ruffed grouse), an official state dog (Great Dane), an official state flower (mountain laurel), an official state insect (the firefly), and an official state toy (everyone knows it's Slinky). But did you know that Pennsylvania has commemorated something else so thoroughly indigenous to the Keystone State that cars bearing Firestone tires are turned away at the state line?

I speak of Pennsylvania's official state pothole. Contrary to the personal experience of locals, the official state pothole cannot be found in the passing lane of the westbound Schuylkill Expressway near Conshohocken. No, Pennsylvania's official state pothole can be found just off Route 6 in Lackawanna County between Scranton and Carbondale in the borough of Archbald. It is the only pothole to have a state park named after it.

But this is no ordinary pothole—it's a glacial pothole. During the ice age, glacial meltwater carrying sand and gravel and rock particles fell like a waterfall hundreds of feet through crevasses in the Laurentide Continental Glacier, forming a pothole in the bedrock beneath. When the glacier finally receded, trees and other vegetation grew on top of it so that you'd never know there was a pothole there in the first place—sort of like nature's asphalt.

The Archbald Pothole would have remained hidden from humans forever, perhaps, if it hadn't been situated in the most heavily mined anthracite region in northeast Pennsylvania. In 1884 a coal miner named Patrick Mahon set off an explosive charge while extending a tunnel, when suddenly tons of water and rock came tumbling down, setting off a panic in the mine. After removing between eight hundred and one thousand tons of stones rubbed round by the glacier, mine inspectors discovered that the miner had opened up the bottom of a pothole about thirty-eight feet from the surface.

In 1887 a fence was built around the perimeter of the pothole and the walls were shored up to prevent collapse as the fame of the pothole spread throughout the geological community, which dubbed Archbald as "a world-class glacial pothole." In 1914 the widow of the landowner turned over a one-acre plot containing the pothole to the Lackawanna Historical Society. In 1940 the county added 150 acres to the site as a park and later turned the site over to the State of Pennsylvania. The Archbald Pothole State Park was officially dedicated in 1964.

Today the Archbald Pothole is a major tourist attraction, unlike the Schuylkill Expressway westbound pothole, the Route 611 southbound pothole, and the Route 309 northbound pothole, all of which continue to attract a fair share of motorist attention because, unlike Archbald, these potholes are actually getting bigger.

The Loneliest Mom
Ashland

The borough of Ashland is located at the convergence of three counties (Schuylkill, Columbia, and Northumberland) in the heart of coal country where Route 61 meets Route 54. The hillside borough of 1.7 square miles peaked in population at 7,045 just before World War II. Since then more than half its population has moved on or died, leaving 2,817 residents, according to the 2010 census. In its heyday—if you can call the Great Depression a heyday—Ashland became the envy of neighboring coal towns and patches because of the dramatic monument to mothers that was built on a hillside overlooking the town and the valley below.

One look at the Monumental Mom statue at the base of Hoffman Boulevard in downtown Ashland tells you everything you need to know about life in Pennsylvania coal towns in the 1930s—it was severe and it was managed from the top down. The mom depicted in the Ashland monument to mothers is not a "Let's bake some chocolate chip cookies!" mom or a "Let me kiss your boo boo!" mom. The eight-foot-tall bronze mother sculpted by Julius C. Loester and erected by the Ashland Boys Association in 1938 more closely resembles the

Not the Mom most of us remember. Ashland's tribute to Motherhood is distant, foreboding, and difficult to see up close.

"Norman! Norman, where are you?!" mom you'd expect to find at the Bates Motel in an Alfred Hitchcock movie.

This is not to say that the Ashland mothers monument is scary. But this mom is distant, guarded, and as welcoming as a medieval fortress. You have to climb thirty-two stone steps from the street (incidentally that's exactly half as many as the Rocky steps in front of the Philadelphia Museum of Art) to reach the top. The two stairways to the statue seem to be guarded by spiky stones embedded like turrets at regular intervals on top of the walls on either side of the railings. A visitor would not even briefly imagine sitting on that wall.

★ ★

After climbing to the top, you are greeted by yet another wall, this one round, which requires you to walk all the way around to the back of the statue to enter the area on the same level with the pedestal. The last wall seems to confirm the impression that the monument's designer, Emil Siebern, wanted visiting pilgrims know that they had jumped through hoops for an audience with Mom. But even there she seems far away. The pedestal, a three-ton block of granite, still leaves the statue unapproachably high above your head—and *she's* sitting. On the pedestal are carved the words, A MOTHER IS THE HOLIEST THING ALIVE, which is not exactly a hugs and kisses sentiment so much as an Eleventh Commandment.

Even in the 1930s the mother figure represented here was something of an anachronism. The sculpture depicts *Whistler's Mother,* the famous 1871 painting by James McNeil Whistler, which wasn't even called that. The portrait's title was *Arrangement in Grey and Black,* which are suitable colors to describe the somber mood of the monument. According to the bronze plaque at the base, readable only if you have climbed all those steps, this monument "honors all mothers past and present and is the only one of its kind in the country." For this mothers around America say, "Thank you."

Fire in the Hole
Centralia

It started, some say, as a trash fire in a landfill located in one of the abandoned coal mines that honeycomb this valley between Big Mountain and Mahanoy Mountain on the edge of Pennsylvania's Western-Middle anthracite field. It was Memorial Day weekend in 1962 when the fire underground was first noticed. It's been burning ever since, like a subterranean forest fire with an inexhaustible supply of fuel. The town above, Centralia, has become a symbol of mankind's futile efforts to bandage the wounds the earth has suffered to serve humanity's needs and greed.

★ ★

Even in its heyday, Centralia was never much of a town, except for the people who called it home. It sat isolated at the end of a lonely stretch of Route 42 through Columbia County. Its nearest neighbors were Ashland in Schuylkill County and Mt. Carmel in Northumberland County. The only reason you would have heard of Centralia, if you've heard of it at all, is because it's been on fire since John F. Kennedy was president.

A visit to Centralia is a visit to a ghost town, except there is no town. There are streets and sidewalks, curbs and stop signs, but most of the buildings are gone. What was once downtown *Centralia* is now an empty intersection. In the first edition of *Pennsylvania Curiosities* I described what I saw in the year 2000: a wooden bench at a former bus stop that mocked the absence of people and a town. On the bench was the name *Centralia* and its zip code, 17927, both of which no longer exist. Across the street were lawn chairs set up under some trees and a sign that said WE LOVE CENTRALIA. The seats are empty because the bench is now gone. The only public building still standing, ironically, is the firehouse with its yellow fire engine polished and ready to respond to fires the crew can still fight in homes that don't exist. There are perhaps half a dozen occupied houses remaining in what was once a town of 1,100 people. Those few scattered homes are owned by people too proud, too old, or too ornery to leave. Where an entire row-house block once stood, now there are single houses, their weak side walls braced by five brick columns resembling outside chimneys.

If you explore the side streets nearest St. Ignatius Cemetery on the south end of Centralia on a summer afternoon like I did, you will find your way blocked by dense underbrush growing over the paved street. Just before the place where nature reclaims what man has left behind, you will see the eerie outline of a human body spray-painted on the macadam like a symbol at a police homicide scene. From there you can see the smoke rising from an open pit uphill at the edge of the fenced-in cemetery, where the fire below continues its spread. Soon the bodies of the long departed will be forced to join the living departed. Even the

The busiest place in Centralia is St. Ignatius
Cemetery, which opens its gates every day to
allow the vanished living to visit the departed.

dead must flee the underground furnace. The pit itself is suitable for a
study by Dante, the first circle, perhaps, of the inferno below. A smoking crater is surrounded by flattened trees that were choked by poison
smoke long before they fell like twigs before the holocaust beneath
them. It's a disturbing reminder of how much human beings have
taken from the earth below Pennsylvania, and how little human beings
can do when the earth decides to take it back.

At first, the state and the federal government tried to fight the fire
by depriving it of oxygen. But the fire was too resourceful, the earth
too seamed with cracks as well as veins of combustible coal. Deadly
gases began seeping into basements. People got sick. The government
tried to vent the gases, but the fire kept moving, silently, inexorably, to
new areas.

Finally, the government began condemning properties and paying people to relocate. According to the Pennsylvania Department of Environmental Protection, close to $40 million was spent fighting the spread of the fire and paying Centralians to move. There were 1,100 people who called Centralia home in 1962. By the year 2000 the number was fewer than twenty. There's no longer a post office in Centralia. The only public building listed in the phone book is the Centralia Fire Department (570-875-0687), but if you call, don't be surprised if there is no answer.

On my last visit to Centralia in October 2012, the state had removed the detour barriers on Route 61 between Ashland and Mt.

There have been six Pennsylvania governors since the fire began beneath Centralia. These protest signs address anger at the sitting governor, Tom Corbett.

Centralia lost its zip code years ago, but these mailboxes
in front of the Fire House are the only remnants of
communication with municipal government.

Carmel that used to steer the curious away from the smoking landscape of a vanished town that once boasted of not one but two Catholic schools, a public grade school and high school, seven churches,
five hotels, and twenty-seven saloons. Now you can drive directly to
Centralia on Route 61 from either direction, but knowing when you've
arrived will be more difficult than in the past.

It has been years since there was "a there, there" along the one
main road to and from Centralia. The one municipal building that
remains—ironically and almost comically—is the Centralia Volunteer
Fire Co. firehouse where the lone yellow fire truck still gleams. In front
of the Municipal Building are two old-fashioned mailboxes identifying one as being for the NTRALIA FIRE CO (note the missing letters) and
the other CENTRALIA BOROUGH. Neither mailbox had anything inside.

There are no memorials to the town, no benches with love notes, no sad signs lamenting the lost zip code. But there was a protest sign posted up by the formerly smoking pit on the south side of town and directed toward the current governor of Pennsylvania, Tom Corbett: "Why must you force these people from their homes to get at the coal underneath? You know the so-called 'fire' was an excuse. How many Centralia people have died after they were forced from their homes? The fire didn't do that, PA did."

The sign is not far from the liveliest place left in Centralia—the cemetery at St. Ignatius, which still opens its gates from 8:00 a.m. until 7:00 p.m. from April to through October and from 9:00 a.m. until 5:00 p.m. from November through March. The cemetery has the only recognizable parking in the ghost town where people still visit the soul of the departed, who outnumber the few still living in Centralia by one hundred to one.

Where the Tongues Forked
Easton

Easton was the scene of two thoroughly despicable treaties negotiated with the Native American Lenni Lenape tribes and the English colonists. In fact, the expression "white man speaks with forked tongue" could well have originated in the Easton treaty known as the Walking Purchase. William Penn was an honorable man in his dealings with the natives, but when he returned to England and turned over the administration to his son, Thomas, the Penn name was tarnished. In 1737 Thomas Penn produced a "lost" treaty negotiated by his father with the Delaware tribe for as much land as a man could walk off in a day and a half. The Indians under Chief Lappawinsoe were leery about the legitimacy of the document but, they reasoned, how much land can a man walk off in thirty-six hours?

What Chief Lappawinsoe didn't know was that the Penns had cleared a trail through the wilderness before the day of the walk, which started from Wrightstown in Bucks County. Not only that, but three of the fastest runners in the colony had been hired to pace off the land in a relay team. By the end of the day-and-a-half "walk," the runners had traveled more than 50 miles and the land within totaled 1,200 square miles, an area almost the size of Rhode Island, which includes most of Pike, Monroe, Lehigh, and Northhampton Counties. The Indians knew they had been robbed. Chief Lappawinsoe complained that the white men "should have walked a few miles and then sat down and smoked a pipe, and now and then have shot a squirrel, and not have kept up the Run, Run all day." But he felt honor bound to abide by the treaty, which was the beginning of the Delawares' westward migration that eventually took them as far as Oklahoma.

The next Easton treaty took place in 1757, following a period of open warfare on the settlers by the Delawares, who by then were clearly aware of how hugely they had been swindled. This time the negotiations were handled by Chief Teedyuscung, and the dirty trick played by the colonial negotiators was to ply the chief with firewater. "It must shock you to hear that pains have been made to make the King [Teedyuscung] drunk every night since the business began," wrote Charles Thomson, a twenty-eight-year-old schoolteacher from Philadelphia who acted as Chief Teedyuscung's personal secretary during the treaty negotiations. "On Saturday, under pretense of rejoicing for the victory gained by the King of Prussia, and the arrival of the fleet, a bonfire was ordered to be made and liquor given to the Indians to induce them to dance," Thomson wrote to a friend. "For fear they should get sober on Sunday and be fit the next day to enter on business, under pretense that the Mohawks had requested it, another bonfire was ordered to be made and more liquor given them."

With Thomson watching his back, Teedyuscung was not swindled in that treaty. Thomson faithfully recorded the chief's words and in gratitude he was given the Lenni Lenape name *Wegh-Wu-Law-Mo-End*, which meant "Man Who Talks the Truth." "It's as true as if Charles Thomson's name is on it" became a popular expression throughout the United States until the Revolutionary period.

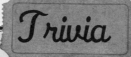

Name Games: The Good, the Bad, and the Ugly

How would you like to grow up in a town called Drab? Or Drain Lick? Or Grimesville? All these are actual names of towns in Pennsylvania. So are Brave and Paradise and Fearnot. Pennsylvania is as full of town names that inspire—Independence, Challenge, Enterprise, Freedom, Energy—as it is town names that, well, don't inspire: Blandburg, Needmore, Slabtown, Slate Lick, Burnt Cabins, Scalp Level, Spraggs. For every Prosperity, there is a Grindstone. For every Hearts Content, there is an Ickesburg. For every Friendsville, there is a Lickingville. For every Crown, there is a Crumb.

Pennsylvania is rich in names like Diamond, Chrome, Gold, and Pearl. It is also saddled with town names like Hungry Hollow, Gravel Lick, Rife, and Seldom Seen. There's Savage, Rough and Ready, Stalker, and Thumptown. There's Shaft and Taxville.

Pennsylvania has town names that seem to be linked by emotion, if not geography. Does Desire lead to Panic? Does Defiance result in Force? Are Fairchance and Fairplay in the same athletic conference? Are Frugality and Economy the result of Effort? Do you have to go through Grimville to find Jollytown? Is Husband a destination for unmarried women from Hope? Do they Ache when they find their Hero is with a Lover? Can they Admire him when they find out she's really from Hooker? Is Progress possible without Endeavor? Is Decorum compatible with Candor? It's all something you have to Hunker down and Muse about, perhaps at one of the Two Taverns.

Pennsylvania has a King and a Queen. It has a Tippecanoe and a Tyler too. It has a Forest as well as a Gump. But for some reason the town of Vim lacks a matching Vigor.

A Mom to Keep You Awake at Night

Frackville

One good mom deserves another. And anyone who makes the journey to Ashland to see the official Mother Monument should make the
twenty-minute drive east on Route 61 to Frackville to see a truly disturbing local landmark. It's called "Pioneer Woman and Child" and it's
located outside Granny's Motel and Restaurant at 115 Coal Street off
Route 61 near the entrance exit ramps for Interstate 81.

The sign in front of Granny's says the hotel was founded in 1876,
the same year the borough of Frackville was incorporated, but since
the fifteen-foot-tall sculpture is made of painted fiberglass, obviously
it wasn't part of the original decor. In fact, it once stood outside a
bakery in Hamburg. What makes this pioneer mother and child tab-
leau so memorable—freaky even—is the level of creepiness it achieves
instantly on so many levels.

For one thing the disturbing fixed and vacant thousand-yard stares
from the powerful blue eyes of both mother and child. The mother
has a sort of Joan-Crawford-in-drag look about her. There's an almost
robotic quality to her posture. She doesn't offer the pie to you so
much as she dares you to eat it. But as scary as mom is, the androgy-
nous and abused-looking child is a candidate for an intervention by
the Department of Human Service. The expression on the face of the
child speaks to an overdose of Ritalin or of being eyewitness to an
Indian massacre.

Whereas the Ashland mom monument only hints at a Hitchcockian-
Oedipal drama, the "Pioneer Woman and Child" looks like the back-
story of Norman Bates's childhood come to life. In fact, the masculine
face on the little girl in the statue looks like a forty-year-old Anthony
Perkins. The head is too big for the body, and the only way we can be
sure it's supposed to be a girl is because she is dragging a doll by its
arm. A *decapitated* doll.

★ ★

Locals have learned to appease whatever superstitions may sur-
round the homicidal countenances on the statues outside Granny's.
After eating in the restaurant, it's considered good luck for departing
patrons to drop a coin down the neck hole of the decapitated doll.

The "Pioneer Mother and Child" statue outside
Frackville has disturbed passersby for years.
Note the headless doll carried by the little girl
who looks like a forty-year-old man.

★ ★

The French Connection
French Azilum

If Marie Antoinette had only said, "You've got a friend in Pennsylvania" instead of "Let them eat cake," who knows what would have
happened in Bradford County? If the deposed queen of France had
made it to the refuge prepared for her and other French nobles in
Pennsylvania, perhaps the village of French Azilum would have been
called "Paris on the Susquehanna." French loyalists arrived in northeastern Pennsylvania in the fall of 1793 to settle the village on the
shores of the Susquehanna about ten miles south of Towanda. As it
was, Marie Antoinette and King Louis XVI lost their heads during the
French Revolution before they could join other fleeing French nobility
in America.

The settlers were assisted in their venture by wealthy Philadelphians
Robert Morris and French-born Stephen Girard, and the village of
Azilum was laid out in a gridiron pattern with 413 half-acre plots surrounding a two-acre market square. By the following spring thirty
rough log-cabin structures had been erected by French settlers, many
of them refugees from the slave revolt on the island of Santo Domingo
(Haiti). The largest of the structures was La Grande Maison, a massive
two-story log structure measuring eighty by sixty feet with numerous
small windows and eight fireplaces. This was supposed to have been
the deposed queen's residence, but after her execution it was used as
a public hall where visiting French dignitaries such as the devious foreign minister Talleyrand and the future French king Louis-Philippe were
entertained.

Following the Reign of Terror and the normalization of the domes-
tic situation in France and Haiti, many of the French loyalists, unused
to the rough life of frontier America, returned home or to the Carib-
bean or to established southern cities such as Charleston and New
Orleans. That, combined with the bankruptcy of American patron
Robert Morris and the invitation by Napoleon Bonaparte for the return
of French exiles, led to the end of Azilum as a functioning French

★ ★

Marie Antoinette never lived to see it, but this is the view
from the Marie Antoinette Lookout of French Azilum on the far
side of the Susquehanna River in Bradford County.

town in Pennsylvania by 1803. There were fifty buildings left behind,
including several small shops, a schoolhouse, a theater, and a chapel.
None of the original structures remains, although a reconstruction of
a 1790s log cabin is on the town's site, as well as the lovely white-
washed LaPorte house, built in 1836 by the son of one of the original
French settlers. The French influence did not vanish completely from
northeastern Pennsylvania following the failure of the Azilum colony.
Among the French refugee families who remained to settle in the area

are the LaPortes, Homets, LeFevres, Brevosts, and D'Autremonts, none of whom, at last sighting, has lost their heads.

The French Azilum Historic Site is now operated by the Pennsylvania Museum and Historical Commission, but the vista of what the area looks like can be seen from the Marie Antoinette Lookout on Route 6 on the east side of the Susquehanna River near Standing Stone Road. (Write to French Azilum, R.R. 2, Box 266, Towanda, Pennsylvania 18848, call 570-265-3376, or visit www.frenchazilum.com.)

Pennsylvania, This Is Your Hometown

Hometown

In 1984 Bruce Springsteen's hit album *Born in the USA* included a haunting ballad called "My Hometown." Things didn't turn out so great for the Hometown in Springsteen's song, which became a metaphor for troubled times facing thousands of communities across the country. "My Hometown" could have been the soundtrack for most of Pennsylvania's coal- and steel-manufacturing towns in the closing decades of the twentieth century. In fact, in the 1982 "Allentown" with a similar theme, singer Billy Joel named names but we won't here. After the song and video became a huge hit and something of an embarrassment to political and business leaders of Pennsylvania's fourth-largest city, Joel revealed that he had chosen to name the song after Allentown, which is neither a coal nor a steel town, because he liked the no-nonsense sound of the name—Allentown. Still, the lyrics resonated locally, as well as nationally, with young people discovering that the American dream doesn't come with a guarantee.

In the three decades since songs like "My Hometown" and "Allentown" captured the bewildered sense of betrayal at the disappearance of traditional industrial jobs, young people have learned their lessons. Sons and daughters no longer expect, nor do they necessarily want, to follow their fathers into the mines or their mothers onto factory floors. What hasn't changed is the penchant Pennsylvanians have for staying put. Among the fifty United States, Pennsylvania leads the nation in a

★ ★

telling statistic. According to the 2000 census, when compared with the population of any other state, a greater proportion of Americans born in Pennsylvania still live in Pennsylvania. Put another way, if you are a native Pennsylvanian, chances are you live in or near your hometown.

George Pinkey is a classic example. For more than sixty years, he has lived in the same town where he once attended elementary school grades one through four in a one-room schoolhouse. His earliest memory here was of sitting on his father's shoulders watching an effigy of Adolf Hitler pass by during a "welcome home" parade for GIs returning from World War II. What separates Pinkey from most Pennsylvanians who have lived their entire lives in the same place is that his hometown is Hometown. "I've been in all fifty states," Pinkey says, "but I've never been in another Hometown."

Neither have I. In fact, I had never been in any hometown but my own until I discovered Hometown, Pennsylvania, on my way to Centralia, a Pennsylvania hometown that is no more. Hometown, Pennsylvania (population 1,500), is a hilltop community of pleasant homes located two miles north of the borough of Tamaqua and about eight miles south of the city of Hazleton on Route 309. Unlike neighboring communities in the heart of Pennsylvania's anthracite-mining region, Hometown looks more like a one-stoplight suburban bedroom community outside Philadelphia or Pittsburgh. There is no "there" there, no downtown with sidewalks, no bench on the courthouse lawn. There is the Beacon Diner, a landmark, and the Hometown Farmer's Market, an even bigger landmark that operates only one day a week (Wednesday 8:00 a.m. to 8:00 p.m.) and attracts customers from one hundred miles away. Hometown is, in fact, a thoroughly unremarkable town except for its remarkably unremarkable name.

I guess when you live in a place called Hometown, you get used to hearing people say the name without meaning the place where you live, the same way someone named Jones doesn't take it personally when people talk about "keeping up with the Joneses." I couldn't get a rise out of most Hometowners I spoke to when I asked

The Hometown Fire Company in Hometown, Pennsylvania, serves as the focal point of community activities in a
town without a single church of any denomination.

for anecdotes, amusing or otherwise, about listing their hometown
address as, well, you know. I was directed toward George Pinkey, a
former township supervisor, as the hometown historian of Hometown
and the surrounding coal region. He has few kind words for the big
mining companies that abandoned their operations, leaving scarred
earth and unemployment in their wake. "When they were done with
us in the 1950s, we were like a sucked orange," Pinkey said. "What
saved Hometown, ironically, was that there was no coal here. All
around us, but not under here."

Hometown was founded in 1828 by a Philadelphia businessman
trying to make a buck from the coal-mining industry by growing food
that fed the mines' horses and mules. These animals never saw the

★ ★

light of day again after they entered the mines. They eventually died underground after pulling countless cars loaded with anthracite. When coal was king, Hometown was a farming community. "I think there's a doctoral thesis somewhere about how many pounds of hay and cabbage and corn it took to produce a ton of coal," says Pinkey. After World War II, when the mines began to close, the farms were sold to developers who built houses and cul-de-sacs and roads that dead-ended for no apparent reason. Hometown became a suburban bedroom community for larger neighbors with fading downtowns. In the process Rush Township, of which Hometown is a part, has become the second-wealthiest municipality in Schuylkill County.

Curiously, or perhaps tellingly, there is not a single church of any denomination in Hometown. On Sunday churchgoers go to their other hometown churches in Tamaqua or Hazleton or Mahanoy City. And afterward on every other Sunday between Labor Day and Memorial Day, upward of two hundred people attend the all-you-can-eat breakfast at the Hometown Fire Company hall. Says Pinkey, "The volunteer fire company is the closest thing we have to a community-wide social organization." Not exactly a church, but still, all you can eat.

You'd Have to Go to Italy to See a Race Like This
Jessup

There's no party like a Scranton party, as the saying goes. But that's just a saying. Nine miles north of Scranton on Route 6 in the borough of Jessup each May on the Saturday of Memorial Day weekend there is literally a party like no other—unless you count the one that's been going on for centuries each May 15 in the ancient city of Gubbio in Italy. Therein lies a story as curious and unique as any you will find in Pennsylvania, the commonwealth of curiosities.

It's called "The Race of the Saints" (in Italian "La Corsa dei Ceri") and it features three teams consisting of dozens of colorfully dressed runners who carry on their shoulders an H-shaped wooden platform holding a fifteen-foot-tall carved oak pedestal weighing four hundred pounds. On top of the pedestals (in Italian *"ceri"*) are thirty-inch-tall statues of three saints of the Catholic Church, two of which you've probably heard of, St. George and St. Anthony. The third, St. Ubaldo, is an obscure (to Americans) saint known as the patron saint of the city of Gubbio (current population 30,000) in the region of Umbria (about midcalf on the right side of the Italian boot). Most of the Italian immigrants who flocked to Jessup in the 1890s to find work in the anthracite coal mines of Pennsylvania came from Gubbio or nearby towns.

The Race of the Saints (which is hardly a race, since St. Ubaldo always wins) commemorates a "miraculous victory" in 1151 when Bishop Ubaldo Baldassini left the walls of the mountain city of Gubbio to meet with the leader of the invading barbarians from the north under Emperor Fredrick I, whose fierce red beard led to his nickname Barbarossa. Somehow Ubaldo convinced Barbarossa not to sack, rape, and pillage Gubbio. But the citizens lost heart when Bishop Ubaldo did not return quickly enough. When he finally arrived with the good news, panic and chaos ruled the city. In order to quickly demonstrate that the bishop was alive, he was hoisted on top of a platform (a *"stanga"* in Italian) where he stood precariously while being carried on the shoulders of men who ran through the panicked streets with Bishop Ubaldo as living proof.

When or why the two other saints were added to the St. Ubaldo Day "Festa dei Ceri" pageant is unclear, as is when the "Race of the Saints" aspect became the public face of the feast day. The costumes worn by the competing saints' teams resemble those worn by participants in the running of the bulls in Pamplona. The three saint teams in Gubbio and Jessup wear white pants with red waistbands, and red kerchiefs (*"fazzoletto"* in Italian) tied around their necks over different colored team shirts—gold or yellow for St. Ubaldo, blue for St. George and black for St. Anthony.

I have seen documentary footage of the Gubbio "Race of the Saints" and it is positively Pamplona-esque in its obvious dangers—heavy objects leaning precariously while carried by running men racing through

★ ★

crowded narrow streets up steep mountain roads. It's a trip or stumble away from serious injury and, worse, toppled saints.

The St. Ubaldo Day race in Jessup is the culmination of an all-day series of religious and family social events. The race begins at 5:30 p.m. and its main route through town starts at the top of Church Street, a fairly steep down slope that runs through the business district. Ten men (and a few women) carry the platforms holding each saint and dozens of teammates run alongside them on both sides to relieve a runner whenever necessary. Relief runners also wait at designated intervals prepared to switch runners as a group. Imagine a baton transfer in a 4-by-4 relay sprint with trained athletes who practice every day for hours. Now imagine your middle-aged brother Bob relieving your tired Uncle Tony during this once-a-year event without either of them tripping and falling over each other. It can be hard to watch sometimes.

That's why there are nine stops during the 1.7 miles of the Corsa dei Ceri "race" through Jessup with fifteen-minute intervals during each to allow both runners and spectators to reposition. At midpoint through the course near where the railroad tracks cross Church Street, the route reverses and the runners must now travel uphill toward the finish line, which, unlike the huge gates of the walled medieval city in Gubbio, is a ten-foot grass embankment outside the Jessup Veterans Memorial Stadium.

Since St. Ubaldo's team always wins, the bragging rights go to the teams who carried their saints with the greatest speed and dignity, the fewest dips and stumbles, no matter what the weather conditions. In Jessup the Race of the Saints goes on rain or shine. Which is not to say it always goes on, period. Since 1914 when the St. Ubaldo's Day event was first celebrated in Jessup as a parade, the "Corsa dei Ceri" took place each year until 1952, when it became a victim of its popularity. That year twenty thousand people attended the race in the small town, causing problems that led to its cancellation for twenty-four years. It was renewed in 1976 during Jessup's Centennial and America's Bicentennial celebration. But in 1990 after thirty thousand people showed up in Jessup for St. Ubaldo's Day, the Race of the Saints event was again cancelled until the year 2000. So far during the twenty-first century the crowds have been kind and manageable during this unique and historic annual event.

The Handprint on the Prison Wall
Jim Thorpe

Sure, I knew the Irish had it rough, I knew they were exploited by the coal mines, and I knew the company store owned their bodies and souls. But until I saw the gallows with the four ropes and the hand-print on the prison wall, I guess I never saw how rough.

Midway up the hill on West Broadway in picturesque Jim Thorpe—the Switzerland of Pennsylvania, according to the welcoming signs—is the Old Jail Museum, formerly the Carbon County Prison, built in 1871 and designed by Edward Haviland, whose famous father gave us and the world the first state penitentiary on Fairmount Avenue in Philadelphia. It was here on June 21, 1877, that four so-called Molly Maguires were strangled to death (one took seventeen minutes to die) from the same scaffold after a shameful trial orchestrated by the president of the Philadelphia and Reading Railroad and prosecuted by his private attorneys based on evidence provided by his private police force.

Twenty-six Mollies in all would hang. They were Irish immigrants guilty of protesting conditions in the coal mines, where a man could earn forty-nine cents for mining a ton of coal and receive a bill for sup-plies at the end of the day. "Bobtail checks," they called them. Tons loaded minus supplies provided equaled $0.00. Then in 1875 they cut the miners' pay by 10 percent.

After surviving a seven-month strike, the owners rewarded the returning miners by cutting their pay another 10 percent. Desperate men do desperate things. There were murders on both sides. Only the Mollies met the gallows.

On the wall of Cell No. 17 of the Old Jail, like a modern-day Shroud of Turin, is a handprint said to belong to one of the Mollies before

★ ★

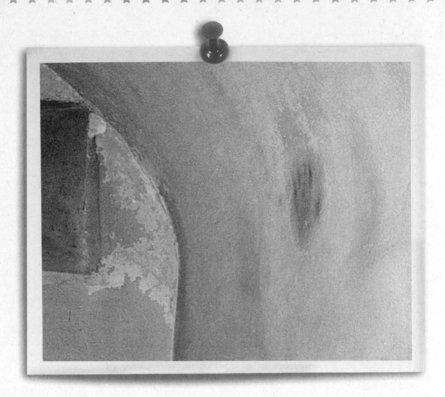

Cell No. 17 of the Old Jail, where the handprint of a miner unjustly sent to his death over a hundred years ago can still be seen on the cell wall.

his execution. He rubbed his hand on the dirt of the floor and held it against the wall until the four fingers and the thumb were clearly outlined. It will remain for the next century, he told his guards in 1877, as a symbol of injustice. They shrugged their shoulders and got on with the business of death. Afterward, they returned to the cell and tried to wash the handprint off the wall, but it wouldn't come off. They wiped it and washed it. Then they painted over it. Then they dug out the plaster and replastered the spot. But always the handprint returned, as real as conscience and just as inexplicable.

In 1975 the *National Enquirer* hired a college professor to perform a spectographic analysis of the handprint to determine its origin and what it consisted of. The professor's report indicated that there was nothing there—no grime, no perspiration, no pigmentation, no nothing. According to the analysis the handprint doesn't exist. But it's there.

The Old Jail Museum itself is open for tours only on weekends. In the dungeon I visited beneath the prison, there was no electricity and only one toilet in sixteen cells used for solitary confinement. Others used buckets emptied only when the prisoner was released. The most startling aspect about the tour is the realization that people were actually serving time here until recent years. The cells for solitary confinement were used until 1980, and the prison remained open until 1995. (Call the Old Jail Museum at 570-325-5259.)

The former Carbon County Prison in Mauch Chunk, where the Molly Maguires were hanged, is now the Old Jail Museum in Jim Thorpe.

★ ★

The Hidden Hooded Man Monument

Mahanoy City

Among its claims to fame, besides being the first town in America with cable TV (and this was in 1948 before most people had televisions of any kind), Mahanoy City (population 4,600) boasts two unique memorials across from each other on Center Street near the Citizens Fire Company. On the north side of the street is what looks like a mom and pop war memorial in the side yard of a white clapboard house surrounded by a white picket fence. Inside that fenced-in yard is a US Army M-60-A3 Patton Tank used in World War II. In front of the tank is a stone with a plaque identifying it as an all-wars memorial to men and women of the Mahanoy Area who served.

The tank turret and cannon face the street. In fact, they're pointing directly at an entirely different memorial across the street. This is either ironic, or perhaps appropriate, because the Molly Maguires always found themselves under the gun—or under the gallows. The Molly Maguire Historical Park is much more discreet than the neighboring tank-brandishing war memorial. Perhaps it is the subject matter—the execution by hanging of twenty-six coal miners in the 1870s. Or perhaps it is the sense of shame and secrecy that still shrouds the events and motivations of those involved. "It was part of that era that was kept quiet," said the vice president of the borough council on the day the park was dedicated in May 2010. "People were afraid to tell their stories because of the times."

It is easy to drive or even walk past the park without noticing it on the corner of Center and Catawissa Streets. There is an eight-foot-high pale stone wall in front of the tiny park. From the street you can't see the statue of the hooded man about to be hanged. The life-sized statue by sculptor Zenos Frudakis shows the man bound hand and foot, standing in front of a gallows. There is no noose, but his fate is clear. What is striking about the statue is the dignity of the condemned man. He stands erect, dressed in his best clothes, his vest buttoned from top to bottom, his suit coat open. He could be on his way to church.

The statue of a man, wrists and ankles bound by ropes, about to be hanged from a gallows, is the central figure in the pocket-sized Molly Maguire Historical Park in Mahanoy City.

On the opposite walls on three sides of the hooded man are etched black granite panels telling the story of the labor strife and violence exacerbated by ethnic and religious tensions between Irish Catholic immigrants and native Protestants of English, Welsh, and German origin. The Molly Maguires were members of a secret organization within a secret organization, the AOH, Ancient Order of Hibernians. They could be described as the radical wing, something like the Provos of the IRA during the 1970s. "History depicts the Molly Maguires as either a band of Irish American martyrs or criminals of labor struggle,"

★ ★

one plaque reads. "Regardless of how history portrays the men called the Molly Maguires, their story provides us with an example of mankind's perseverance in the face of trial and tribulation."

During the era from 1862 to 1879 there were murders on both sides throughout Pennsylvania's anthracite coal region in towns like Centralia, Shenandoah, Summit Hill, Shamokin, Mahanoy City, Tamaqua, Audenreid, and Lansford. But only Molly Maguires met official justice at the end of a rope. After the Molly Maguires were infiltrated by an undercover Pinkerton detective, James McParland, his testimony in court led to the executions of ten Mollies on a single day, June 21, 1877—six in Pottsville and four in Mauch Chunk (now Jim Thorpe). By 1879 another ten convicted Mollies had become hooded men.

In 1970 Sean Connery and Richard Harris starred in a popular film version of those events. In the movie *The Molly Maguires*, Connery played the role of John "Black Jack" Kehoe, a Molly leader who was executed. Harris played the role of the Pinkerton spy McParland. At the end of the movie Kehoe is about to hang, and McParland comes to visit him in his cell. They almost act like friends, the doomed Kehoe joking like it was all a good time before he was betrayed. Finally he asks, "What are you doing here?" McParland doesn't reply. "Is it forgiveness? "And right before Sean Connery lunges at Richard Harris, the condemned man says, "I never could stand the sight of a man carrying a cross."

On a plaque on the wall of the Molly Maguire Historical Park the name of the chairman of the advisory board is listed as "Sir Sean Connery."

Home of the Martin Guitar

Nazareth

"America's Guitar" is made in Nazareth, which historically is well known for the quality of its woodworkers. I'm speaking of Nazareth, Pennsylvania, of course, which is six miles from Bethlehem, an American city that historically was known for its production of steel until its

Home to America's Guitar, the C. F. Martin
headquarters in Nazareth.

luck ran out. The enormous Bethlehem Steel plant is now a casino.
Explain that your grandchildren. But the fine tradition of woodwork-
ing continues in the borough of Nazareth, home to C. F. Martin & Co.
where fine guitars and other stringed instruments have been manufactured continuously since Christian Frederick Martin Sr. set up shop in
the Lehigh Valley in 1839. The Martin guitar story is a family story that
unfolds over six generations from birth of the first C. F. Martin in 1796
in Markneukirchen, Germany, to the current CEO Christian Frederick
Martin IV, who oversees production by six hundred employees at the
198,000-square-foot factory that is open for tours and includes an
impressive guitar museum.

★ ★

**On the Martin Guitar factory tour you will see guitars
made the old-fashioned way—as well as with robots.**

So beloved is the Martin brand name to professional musicians that
the name "America's Guitar" is only the beginning of the accolades. If
Eric Clapton had his say, the Martin brand might be called "Heaven's
Guitar" or maybe "Reincarnation's Guitar." On the wall of the guitar
museum is a quote from Clapton: "If I could choose what to come
back as, it would be a Martin OM-45." I guess you have to be an afi-
cionado to appreciate that. But there is no doubt of the impact Martin
guitars have had on popular music since the introduction of the Dread-
nought or D size guitar series in 1929.

**Some of the famous guitars on display
at the Martin Guitar Museum.**

Since then the Martin guitar has been a staple of musicians in every genre of American music decade after decade, from cowboy performers like Gene Autry and Montana Slim, to country crooners like George Jones and Johnny Cash, to folk artists like Joan Baez and young Bob Dylan, to rock and rollers like Elvis and Rick Nelson. To make that point, the walls in the entry lobby of the Martin Guitar visitors' center, factory, and museum are lined with dozens of LP record album jackets and CD box covers featuring performers playing Martin guitars, from Donovan to Steven Stills, to Simon and Garfunkel to the Smothers Brothers.

Inside the museum are one of a kind instruments, including the D-100, the one-millionth Martin guitar produced, which has a chandelier-sized mother-of-pearl inlay covering the back, as well as the double-necked six- and twelve-string guitar prototype made for Eric

Continued on page 228

How Jim Thorpe Came to Pennsylvania

In the light of day on a September afternoon, the town of Jim Thorpe glows with a rust red from the Carbon County courthouse. The building was built with stone quarried from the mountain called Mauch Chunk ("Bear Mountain" to the original inhabitants, who called themselves Lenni Lenape, which in their tongue meant "original inhabitants"). The town itself was called Mauch Chunk until 1954, when the body of the greatest American athlete, Jim Thorpe, was interred there in exchange for its original name.

No small irony there—an Indian name changed to honor an Indian with a European name. On May 28, 1888, in what was still called Indian Territory, now called Oklahoma, a nine-and-a-half-pound baby boy was born to a member of the Thunder Clan of the Sac and Fox tribe. He was born at sunrise. His mother named him *Wa-tho-huck*, meaning "Bright Path." His father, Hiram Thorpe, a direct descendent of Chief Black Hawk and an accomplished athlete in every sport he endeavored, named his son James.

The story of Jim Thorpe, All-American, is better known to most people through the movie by that name, starring Burt Lancaster. But Jim Thorpe was a real person and his athletic exploits led him to be named the best athlete of the first half of the twentieth century in a poll by sportswriters in 1950. Thorpe broke into the American consciousness in 1907 when he came to Pennsylvania's famous Carlisle Indian Institute and made it even more famous by playing football under the coach who would himself become a legend, Glenn "Pop" Warner. Playing in a game against national football power, the Army team, Thorpe scored on the opening kickoff, which was called back due to a penalty. On the ensuing kickoff Thorpe ran for another touchdown on Carlisle's way to a twenty-seven-to-six victory. "He was able to do everything anyone else could do but he could do it better," said Army cadet Dwight D. Eisenhower, who Thorpe put out of the game with a crushing tackle that ended Ike's football career. "There was no one like him in the world."

In 1912 Thorpe won two gold medals at the Stockholm Olympics in the decathlon and pentathlon. He met King Gustav V of Sweden, who shook Thorpe's hand and said, "You, sir, are the greatest athlete in the world." That is the quote that appears on Jim Thorpe's tomb, located a couple of miles outside of downtown Jim Thorpe on North Street (Route 903). Thorpe played professional baseball for the Giants, Reds, and Braves. He was the highest-paid player in the National Football League, of which he served as president from 1920 until 1926. He could do everything on a football field, including kick. On a return to Carlisle in 1941 at the age of fifty-two, Thorpe stood in the middle of the field and drop-kicked a football over the goal. He then turned and placekicked a field goal over the other end zone—wearing street shoes.

Final resting place for "the greatest athlete in the world."

When he died in 1953, a newspaper editor in Carbon County seized upon the idea of bringing Jim Thorpe's body to the towns of Mauch Chunk and East Mauch Chunk, which would merge and change their names to Jim Thorpe. Thorpe's widow agreed to move his body to Pennsylvania, and in 1954, one hundred years after the founding of East Mauch Chunk, the athlete's body was buried there. The Jim Thorpe Memorial has been augmented in recent years with a sculpture garden and metal placards telling stories from his life.

Continued from page 225

Clapton. So many guitars, so little time. The museum also includes a workshop resembling the one where the original Martin guitars were painstakingly manufactured by individual craftsmen in the 1800s. During the factory tour—which is free and you are allowed to take photos—you see that the days of the handmade Martin guitar have been replaced by many hands in an assembly process that includes robots and lasers as well as old school low-tech tools such as spring-loaded wooden clothespins, which are used by the hundreds during the rim assembly process done by hand.

What is also evident while watching the hundreds working on the factory floor is the sense of craft each person brings to his or her portion of the guitar-making process, whether it's operating a laser cutting tool or applying a hand polish to the finished product. There is an evident seriousness about the individual guitar each person has the responsibility to produce. You really don't get to see that much anymore in America, something being made from scratch, from a rough piece of lumber to an exquisite musical instrument. There is a pride in that you can sense at the Martin guitar factory, where you are reminded of what it looked like when America was a nation of makers rather than merely a nation of consumers. For information and tour times call Martin Guitar Museum, Factory Tour, and Visitors' Center at (610) 759-2837 or visit www.martinguitar.com.

Jayne Mansfield: Never Quite Marilyn Monroe
Pen Argyl

Under a steel gray January 2012 sky with the rounded hump of dark Blue Mountain behind, I saw Jayne Mansfield for the first time. It was a heaving white bosom against the darkness of the background. A heart-shaped white marble tombstone cleaving the winter bleakness around Pen Argyl. "What are those?" my daughter Molly had asked minutes earlier, pointing to the huge cone-shaped slag heaps of junk rock you see outside of Pennsylvania coal towns. Given what we were

Always decorated with colorful plastic flowers is the heart-shaped tombstone of Hollywood blonde bombshell Jayne Mansfield in Pen Argyl.

trying to find, they looked like huge barren breasts, dark and lifeless. And in the midst of this gloom, Molly spotted Jayne's boobs across a cemetery of tombstones.

Not knowing that the road within the cemetery looped around and would have left us right in front of the tomb of America's second most famous blonde bombshell of the mid-twentieth century, I stepped out of the car ("Molly, do you want to come? Please? Come on, it's only a

★ ★

little way and we've driven so far. Don't you want to see what it looks like up close?") and then I walked alone across fifty yards of earth above the frozen faithfully departed to gaze at the carefully tended burial plot of Jayne Mansfield, with bright pink and fresh plastic flowers in decorative urns on either side.

In the 1960s the name of Jayne Mansfield was certainly more famous as an actress than the name of her more accomplished actress daughter, Mariska Hargitay, is today. After all, daughter Mariska, has represented two things—Law and Order—for more than a decade in her role as Det. Olivia Benson in the popular crime series *Law and Order: Special Victims Unit.* The two things most associated with her mother Jayne are Bada-Boom and Bada-Bing.

Jayne Mansfield was a Bryn Mawr girl. Literally. She was born in Bryn Mawr Hospital on April 19, 1933. By the time she died in a late-night car crash on the road from Biloxi, Mississippi, to New Orleans, Louisiana, on June 29, 1967, she'd spent most of her life away from her home state. But she is buried in Fairview Cemetery outside Pen Argyl in Northhampton County, where her mother's family still lives. Jayne Mansfield was the poor man's Norma Jean, a not-quite Marilyn Monroe. She was famous mostly for two things, which she showed off at every opportunity.

Mansfield arrived in Hollywood in the mid-1950s and got her first job after writing "40-22-34" on a card she left in a producer's office. Never a star but always an attraction, Jayne Mansfield once said, "I decided early in life that the first thing to do was to become famous—I'd worry about acting later." Jayne lived up (or down) to her ambitions. While trying to break into the movies, she won a series of beauty contests with names like Miss Negligee, Miss Nylon Sweater, Miss Geiger Counter, and Miss Tomato. She appeared in a legitimate hit movie, *Will Success Spoil Rock Hunter?,* but mostly she is remembered as a heaving bosom in various low-budget foreign movies like *The Loves of Hercules* starring her muscleman husband, Mickey Hargitay.

In 1964 when the Beatles arrived in the United States on their first tour, they were asked which American celebrity they would most like to meet. The lads chose Jayne Mansfield. Upon meeting them, she asked the mop-topped John Lennon if his hair was real. He replied by looking at her breasts and asking, "Are those real?"

In the end, Jayne Mansfield's career in Hollywood was all but over. She was appearing at a supper club in Biloxi when she died in a car crash, in which—contrary to widely held belief—she was not decapitated. A blonde bouffant wig she was wearing was thrown from the vehicle, which started the rumors. Like the swimming pool outside her Sunset Boulevard home and the bed inside it, Jayne Mansfield's tombstone is in the shape of a heart. The inscription beneath her name reads, WE LIVE TO LOVE YOU MORE EACH DAY. (Fairview Cemetery, Middletown Road just outside of Pen Argyl.)

The Day the Earth Ate the River
Port Griffith

If Don McLean wrote an epic song about the Pennsylvania coal industry along the lines of "American Pie," the date January 22, 1959, would be remembered as "the day the music died." That was the day the earth swallowed the river and old King Coal drowned.

It happened in Port Griffith, one of the towns "up the line" as they say in Wilkes-Barre, meaning the Wyoming Valley communities along the Susquehanna River north of it and south of Scranton, where the same towns become "down the line." There were eighty-one miners at work that day in the Knox Coal Company's two mine shafts, one of them a nearly exhausted dig in the Pittston Vein, which ran alongside and underneath the Susquehanna River. Soon it became an underground branch of the Susquehanna. At 11:20 a.m., the river broke through the roof of the mine, sending a virtual Niagara Falls into not only the Knox mine but into all the other mines that honeycombed the valley. Most of the miners escaped, but twelve were swept away.

★ ★

The hole in the river formed a giant whirlpool that sucked 2.7 million gallons of water per minute into the mines. Attempts were made to plug the hole with fifty-ton coal cars, called gondolas, that were dumped into the river. Sixty gondolas were sucked into the whirlpool and vanished like toys down the bathtub drain. It took another four hundred coal cars plus 25,000 cubic yards of earth, rock, and boulders before the hole in the river stopped gulping after three days. During that time more than 10 billion gallons of water poured into the mines. The Knox Mine Disaster, as it has been known ever since, marked the end of deep anthracite mining in the region. It was Pennsylvania's wreck of the *Edmund Fitzgerald,* and like Lake Superior, the Susquehanna never gave up her dead. The bodies of the twelve miners were never found.

In the aftermath the web of greed and corruption that caused the Knox Mine Disaster was uncovered. State mine inspectors had turned the other way as Knox Mine officials ordered their miners to dig shafts more than 125 feet past the "stop line" beneath the Susquehanna. When the river burst through, only six feet separated the mine roof from the riverbed. One of the founders of the Knox Mine, John Sciandra, was the boss of the northeastern Pennsylvania organized crime family. A secret partner in the Knox Mine was an official with the United Mine Workers Union. The level of corruption by government inspectors, the betrayal by union leaders, and the criminal greed that drove it all were exposed in the trials of ten people indicted in the aftermath of the Knox Mine Disaster. However, only three served jail time.

In front of St. Joseph's Church in Port Griffith stands a tombstone engraved with the names of the twelve men who perished in the Knox Mine Disaster. Every January 22, a memorial service is held at the church not only for the twelve dead miners, but also for the death of the coal industry. In the wake of the mine flooding, 7,500 jobs were lost in towns up and down the line.

Hot New Beer Is America's Oldest
Pottsville

One of Pennsylvania's most popular beers was an overnight success, comparatively speaking. A decade or so must seem like the day before yesterday to a company that's been brewing beer for more than 170 years. Before there was a Bud for you or a Schaeffer to sing about, before Miller even had life, let alone a high life, there was a Yuengling Brewery in Pottsville. Founded in 1829 by David G. Yuengling, the family-owned business is America's oldest brewery and was so designated by the National Registry of Historic Places during the Bicentennial celebration in 1976.

To have survived all that time, the Yuengling Brewery had to overcome a hurdle that put most of its competition out of business for good: the Eighteenth Amendment to the Constitution, better known as Prohibition, which became law in 1919. Yuengling responded by switching over to the production of an almost nonalcoholic brew called near beer. In 1920 the company opened a dairy next to the brewery. Somehow, the company survived until 1933 when Prohibition was repealed. To celebrate the victory of "wets" over "dries" at the polls, Yuengling produced its first real beer in more than a decade and called it Winner. (A truckload of Winner beer was shipped to new president Franklin D. Roosevelt as a welcome to the White House.)

For most beer drinkers outside of central Pennsylvania, Yuengling remained the answer to a trivia question (What is America's oldest . . . ?) until the fifth generation of Yuenglings transformed it from a beloved regional beer into a nationally known brand name. Richard L. Yuengling purchased the company from his father and uncle in 1985 and immediately began marketing the product to younger customers. The result has been a 400 percent increase in sales. Yuengling's Black and Tan—half porter, half lager—was an immediate hit among urban sophisticates in Philadelphia and Baltimore. Soon Yuengling lager had become a staple in bars where just a year before people didn't know how to pronounce it (for the record, it's *YING-ling*). To this day, the order of "lager" will get you a bottle of Yuengling in most bars.

★ ★

In 1998 Yuengling brewery began the largest expansion in its seventeen-decade history with the construction of a new brewery in Tampa, Florida, of all places. The original brewery at Fifth and Mahantongo Streets in Pottsville is still the greatest, however, and tours are conducted twice a day Monday through Friday and three times a day on Saturday during the summer months. For more information call (570) 622-4141 or visit www.yuengling.com.

The Best NFL Team You Never Heard Of
Pottsville

During the third quarter of a long and lousy Monday night football game on October 13, 2003, the St. Louis Rams scored a rare safety on their way to a thirty-six-point shutout over the Atlanta Falcons. The two-point safety made the score nineteen to zero, and there being little else of interest to discuss in the contest on the field, the ABC statistics crew put together a graphic showing the five NFL teams that had allowed the most safeties in a single season. Finishing third on the all-time list, with four safeties during the 1927 season, were the Pottsville Maroons. ABC commentator John Madden, who knows a little football, looked at the graphic and said, "Pottsville? Where's that?" After a moment Madden's broadcasting boothmate Al Michaels replied, "Pennsylvania, I think." You could almost hear the scratching of heads on national TV. Finally some director gave them the answer over their headsets, but Madden didn't pretend he knew it all along. "I'm embarrassed," he said. "I should know this." And perhaps he should have known, considering that during his playing days Madden was an offensive lineman for the Philadelphia Eagles, the closest NFL city to Pottsville.

What Madden and Michaels didn't tell Monday-night-football viewers was that the Pottsville Maroons were not only a member of the National Football League; the team from tiny Pottsville with homegrown players from Coal Country was an NFL powerhouse. In fact,

Pennsylvania's "other" NFL championship-winning team was denied its place in the record books on a technicality. The Maroons should join fellow Keystone State NFL championship teams like the six-time Steelers (1974, 1975, 1978, 1979), three-time Eagles (1948, 1949, 1960), and the 1926 Frankford Yellow Jackets, which was the NFL franchise in Philadelphia before the Eagles were founded. On December 6, 1925, the Pottsville Maroons defeated the Chicago Cardinals, in Chicago, by a score of twenty-one to seven to win the NFL championship. No one disputes that the Maroons from Pottsville (population 16,000) won the match against the Cardinals from Chicago (population 16,000-plus-five-million).

But the rightful champions got hosed by the NFL rules committee in a ruling that stripped the Maroons of the title. The dispute—in a nutshell—is over the NFL's decision to suspend Pottsville at the end of the 1925 season for agreeing to play an exhibition game against Notre Dame University the week *after* the Chicago Cardinals game. The issue was not the opponent but the venue, Shibe Park (later Connie Mack Stadium) in Philadelphia. League rules at the time forbade one team from encroaching on another team's core fan base (or in today's terminology, "media market"). The owner of the Frankford Yellow Jackets—which won the championship a year later—protested to the league that those mighty Maroons from Pottsville were muscling in on the Yellow Jackets' humble hive of fans. The subsequent suspension led to the Cardinals being declared the NFL champions in a postseason awards ceremony in which the Cardinals' owner refused to accept the championship trophy. This has never prevented the Cardinals from listing their 1925 NFL Championship on the team's resume in whatever city the Cardinals happen to have called home over the last eight decades (Chicago, St. Louis, Phoenix . . . wherever!).

However, for Pottsville, this was their last shot at the Bigs. Never again would a Pottsville sports team, professional or amateur, win a national title. And this was the National Football League, and it was the championship game, and Pottsville did beat Chicago straight up.

So why doesn't Pottsville at least get an asterisk in the record books, if not a championship trophy?

As you might imagine, this issue is of keenest interest to sports fans from the city of Pottsville, the county seat of Schuylkill County and formerly a literary capital back when novelist John O'Hara wrote tales of its intrigues and class distinctions for a nation still interested in places like Pottsville. Today an NFL team called the Maroons from a coal town the size of Pottsville seems as impossible to justify as an NFL franchise named for the meat-packing industry in some small Midwestern factory town like, say, Green Bay, Wisconsin. And yet the Maroons were as real as the Green Bay Packers (who lost thirty-one to zero to the Maroons in the 1925 Thanksgiving Day game played in Pottsville— Brett Favre was the backup quarterback that day). A few years later the Maroons, like the Cardinals, moved to another city. Unlike the Cardinals the Maroons name and the franchise died in Boston in 1930.

And so recognition of the Pottsville NFL championship lies, for want of a better word, marooned by NFL history books. Pennsylvania's Historical and Museum Commission has marked the Maroons' achievement with a lawyerly worded blue and yellow historical marker in downtown Pottsville. It reads, "In 1925 the Maroons compiled a record widely believed as the league's best. They climaxed their season by defeating Notre Dame in a well-publicized pro-vs.-college match in Philadelphia—but were denied the league championship in a controversial league decision."

Notre Dame fielded the Four Horsemen that day beneath a steel-gray December sky in 1925. The pros from Pottsville beat the fabled backfield from South Bend 9–7 in an exhibition game that cost them the national title. The following season the Maroons outscored their opponents by a remarkable 409 to 31 points, including seventeen shutouts over a twenty-game schedule, and still managed to finish third in the NFL standings behind the Frankford Yellow Jackets and the Chicago Bears.

Hollywood Gives Scranton a Thumbs-Up

Scranton

If you love Pennsylvania, you've got to love what happened in Scranton during the last weekend in October 2007. Despite two days of almost constant rain on Friday and Saturday, the capital city of NEPA (Northeastern Pennsylvania) won the hearts and minds of Hollywood during the three-day Office-Con, a gathering of cast, writers, producers, and thousands of fans of the NBC hit comedy *The Office*, which is set, even if not actually shot, in Scranton, Pennsylvania. The almost

Did you get the memo? Paper is NOT dead!

funereal weather didn't hinder the enthusiasm of the estimated five thousand fans from all over the country and world whose devotion to the quirky comedy about the office employees of the fictitious Dunder Mifflin Paper Company had brought them from as far away as Australia to have a chance to mingle with the cast. And fans were delighted to be there with or without all the show's stars at what seemed at the time likely to become to become an annual event. And when the skies cleared into brilliant sunshine around 4:00 p.m. Saturday afternoon, it was like the buoyant karma of the gathering had won the battle with nature. From the hilltop campus of the University of Scranton, where the Office Convention was headquartered, downtown Scranton seemed to gleam in a halo of golds and russets from the tree-crowded hillsides.

It looked every bit as beautiful as *The Office* executive producer Greg Daniels described it during a crowded press conference where he became perhaps the first person, with a straight face anyway, to compare hardscrabble Scranton with the mythical Emerald City. "As we drove into Scranton for the first time, it was like arriving in Oz after reading about it all those years," Daniels said. "The surrounding area is so much more beautiful than the dusty brown lots in Van Nuys (California) where we create our show."

The Office has made famous an old saying that a Scranton cop told me dates back to the days of vaudeville: "There ain't no party like a Scranton party, 'cause a Scranton party never ends." And *The Office* cast partied like it was still 1999. They sang karaoke late at night, they jammed onstage with the local band, the Scrantones. Philly-born Kate Flannery (who plays Meredith) joined the band to sing along to the "Pennsylvania Polka," and Ed Helms (who plays Andy) summed up the cast's experience: "It's like we're the Beatles in Scranton." And in a way this quirky TV comedy series did for Scranton what the Beatles did for Liverpool and what *Rocky* did for Philadelphia. It's making a hometown suddenly feel special in the eyes of the world for being what it's always been—itself.

Deep below Scranton

Scranton

Tony Donofrio has an upstate Pennsylvania voice that could crack slate, even here, 250 feet underground in the Lackawanna Coal Mine outside Scranton. Tony is our tour guide and his voice does not require amplification. It is a high-pitched, high-speed voice with wide-nasal Midwestern A sounds, perfect for a bunch of beefy guys sitting around a table in Chicago toasting "Da Bears!" Tony has been a coal miner since 1964, when the coal industry in this part of Pennsylvania was already on its last legs. You can tell he'd rather be digging coal than giving tours, but you can also tell that he takes pride in giving tours to people who shake their heads at the thought of human beings spending their working lives in perpetual darkness and danger. "It's not for everybody," says Tony of the miner's life; twenty people in the tour group nod.

The tour takes about an hour, more than enough time to convince even hardy souls that working life aboveground has its sweeter pleasures. For instance, there are no monkey veins in most surface jobs. Monkey veins are seams of coal so narrow that miners must crawl on their hands and knees or squat-walk like lesser primates. Assignment to a monkey vein was awarded by the labor union law of natural selection based upon seniority. The more seniority, the less monkey walking. Most of the Lackawanna Coal Mine tour is through roomy and well-lighted chambers, but at some point during the tour, Tony or one of his cohorts will kill the lights just long enough to demonstrate the claustrophobic effects of an optical condition known as pitch black. "Hear that?" asks Tony, banging an iron rod onto the tunnel roof overhead. "That's solid. That's the sound a miner wants to hear. Now hear this?" he asks, demonstrating the sound a miner doesn't want to hear overhead, a muffled dull *thunk* rather than the solid ping of iron on rock. Thunk means something's wrong, a cavity no dentist can fill.

The story of the Lackawanna Coal Mine is the story of Scranton. The city took its current name in 1851 from the founders of the Lackawanna

That hand sticking up is supposed to be a miner trapped in a cave. Tour guide Tony Donofrio can push a button that makes the hand move, scaring the bejabbers out of visitors to the Lackawanna Coal Mine tour.

★ ★

Iron and Coal Company, established in 1840. George W. and Seldon Scranton discovered that the black diamond heat of burning anthracite did wonderful hardening things to nails and, later, rails. The expression "hard as nails" may have been around for a long time, but Scranton made nails harder, stronger. By 1900 one out of six miles of railroad tracks laid in the United States was forged steel from Scranton.

The owners of the region's coal mines felt they were the stewards of God's abundant gifts underground. They were, in their own words, "Christian men to whom God in His infinite wisdom had given control of the property interests in this country!" A young man named Henry Ford wanted to build an automobile manufacturing plant in Scranton, but the coal barons at play in the fields of the Lord felt such employment opportunities would only confuse their childlike workers, not to mention cut into profits by creating a competitive wage situation among prospective employees. Ford looked elsewhere, and Scranton looks back in regret, or perhaps relief, that it did not become Pennsylvania's Detroit.

After all, being Pennsylvania's Scranton was difficult enough. In 1897 union-minded miners in Lattimer outside of Hazleton protested wages and conditions and were answered with a hail of bullets from sheriff's deputies that killed nineteen outright and wounded another forty-nine. The Lattimer Massacre led to the rise of a young labor leader named John L. Mitchell, who was elected president of the United Mine Workers union two years later at the age of twenty-nine. Mitchell, whose statue stands in front of the Lackawanna County courthouse in Scranton, led the mine workers in a bitter and passionate and seemingly never-ending strike in 1902. It was the longest strike in labor history until that time—165 days or twenty-three weeks or five and a half months—requiring the personal involvement of President Theodore Roosevelt to settle it. It transformed the labor-management landscape, prompting laws to protect the rights of working men and their families.

Continued on page 244

If Joe Biden Had Grown Up in Wilkes-Barre, Would He Be Vice President?

Vice President Joe Biden's roots in Scranton have been something of a mixed blessing for his hometown. For all the positive publicity generated by Biden's fond connection with the capital city of Northeast Pennsylvania, it is the *Saturday Night Live* skits featuring Jason Sudeikis playing Joe Biden as a loose cannon that gave many Americans an indelible comedic impression of Scranton. The two most famous examples were the *SNL* skits following the vice presidential debates in 2008 and 2012.

In the first debate, then Senator Biden of Delaware was matched up with his Republican opponent, then Alaska Governor Sarah Palin. At the time of the *SNL* spoof debate, Palin was at the height of her *SNL* fame as portrayed by virtual look-alike Tina Fey. But it was Sudeikis's Biden who stole the show with his objection to Palin referring to him as a Washington insider."You know I get tired of being called an insider," Biden began. "I come from Scranton, Pennsylvania, and that's as hardscrabble a place as you're ever gonna find. I'll show you around sometime and you'll see. It's a hellhole. An absolute jerkwater of a town. You couldn't stand to spend a weekend there. It's an awful, awful, sad place filled with sad desperate people with no ambition. Nobody, and I mean nobody but me, came out of that place. It's a genetic cesspool. So don't tell me that I'm a Washington insider because I come from the absolute worst place on earth. Scranton, Pennsylvania. And Wilmington, Delaware, isn't much better."

Many Scrantonians were laughing through their tears at that humiliating tribute on national TV. And that was just the beginning of the Biden salvos of mock praise to Scranton on *Saturday Night Live*. In so many skits featuring the vice president, Scranton got a shout out much like "beautiful downtown Burbank" got on Johnny Carson's *Tonight Show* over the years. But it was hard to top the Dante's *Inferno* reference made during the *Saturday Night Live* skit spoofing the 2012 vice presidential debate between Biden and Wisconsin Congressman Paul Ryan, in which the vice president (Sudeikis, again) raised (or perhaps lowered) the bar in terms of criticism of his hometown.

Ryan, played by *SNL* cast member Taran Killam, said, "Vice President Biden and I come from very similar places. I'm from Janesville, Wisconsin, and he's from Scranton, Pennsylvania. Do you know what the unemployment rate in Scranton is right now? It's 10 percent. I'd like to know what Senator Biden would say to the hard-working people of towns like Janesville and Scranton."

Sudeikis, who owns the Biden impersonation franchise, answered, "I know what I'd like to say to my friend and to the people of Janesville. Things may be bad where you live, but I guarantee you it's a paradise next to the burning coal heap that is Scranton, Pennsylvania. You know that show, *The Walking Dead*? It would make a good tourism ad for Scranton, Pennsylvania. If you went to the lowest circle of hell, you'd still be forty-five minutes outside of Scranton. I grew up there; I love it. It's the single worst place on earth."

Despite that national laughingstock moment, Scranton voters supported the Democratic ticket featuring their shoot-from-the-lip native son for vice president on Election Day by a 63 percent to 37 percent margin. The same was not true in Ryan's hometown of Janesville, Wisconsin, where in November 2012 Ryan lost in Janesville for the first time in his eight races for the House of Representatives. He lost the vote for Congress in Janesville by 10 points and at the same time lost by 25 points on the Republican ticket for vice president. As one columnist noted about the election results from the hometowns of both vice presidential candidates, "Obviously the people of Scranton know a joke when they see one. And so do the voters of Janesville. "

★ ★

Continued from page 241

The need for such laws is apparent here, 1,200 feet downhill from the opening of the Lackawanna Coal Mine. That's where we meet a child, actually a mannequin of a child, who could be seven years old but looks younger. The little boy is called a nipper. His job was to open and close doors to allow coal cars to pass and ventilation to circulate. "This nipper," said Tony, "had this much light to work with for eight, ten hours a day." Think of a Zippo lighter illuminating a subway concourse. That's how much light his coal oil headlamp could muster. Even by 1908, four years after the strike, one out of four mine workers was a boy between the ages of seven and sixteen.

The skies above Scranton foundries glowed twenty-four hours a day until the Pennsylvania iron ore gave out. Coal was king for another generation, but peak production came in 1917 during the First World War. Nothing has been the same since the Knox Mine Disaster of 1959. But one thing is true in Scranton, Wilkes-Barre, Hazleton, Shamokin, and wherever else God's self-appointed stewards harvested the wealth below the earth—childhood is no longer as dark as it once was. (Lackawanna Coal Mine is open daily 10:00 a.m. to 4:30 p.m. April through November. For more info visit www.theminegame.com.)

The First War Between the States

Wilkes-Barre

At about the same time that Charles Mason and Jeremiah Dixon arrived in Philadelphia to begin the survey that would settle the boundary dispute between Pennsylvania and Maryland in 1763, settlers from Connecticut began arriving in the Wyoming Valley of northeast Pennsylvania. Not only did they claim that the land belonged to them; they claimed that the land was part of the colony of Connecticut. Now, it's understandable that there could be some rival claims to the same land by adjoining colonies such as Pennsylvania and Maryland, especially when there are no natural boundaries like rivers to mark where one state ends and another begins. But how the heck do settlers from

★ ★

Connecticut leapfrog over New York, land in Pennsylvania, and call it home?

Needless to say, there was a king involved. In fact, it was the same King Charles II who in 1681 granted William Penn the land in the New World that would become Pennsylvania. Unfortunately, nineteen years earlier in 1662, King Charles II had granted portions of northeastern Pennsylvania to the colony of Connecticut. Like the border dispute with Maryland, the land feud between Pennsylvania and Connecticut sim-mered for almost a century before being resolved. Unlike the dispute with Maryland, which was settled with the border survey that became famous as the Mason-Dixon Line, the issue of Connecticut Yankees in Pennsylvania was resolved the old-fashioned way, in a series of bloody but historically obscure battles called the Yankee-Pennamite Wars.

Pennamite was the Biblical-sounding name (think Philistines) that the proper colonists from Connecticut called their Pennsylvania neigh-bors. In 1762 the first Connecticut settlers arrived in the area around Wilkes-Barre. A year later the Yankees were driven out of the region by the Lenni Lenape in a massacre sparked by the murder of their Chief Teedyuscung, which they blamed on the new settlers. When the Yankees returned in 1769, they found that their Pennamite rivals had taken over their lands and built a fort to defend their hold on the land. Thus began the first Yankee-Pennamite War (1769–1771).

The Yankees, like their American League baseball team namesake, were pushy overachievers who attracted the immediate dislike of everyone they encountered. The word *Yankee* originated as a deroga-tory term used by the Dutch already settled in New Amsterdam (later New York) to describe the newly arrived English settlers in Connecti-cut. The American equivalent to Yankee would be "Johnny-come-lately," although the literal Dutch Jan Kaas means "John Cheese." These Connecticut Yankees not only claimed ownership of already-settled land in Pennsylvania, but they also claimed that King Charles II gave them title to the north-south band of land as wide as today's Connecticut and

Continued on page 248

Why, Oh Why, Wyoming?

The state of Wyoming is named after Pennsylvania's Wyoming Valley. Why, one would wonder, would a territory carved out of the then-territories of Dakota, Utah, and Idaho in 1868, and eventually granted statehood in 1890, be named for a relatively unknown valley two thousand miles away? All of those territorial names were Indian in origin, but Wyoming is an eastern American Indian name, the language equivalent of giving a French province a Russian name. In Algonquin the word *wyoming* means either "large prairie place" or "mountains and valleys alternating" depending on whether you are using the French translation or the Russian.

The name Wyoming was famous in nineteenth-century America because of an eighteenth-century American massacre made more lyrical, if not more famous, by a Scottish poet named Thomas Campbell. In 1809 Campbell wrote an epic poem, "Gertrude of Wyoming," about a Revolutionary War battle on Pennsylvania soil that, I'm sure, most Pennsylvanians have never heard of. (I base that on the fact that I had never heard of it, and I'm the Pennsylvania guy writing this book.) In the 1800s Gertrude of Wyoming was as famous a name as Monica Lewinsky and for pretty much the same reasons—she was a famous victim everyone knew about, and nobody wanted to be in her shoes—although more people admired Gertrude. She was the fictional heroine of a horrific ordeal. During the Revolutionary War the Wyoming Massacre outside Wilkes-Barre was the British equivalent of the My Lai Massacre during the war in Vietnam.

On July 3, 1778, a force of four hundred keen but poorly trained Pennsylvania citizen militia, most too young or too old to be proper soldiers, advanced under General Zebulon Butler from a fortified position to meet the forces of British general John Butler, a distant relative, and his Iroquois allies under Chief Sayenqueraghta. It was a scene out of a movie. Think of the massacre of the British and Americans by the Indians in the Daniel Day Lewis version of *Last of the Mohicans.*

The continentals were drawn into a trap. While advancing on a line of apparently retreating British soldiers after a brief engagement, the Americans were attacked on both flanks by hundreds of Iroquois warriors crouching in the high grass. The untrained farmer soldiers panicked. Some fought. Some ran. They all died. Men were roasted alive in sight of the American fort where the remaining garrison huddled with the women and children. At midnight under firelight, an old white woman, who had been captured by the Iroquois as a child and later married to a chief, walked in a circle and personally executed between sixteen and twenty American soldiers with a tomahawk. She was known as Queen Esther and said to be the daughter of a Frenchman named Montour, as in Montour County.

When the soldiers were sacrificed, the Iroquois turned their attention to the women and children and remaining men fleeing Forty Fort. Gertrude of Wyoming was one of them. The event became the story that became the poem that became the metaphor for America's brave resistance and eventual triumph over British tyranny and Native American savagery on the frontier. At least, that was how it was seen in 1868 when Wyoming got its name. But then again, consider the options. Would you want to live in a state named Gertrude?

> And tranced in giddy horror Gertrude swoon'd;
> Yet, while she clasps him lifeless to her zone, Say, burst they,
> borrow'd from her father's wound,
> These drops?—Oh, God! the life-blood is her own!

★ ★

Continued from page 245

extending all the way to the Pacific Ocean. Pennsylvania's acting governor, Richard Penn, grandson of founder William Penn, wrote a letter
describing the invasion of the colony by the Yankees as an "insolent
outrage by a set of men who had long bid defiance to the laws of the
country." Then he came as close as a Quaker can come to ordering his
colonists to take up arms to repel the invaders. They did.

There were two or three wars, depending on which historian you
believe. All agree that the combatants took time out to join forces
against the British during the Revolutionary War. Hostilities recom-
menced after the Continental Congress court of arbitration ruled in
1782 that the Wyoming Valley belonged to Pennsylvania. But the
Connecticut settlers wouldn't leave, and in 1784 the Pennamite forces
burned the Yankee stronghold of Wilkes-Barre. Connecticut and Ver-
mont sent reinforcements to fight the Pennamites. It was truly a war
between the states. What a mess.

The entire issue wasn't settled until 1799, when the Pennsylvania
Legislature passed the Compromise Act to settle the claims of Connecticut. In the end the Connecticut influence in Pennsylvania includes
the towns of Wilkes-Barre, Plymouth, Kingston, Pittston, Hanover, and
Forty Fort (named after the Connecticut plan to establish townships
that could support and protect forty families). The Yankee-Pennamite
Wars were more like skirmishes between rival militias, and the total
casualties numbered in the hundreds rather than thousands, but who
knew that Pennsylvania and Connecticut actually fought a war against
each other? Pennsylvania won, of course. Otherwise we'd all be speaking Yankee.

4

North Central

Democratic political strategist *James Carville, who managed success-ful campaigns for Bob Casey for Pennsylvania governor and Harris Wof-ford for US Senator from Pennsylvania and Bill Clinton for president, famously described Pennsylvania as being "Philadelphia and Pittsburgh with Alabama in between." By that he meant, well, you know what he meant. In a word, Pennsyltucky, which is an insult to both states. Geo-graphically this politically conservative "in between" area is represented by a big T-shaped section across the northern tier of counties and down the center of the state. That has proven to be true in most elec-tions. But if there is a conservative rural "heart of Dixie" in the Keystone State, it can be found in North Central Pennsylvania. Not that that's a bad thing. Especially if you happen to be a deer. Because despite the per capita percentage of hunters in Pennsylvania compared to any other state, deer outnumber the humans in heavily forested sections of North Central.*

Perhaps incongruously, this region is also the home of Pennsylvania State University, the pride of the commonwealth and a recognized symbol of academic excellence and integrity combined with athletic success. And in an instant all that sterling reputation was irreparably tarnished in an almost inconceivable way—failure to protect children from a sexual predator. Following a grand jury report in November 2011 detailing the administration's failure to prevent former assistant

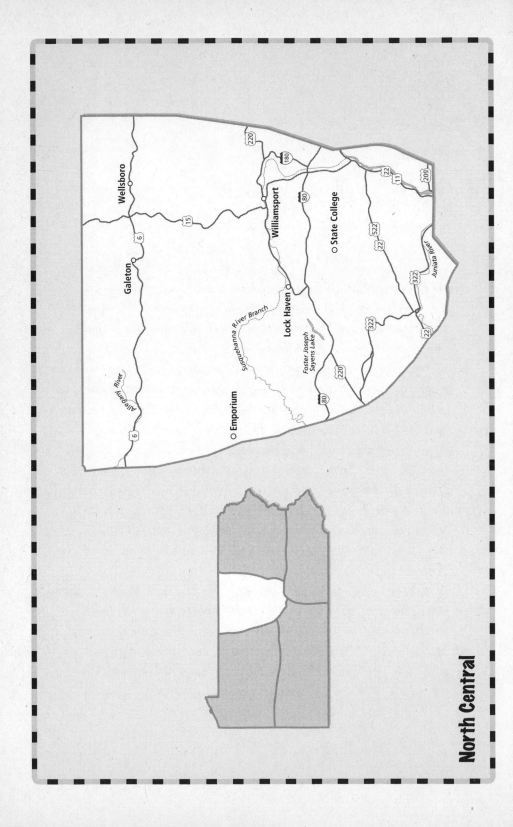

★ ★

football coach Jerry Sandusky's sexual abuse of young boys, legendary football coach Joe Paterno was fired only to die of cancer within
weeks. As of this writing the ousted president of Penn State, Graham
Spanier, faces criminal charges of perjury, obstruction of justice, and
endangering the welfare of children.

The boundaries of North Central Pennsylvania include all or parts of
Potter, Tioga, Lycoming, Clinton, Centre, and Cameron Counties from
the New York border to State College. It is an area fifty times the size
of Philadelphia with one-fifth as many people. It was the center of
Pennsylvania's lumber industry in the mid-1800s, and its largest river
town, Williamsport, with twenty-nine sawmills, boasted of having
more millionaires per capita than any other city in America. You can
hear the story at the Pennsylvania Lumber Museum off scenic Route
6 in Galeton in Potter County, which calls itself "God's Country." By
1920 the forests of North Central were stripped bare and the loggers
simply moved on, leaving it to the state and national governments to
begin the conservation efforts that have restored the green to Penn's
Woods.

★ ★

Potter County KO's Cameron County as Divorce Capital
Emporium

If you look at the Pennsylvania Statistical Abstract (and I recommend that you do, it's *fascinating* reading), you'll find Pennsylvania broken down by numbers. For instance, 6.2 Pennsylvanians per thousand get married each year, and 3.3 per thousand get divorced (usually not the same people). Some counties' divorce rates are lower than the state average. Delaware County, for instance, has a divorce rate of 1.5 per thousand, the lowest in the state. Philadelphia is second lowest, with a divorce rate of 2.1.

Most counties fall into the mid-twos, with only Greene and Wyoming Counties cracking the fours, with divorce rates of 4.2 and 4.3, respectively. Then we come to tiny (by population) Cameron County in north central Pennsylvania. According to the state statistics for 1995, the year people first took notice, Cameron County has a divorce rate of 874 people per thousand.

That's not a typo. Cameron County was "Divorce Capital of Pennsylvania" until 2009 when neighboring Potter County took the lead in the divorce business. "We're a lot higher than we were then," said Cameron County prothonotary David J. Reed, referring to the 1995 divorce statistics. "We handled more than 8,000 divorces in the year 2000." That would be 8,000 divorces in a county with a population of 5,800 for a divorce rate of more than 1,600 per thousand! That's a heap of marital discord.

The divorce business is so brisk that when you call the prothonotary's office (that's where divorce papers must be filed) at the county courthouse in Emporium, the recording gives you a menu of seven choices, the first two of which are divorce related. This has nothing to do with the rocky state of matrimony in Cameron County. It's because what Elkton is to Maryland, what Las Vegas is to Nevada, Emporium is to Pennsylvania, except people come to Emporium to get divorced instead of married. Unlike Elkton or Las Vegas, couples don't actually have to come to Emporium to end their marriages. Only the paperwork is necessary.

It all started in the early 1980s after Pennsylvania adopted a no-fault divorce law. Mike Davis, a lawyer in Pittsburgh, wanted to cash in on the new opportunity by offering a "simple, uncontested" divorce in the fastest time. The problem was that the courts in Allegheny County were clogged, and a petition for divorce could take weeks, even months. So the enterprising lawyer started approaching the courthouses in less-populated counties to see if they would process the divorces. First Davis approached Potter County (population 16,717) and Potter County told him to take a hike. So Davis came to Emporium in neighboring Cameron County, and you might say, it was a marriage made in heaven.

Each week, hundreds of divorce petitions from all over Pennsylvania pour into the Cameron County Prothonotary Office, where they are processed and then signed by a visiting judge from Elk County. The court filing fees are a major source of income for the county. In fact, the divorce-court fee income is almost half of what Cameron County reaps in property taxes. Of course, Cameron County isn't exactly advertising the fact that it has become the "Divorce Capital" of Pennsylvania. "I'd say it's a surprise to most people around here when they hear about it," says David Brown, publisher of the *Cameron County Echo*, the weekly newspaper. "It's pretty much a well-kept secret."

As big a secret was that Potter County, which originally scorned the divorce mill offer, reconsidered after recognizing the income possibilities and agreed to process out-of-county divorces in its prothonotary office. By 2009 Potter had surpassed Cameron in divorces filed from the same law firms that had been Cameron's bread and butter. In that year Potter County Courthouse in Coudersport processed more than 6,000 divorces compared to fewer than 4,000 in Cameron County. The irony of ironies is that the new Divorce Capital of Pennsylvania advertises itself as "God's Country."

★ ★

When Lumber Was King in Pennsylvania

Galeton

It has been written that when William Penn landed in Pennsylvania in 1682, his colony was so thickly forested that a squirrel could run from Philadelphia to Pittsburgh without once setting its feet on the ground. So it's really no leap of imagination to understand how one of Pennsylvania's first and greatest businesses was the lumber industry. Most of the original forest that once carpeted the commonwealth has been cut down at least once. In fact, Pennsylvania's huge state forest system was born in the first half of the twentieth century from lumbered-out mountains left barren by the lumber companies that had swept through and moved on in search of more trees. Imagine the leafy rolling mountains we see today throughout central and northern Pennsylvania without a single living tree to bend in the wind.

Much of the growth of mature trees in Pennsylvania is the legacy of the Civilian Conservation Corps (CCC), one of the so-called alphabet-soup agencies set up by the federal government during the Great Depression to put millions of unemployed men to work. Between 1933 and 1942 the CCC planted 200 million new trees in the nation's forests, and Pennsylvania has living proof of those efforts. The story of the CCC is among those told at the Pennsylvania Lumber Museum on Route 6 in Potter County, not far from Galeton, where one of the largest sawmills in the world was located when lumber was king in Pennsylvania. The Lumber Museum tells the story of the "woodhicks," the seasonal lumberjacks who worked from November until April in the lumber camps that dotted the forested landscape of Pennsylvania.

Woodhicks worked from 5:00 a.m. until lights out at 9:00 p.m. six days a week. They lived in bunkhouses in camps of sixty men and worked through the cold and snow, cutting down trees and hauling the lumber to train cars traveling on tracks laid by the lumbermen. It was hard work performed by hard men who lived in close quarters and rarely bathed. They hung their wet socks and long johns on

**More deer than people live in sparsely populated
Potter County (16,000 people over 1,100 square
miles), which calls itself "God's Country."**

clotheslines strung near the bunkhouse woodstoves and, as the self-guided tour booklet notes, "the stench of steaming clothes added to body odors is left to your imagination." Also left to the imagination was the lumber industry in Pennsylvania, which one hundred years ago produced the majority of the white pine and hemlock boards used by builders and cabinet makers in the United States.

For more information call the museum at (814) 435-2652 or visit www.lumbermuseum.com.

★ ★

Home of the Growler

Lock Haven

Lock Haven, contrary to popular perception, was not named because the town's residents leave their doors unlocked. Even today, that could be said of more Pennsylvania towns than would care to admit it. Others suggest that Lock Haven got its name from its founder, Jerry Church, who was a loon and should have been "locked away"

Whatever you do at the Texas Lunch restaurant in Lock Haven, don't order a hoagie.

because he lived in a tree house when everyone else had their feet
set firmly on the ground. This, of course, is a gross exaggeration. Jerry
Church didn't live in a tree house. He had his law offices in a tree
house eleven feet off the ground overlooking the Susquehanna River.
He felt it was cheaper than advertising for clients.

Subsequent generations would recognize Jerry Church's eccentricity
for the genius it was. While the rest of Lock Haven was underwater
from regular Susquehanna River floods, Jerry Church's feet would have
been dry from his law office perch even during Hurricane Agnes in
1972, after which a dike was built through downtown.

At any rate it was Jerry Church, lawyer and land speculator, who
founded Lock Haven in 1832, giving it a name that was bound to
attract canal boats operating along the west branch of the Susquehanna in Clinton County. The canals in Lock Haven connected the
Susquehanna with Bald Eagle Creek. Church had to quit school at the
age of fourteen after attempting to kiss his teacher. He worked for
two years after that making shingles and then quit, noting in his mem-
oirs that hard work did not agree with him and hurt his feelings.

With Jerry Church as a founder, Lock Haven was bound to have
some eccentric institutions, and one of them is Texas Lunch, the all-
night diner that is known for growlers the way South Philly is known
for hoagies.

The growler, so named because your stomach supposedly growls
after eating one, is basically a chili dog with a special recipe. The
original Greek owners of the restaurant called their special sandwich
a Texas hot dog; they discouraged use of the nickname by charging
an extra twenty-five cents to any customer ordering a growler rather
than a Texas hot dog. The current owners have embraced the name,
and waitresses wear T-shirts identifying Lock Haven's Texas Lunch as
"Home of the Growler." The restaurant is at 204 East Main Street. Call
(570) 748-3522.

Rivals Since Birth

Pennsylvania has always had a certain attitude—I refuse to call it an inferiority complex, it's more like a healthy revulsion—toward New York. Well, lah-dee-dah, so what if your big city just surpassed our big city to become the biggest city in America in 1800? We Pennsylvanians, with our Quaker tolerance, German steadfastness, and frontier spirit, barely noticed. And that Erie Canal that linked the Great Lakes with the Atlantic Ocean through New York Harbor in 1825 and guaranteed New York's commercial dominance over Philadelphia, we couldn't help but notice that. And when New York went on to become the most powerful, successful, glamorous, and influential city in America and the world, well, wasn't that nice for New York?

Of course, for Pennsylvania it was like swallowing sulfuric acid and then being asked if we'd care for another drink. Those damn Yankees! We've loved to hate them for two hundred years. Where we Pennsylvanians were pleased to snuggle into the heart of America by calling ourselves the "Keystone State," our northern neighbors declared their modest aspirations by declaring New York the "Empire State." They were like rich in-laws who described your best expensive china as "quaint." The emotional difference between New York, the state, and New York, the city, is lost on most Pennsylvanians, except for those who live in harmony, most of the time, with their nearby New Yorker brethren who dwell in caves and huts and such along the 320-mile border separating the least populated regions in both states. Whether by accident or divine design, there are more deer than people found in the six northern-tier Pennsylvania counties that form the straight edge along the topographically invisible line defining New York's southern boundary. Even at the business end of the border on the east, where the Delaware River emphatically divides the two states, the mighty rival metropolises staring across the water at each other are Matamoras, Pennsylvania, and Port Jervis, New York, hardly a showdown between the Eagles and the Giants.

Historically, Pennsylvania's pride has been bruised by New York's size—both the city and the state. New York State is only 4,000 square miles bigger than Pennsylvania (49,576 to 45,333), and New York's population advantage of five million can be explained in a song. "You take Manhattan, the Bronx and Staten Island, too . . ." and what's left of New York City is still bigger than Philadelphia. Fortunately, since the beginning both states had neighboring New Jersey to pick on like a younger brother. The face New Jersey shows Philadelphia is Camden, New Jersey's poorest city. The face New Jersey turns to New York City is Hoboken. The poor Garden State never had a chance to impress its larger, prettier, more important neighbors. Benjamin Franklin described New Jersey's civic predicament—"like a barrel being tapped at both ends"—as being stuck between Philadelphia, then the largest city in America, and the already thriving seaport of New York. Hence were born the first Jersey jokes.

These natural-gas-fueled street lamps burn twenty-four hours a day in Wellsboro, the Tioga County seat.

The rivalry between New York and Pennsylvania is not so much one sided as it is more deeply felt by inhabitants on the western shore of the Delaware. And Pennsylvania hates admitting that! These days the battle of pride between the states is passionately joined by New Yorkers only when important issues are on the line, such as the outcome of a Sixers-Knicks or Penguins-Islanders or Steelers-Jets or Flyers-Rangers or Pirates-Mets game. Need I mention how Pennsylvanians feel about the Y-word?

Say It Ain't So, Joepa
State College

On the Monday morning after Joe Paterno died in January 2012, I awoke before daybreak and began a long and dreary winter drive to State College to pay my respects in front of the statue to the now disgraced but forever legendary Penn State football coach. I stopped for a travel cup of coffee at the local Wawa and bought two copies of that day's *Philadelphia Inquirer* with the front-page banner headline, "Lion At Rest." I would lay one copy of the newspaper in front of the Paterno statue in front of Beaver Stadium, one memento among thousands that ringed the statue that morning.

It was a drive made for contemplation. The dark, wet skies over West Philadelphia gave way to the claustrophobic tunnel vision of the Schuylkill Expressway and the Pennsylvania Turnpike. There was fog everywhere and when dawn did arrive it merely turned the fog brighter and more impenetrable. At times it seemed like mine was the only car on the highway for mile after lonely mile.

The weather suited the mission. Without any visible landscape to distract me I was in a cocoon of private thoughts. Chief among them being: Why am I doing this? That question echoed in my mind for hours and hundreds of miles until the answer took on a musical rhythm in the form of Paul Simon singing "Graceland": *"For reasons I cannot explain, some part of me wants to see Joepa, Joepa."* Young and old called him by that nickname, Joepa. The only word more endearing was "Coach."

The simple truth was I wanted to see the statue before it was removed, which it was suddenly by workmen early one Sunday morning, seven months to the day after Paterno died of cancer at the age of eighty-five. I wanted to see the statue in the context of grief and adoration in what would be a window of deference of harsh judgment for Paterno's role in the Sandusky child sex scandal. That window seemed to have slammed shut months later with the appearance of an airplane over the Penn State campus carrying a towed message that

On the day after Penn State football coach Joe Paterno died amidst the Sandusky child sex abuse scandal, thousands paid their respects by leaving mementos around the bronze statue of Paterno outside Beaver Stadium.

was as ominous as a great white shark's dorsal fin in the water: "Take down the statue or we will."

I also wanted to stand in front of the Paterno statue as an act of genuflection before a human symbol of a united State of Pennsylvania. There are very few men—name one other than Paterno—whose lives represented the achievements celebrated by the entire state, rather than a city or region. Paterno was the pope of Pennsylvania. Venerated, appreciated, and symbolic of a larger institution that was recognized for—what's the word?—goodness. Until the staggering betrayal revealed in the last months of his life and the permanent stain on his legacy, Joe Paterno represented an uncommon goodness that was the pride of Pennsylvania.

And now that was gone. And I knew that as I drove past fog-shrouded Harrisburg, crossing the Susquehanna, and then paralleling the invisible winding course of the Juniata River northwest to Lewistown, where the fog finally broke, and over the snowy mountain roads to Penn State on a bleak Monday morning.

At a Dunkin' Donuts I picked up a copy of the daily student newspaper, the *Collegian*. On the cover was a full-page photo of a twenty-three-year-old Joe Paterno, newly arrived as an assistant football coach at Penn State, not much older than his players. More than fifty years later, that image of Coach is what the editors wanted students to have as their mind's eye memory of Joe Paterno in life.

At the statue people stood silently in small groups or by themselves. I saw a mother crouched behind two young children whispering about the man who was the statue. Someone, a student probably, had draped an American flag around the bronze shoulders along with a blue and white knit Penn State scarf.

I laid the "Lion at Rest" edition of *The Inquirer* at the edge of the expanding circle of memorabilia and good wishes. I started taking pictures. After perhaps twenty minutes I noticed that a Penn State maintenance man and a campus police officer had removed the American flag from where it had been improperly draped. Wordlessly, but with the dignity of ceremony, the two men stood across from each other and folded the flag in proper triangular fashion. Then they placed it inside a clear plastic sleeve and laid the Stars and Stripes carefully at the clay feet of the bronze god who was soon to be swept away.

The Millionaires of Williamsport

The mascot of my alma mater, Lower Merion High School, is a bulldog. I suppose that had something to do with tenaciousness and "Grrrrr" and all that, but as far as I know, Lower Merion Township wasn't infested with bulldogs at any key period in its development. The same cannot be said of Williamsport and millionaires. At one time in the mid-1800s, Williamsport was home to more millionaires per capita than any other town in the United States. The wealth was literally flowing down the Susquehanna River from the lumber trade born of the thick forests of central Pennsylvania. I have visited other Pennsylvania towns that make the same millionaires-per-capita claim, specifically Jim Thorpe (then Mauch Chunk), but only Williamsport has institutionalized the title by naming its high school teams "The Millionaires."

As you might imagine, a Millionaire mascot should look like a millionaire, and Williamsport's does. Think of the guy on the Monopoly box when he was fifteen years old. No need for a monocle, but decked out in top hat, white gloves, and cane, perhaps with a black cape on a windy day.

Little League Baseball
Williamsport

Among Pennsylvania's many exports to the world—a constitutional republic, the Slinky, steel, anthracite, Frankie Avalon, and Crayola crayons—perhaps the most successful has been Little League Baseball. Some thirty million people around the world have played Little League since it was invented in 1939 by a lumberyard clerk from Williamsport named Carl Stotz. Among them is the current president of the United

Williamsport, Pennsylvania, the birthplace of Little League
Baseball—one of the state's most successful exports.

States, George W. Bush, who played catcher for the Little League team
in Midland, Texas. (Al Gore didn't.) Bush is the first president to have
played Little League; his father has the distinction of being the first Little League volunteer coach to become president of the United States.

Little League has been a hit around the world since Carl Stotz solic-
ited sponsorship from local businesses to start a youth baseball league.
It was Stotz who drew the dimensions of the Little League baseball
diamond to be two-thirds the size of the regular baseball field (sixty

feet from base to base rather than ninety, and forty feet from the pitcher's mound to home plate rather than sixty feet, six inches).

In 1939 there were three Little League teams sponsored by Williamsport area companies: Lycoming Dairy, Lundy Lumber, and Jumbo Pretzel. By 1999 the game invented in a Susquehanna River town was being played in Burkina-Faso, an African country with a population less than Pennsylvania's and the one-hundredth nation to join the Little League. Today there are more than twenty thousand Little League programs operating worldwide.

The original home of Little League stands on West Fourth Street in Williamsport, across the street from the Pittsburgh Pirates' minor-league baseball club, the Crosscutters, named in honor of Williamsport's famed history in the state's lumber industry. It was on this field that the first twelve Little League World Series were played, from 1947 through 1958.

Since then the World Series has been played across the river in the Howard J. Lamade Stadium in South Williamsport, adjacent to the Peter J. McGovern Little League Museum. Carl Stotz, the founder and first commissioner, was forced out of his position in 1956 when he filed suit in federal court seeking to prevent the expansion of the league. Clearly, he never envisioned the worldwide organization nor the live network TV coverage of the Little League World Series that has accompanied the championship game since 1960.

The main room on the first floor of the Little League museum resembles a baseball playing field, complete with white baselines painted on the floor and a home plate with a mannequin catcher and umpire standing behind it. The room literally shrieks "Play ball!" but a sign at the front door advises visitors, no bats or gloves allowed in the museum. The exhibits behind glass show every Little League World Series Championship team photo since 1947. That year's Williamsport all-star team wore mismatched uniforms from a local VFW, Sears, Hossers, and 40 & 8 business sponsors. The 1948 Champions from nearby Lock Haven all wore uniforms sponsored by Keds. In 1957

Monterrey, Mexico, became the first of several foreign teams to win the Little League World Series and the first team to repeat the following year.

The Little League Hall of Excellence is a separate room showing large photographs of Little League alumni who have gone on to make a name for themselves in sports and other endeavors. They include major-league all-stars Mike Schmidt and Tom Seaver, former NBA star and US senator Bill Bradley, movie star Tom Selleck, author and columnist George Will, and humorist Dave Barry.

While I was visiting South Williamsport, construction was under way for an expansion of the stadium complex (a record 41,200 people crowded into Lamade Stadium to see the 1998 championship game won by Toms River, New Jersey, over Kashima, Japan). Today the expanded stadium can accommodate ten thousand in seats around the infield with room for thirty thousand more people on the hillside beyond the outfield fences. If you make it to see the Little League August Classic, make sure to take a trip across the Susquehanna River to West Fourth Street in Williamsport to see the little field where Carl Stotz started it all.

5

Northwest

Northwest Pennsylvania is *the story of oil. Everyone knows the story of how oil was "discovered" in Pennsylvania in 1859 by Edwin Drake, who drilled the first well near Titusville. It was his drilling technique that made history, if not money for Drake, who died, in the preferred term of the day, "penniless." The biggest boom and bust happened at the town of Pithole, whose population jumped to 15,000 then down to 261 in just a few years.*

In the Northwest wooden oil derricks covered hillsides as densely as the trees that used to stand there from Lake Erie and the New York border on the north to the Ohio state line on the west. Oil is still being produced in the Northwest from thousands and thousands of wells throughout the region. And the towns without oil wells are growing groundhogs. Well at least one is. Punxsutawney in Jefferson County has become internationally famous as the Groundhog Day capital of the world. Even before the major hit movie starring Bill Murray, Punxsutawney was known as the place to be on February 2. Since 2004 the official spokesrodent for the Pennsylvania Lottery has been Gus, "the second most famous groundhog in Pennsylvania." Meanwhile, I can guarantee that the most disturbing natural phenomenon that you can witness on the shores of a body of water shared by Pennsylvania and Ohio takes place on the Pennsylvania side of the Pymatuning Reservoir in a town called Linesville, where the sign at the city limits reads, WELCOME TO LINESVILLE. *FOUNDED 1824. WHERE THE DUCKS WALK ON THE FISH. You have to see it to believe it. And once you've seen it, you still won't.*

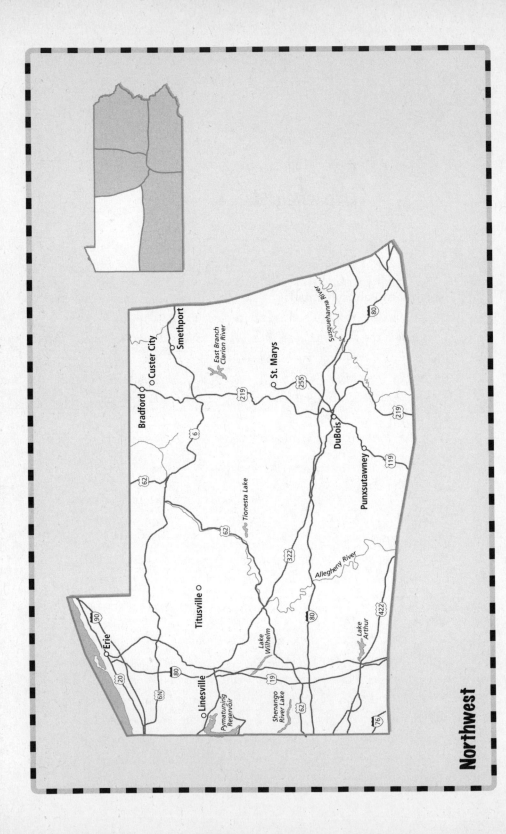

Northwest

Cold Town, Warm Hearts

Bradford

It's August and the heater is turned on in the house where I'm writing this. The heat is always on here—January or July, it makes no difference—because as hot as it can get during the day, it can get colder than you'd imagine here at night. "Here" is upstate Pennsylvania. It's so upstate that Buffalo is closer than Pittsburgh and Canada is closer than a foreign country has a right to be. I am not so much in the middle of nowhere as on the edge of nowhere. "Nowhere" would be the next-biggest town, Bradford, which only the jurisdictional reality of the New York state line two miles north prevents from being part of the vast Seneca Indian reservation. Therefore I am on the edge of Bradford, shivering during the late summer in the village of Lewis Run in McKean County. Bradford (COOL TOWN, WARM HEARTS reads the sign on the side of an oil refinery tank in the middle of town) has the teeth-chattering distinction of being the AccuWeather-certified coldest place in the state. "The Icebox of Pennsylvania," Bradford has been called, a title shared with neighboring upstate towns of Kane and St. Mary's, each of which claims to be colder than the other. Lewis Run runs even cooler. This I am told inside the Lewis Run home of L. A. "Larry" Rotheraine, a warm-blooded Philadelphia boy gone cold country.

There aren't many people where Rotheraine lives now—something like forty-eight people per square mile, compared to the big city downstate where the population density is 11,745 per square mile. What there are per square mile are mountains, lots and lots of mountains, those rolling green Pennsylvania tree humps that rise and fall endlessly in these parts and much of the rest of the state. But for whatever reason the mountains in McKean County and the prevailing winds from the northwest create uniquely cooler atmospheric conditions. Already in mid-August the leaves are turning on some trees. "Seven years ago our first frost came on August 21," Rotheraine said, oddly, almost like it's a good thing.

Rotheraine watches for frost the way a card counter watches for face cards in Atlantic City. That's because this big-city boy is the most successful gardener in McKean County and perhaps in the state of Pennsylvania. For the last fourteen years, Rotheraine has been the master gardener at Evergreen Elm Inc., a provider of services to mentally challenged adults in Bradford, where Rotheraine teaches and encourages groups and individuals as they help him work an extraordinary garden covering a mere two-thirds of an acre. One Saturday night I watched as Rotheraine and three of his eager protégés collected their prizewinning vegetables on the last day of the weeklong McKean County Fair. "Who's got their long johns on?" asked the radio personality introducing the featured country-western band on the main stage, while Rotheraine and his veteran prizewinning assistants toured the midway on a night when temperatures would drop into the low forties. If McKean County is the icebox of Pennsylvania, then Rotheraine's garden is the vegetable bin. That night Evergreen Elm gardeners had entered thirty different vegetables and won thirty ribbons—twenty-two blue, five red, and three white. At the 2003 McKean County Fair, Rotheraine and his clients actually lost . . . well, finished second, anyway, in one vegetable competition. They won the top prize awarded in every other category. (Yawn.) They've been virtually sweeping the top prizes at the fair for so long that Evergreen Elm decided to limit its entries just so someone else could get a chance to win the blue.

What's Rotheraine's secret? It's called biodynamic gardening, a compost-intensive process pioneered by the influential and controversial scientist-writer Dr. Rudolf Steiner (1861–1925), whose spiritualistic concepts of planting and growing vegetables sound like voodoo to traditional agriculturalists. But the proof is in the ribbons and, more impressively, in the yield. Evergreen Elm's garden produces three to four times the average yield for onions, cabbages, beets, carrots, peppers, squash, and other vegetables. The cherry tomatoes can yield as much as forty times the average; a single plant can grow to fifteen feet and produce two thousand tomatoes a year.

Master gardener Larry Rotheraine stands next to one of his remarkable cherry tomato plants that yield two thousand tomatoes per season.

I don't pretend to understand how he does it, but I will go on record as saying that the best tomato I ever ate was out of Evergreen Elm's garden. It was like I finally tasted a real tomato for the first time, meaty, flavorful, and juicy without being drippy. But then, I pour ketchup on my scrambled eggs. A more distinguished and discriminating judgment comes from Diarmuid Murphy, executive chef at Glendorn, an exclusive 1,280-acre estate near Bradford that caters to guests with gourmet palates. After the young Irishman's appointment to the top food preparation post in 2002, he was invited by Rotheraine to the Evergreen Elm garden for a tour and vegetable tasting. Ever since, Glendorn's Murphy has purchased as much of the garden's produce as Evergreen Elm is willing to sell. "Across the board, these vegetables blow away every vegetable I've ever tasted," said Murphy, shortly after returning from a James Beard Foundation dinner in Oklahoma. Evergreen Elm's biodynamic vegetables had been the talk of the table among the fine-food professionals at this dinner.

It all makes you wonder what Rotheraine could do in a warmer climate where the frost doesn't paint the pumpkins until Halloween. "I could grow more in a warmer climate, but I couldn't get the quality of seeds I get from this cold," Rotheraine said of what he calls his Highlands Star Seeds. "Besides, I love it here. This is my home now. These people are my family." For L. A. Rotheraine, home is where the heat isn't. For more information visit www.rotheraine.com.

Zippo Dee Doo Dah
Bradford

At one time or another in your life, you've probably owned a Zippo lighter. Your Zippo may have had a design, decoration, commemorative decal, or advertisement on the front of it (mine has gears and the Harley-Davidson Motorcycles logo), but I guarantee that yours had the same thing written on the bottom as mine does: ZIPPO, BRADFORD, PA.

Bradford has been the home to Zippo lighters since the beginning, and the beginning was a summer night in 1932 during a dinner dance

The Most Famous Town That Doesn't Exist

Since the international success of the movie *Saving Private Ryan*, Pennsylvania has become a symbol of the home of the citizen soldier. Who can forget the final scene of a now old and gray James Francis Ryan standing at attention and saluting in front of a white cross at the American military cemetery in Normandy? The camera then pushes in to show the name on the cross, CAPT. JOHN MILLER, PENNSYLVANIA.

In the movie the American soldiers under his command have bets on what Captain Miller (played by Tom Hanks) did in civilian life and where he lived. In one of the most gripping scenes in the movie, he reveals that he's an English teacher at Thomas Alva Edison High School in Addley, Pennsylvania.

In fact, there is no Addley, Pennsylvania. It was a name made up by *Saving Private Ryan* screenwriter Robert Rodat, who grew up in New Hampshire.

at the Bradford Country Club where well-to-do Bradfordians, most of whom were in the oil business, gathered to complain about business during those darkest early days of the Great Depression.

A forty-seven-year-old oilman named George Blaisdell had almost been wiped out by falling crude oil prices, and to escape the depressing talk, he stepped out onto the balcony for a smoke. There stood Dick Dresser, an elegantly dressed young man from a wealthy family, trying to light his cigarette with some kind of cheap-looking foreign lighter. When the little wheel on the top of the lighter struck the flint and sparked the wick into flame, a lightbulb went on in Blaisdell's

Even the streetlights look like Zippo lighters in Bradford.

head. What if he could manufacture a better windproof lighter that could be used in one hand? Zippo dee doo dah!

The first Zippo lighters were boxier in shape, a half inch taller and a quarter inch wider than current models, but that's about the only difference. In the first month Blaisdell's company produced eighty-two units designed to sell for $1.95 each. Total sales that first month were $69.15. Blaisdell needed something else, something unique to attract attention to his product. He came up with what he called a "forever

★ ★

guarantee," a lifetime replacement or repair warranty that continues to this day.

Today you can view returned Zippo lighters being received and repaired and shipped off by the virtually all-female crew of employees at the Zippo Repair Clinic at the Zippo Lighter Museum in Bradford. One display case at the museum contains a variety of mangled lighters that have been returned over the years. The list of the causes beneath the damaged lighters includes garbage disposal, bulldozer, power mower, ice crusher, and cocker spaniel.

To get to the Zippo museum, visitors must first walk through the Zippo gift shop, where lighters that once cost $1.95 now retail for $35.95. There are Zippos with World Wrestling Federation stars like Stone Cold Steve Austin and the Undertaker. There are Jeep, Ford, and Chevy Zippos. There are Elvis, Beatles, and Kiss Zippos. There's even a *Titanic* Zippo, one of thousands of specialty collectible models manufactured over the years. Outside the Zippo Visitors Center, the streetlights in the parking area and along Zippo Drive are shaped like flaming Zippo lighters.

Incidentally, Blaisdell, who died in 1978 at the age of ninety-three, chose the name Zippo because he was delighted by the sound of a new invention by another Pennsylvania manufacturing company. The Talon Company had revolutionized the clothing industry with a new type of easy-to-use-with-one-hand metal fastener. They called it the zipper. (For more information call the Zippo Visitors Information Center at 814-368-2700 or check out www.zippo.com.)

Oil's Well That Ends Well
Custer City

The question was worth $125,000. "In what state was the first oil well drilled?" asked Regis Philbin. "(A) California, (B) Oklahoma, (C) Pennsylvania, or (D) Texas." The contestant on *Who Wants to Be a Millionaire* used one of his lifelines, a call to a friend, to be sure of the answer that anyone from Oil City to Wellsboro could come up with

★ ★

in a heartbeat. It was up in Titusville in Crawford County that Colonel Edwin Drake discovered oil on August 27, 1859, by drilling a well sixty-nine feet into the ground that produced twenty barrels of crude oil a day. It was the first time that oil had been obtained in substantial quantities, and it set off a mad rush of drilling and speculating that turned Oil Creek into "The Valley That Changed the World." The Pennsylvania oil rush was *Who Wants to Be a Millionaire* for keeps, but Drake went broke due to competition and falling oil prices. When he made his discovery, oil was selling for twenty dollars a barrel. By 1861 you could buy a barrel of oil for a dime."Oil is just now on a boom. Everybody talks oil, and the visitor must talk oil or endure the unconcealed pity of all around him," wrote Colonel A. K. McClure in the *Philadelphia Times* after a visit to Bradford in May 1883. "The houses as a rule are pitched together like a winter camp, with here and there a solid brick edifice to mock the makeshift structures around it. The oil exchange is a beautiful building, and looks as if it was expected that oil gambling would continue, even after the day of doom, regardless of the shifting of oil centers." McClure described the kind of Black Gold Fever that fueled the mad bidding on oil futures at the exchange, the same type of dime-for-a-dollar "buying on margin" speculation that led to the stock market crash of 1929. "They sold oil by the million of barrels, without a speck in sight, and with only a small percentage of margin money to give substance to the hazard. Five million barrels, and even more, are sold in a day, and speculators make one day to lose the next." After oil was discovered in Bradford in McKean County in 1872 at the imposing depth of 1,200 feet, the greatest oil field in American history went into operation. The Bradford Oil District included all of McKean County and part of neighboring Cattaraugus County, New York. In 1878 the Bradford field produced 6.5 million barrels of oil, 42 percent of the total oil production in the United States. By 1883 Bradford was producing 23 million barrels of oil each year, an incredible 83 percent of American oil production.

Not only was Pennsylvania crude oil plentiful; it was special. The "miracle molecule" found only in Pennsylvania Grade crude oil makes

There are ninety thousand (NINETY THOUSAND!) oil wells in McKean County alone. This is the kind of staggering statistic memorialized at the Penn-Brad Historical Oil Well Park.

it the best lubricating oil in the world. Unlike asphalt-based oil found everywhere from Texas to Saudi Arabia, Pennsylvania crude is paraffin based. This makes it waxier than other crude oil, a difference you can see. Pennsylvania crude isn't black; it's greenish amber in hue, almost the color of tea.

You can see it for yourself at the Penn-Brad Historical Oil Well Park and Museum located on Route 219 between Bradford and Custer City, not far from where the first oil well in the area was sunk. The seventy-two-foot-tall wooden derrick is an exact replica of the 1890s standard rigs that dotted the surrounding countryside and mountains like trees by the hundreds. What you'll learn at the Penn-Brad Oil Well Park and Museum is that oil wells weren't drilled so much as pounded into the ground. The drill bit was a solid iron cylinder more than six inches in diameter and seven feet in length, weighing up to eight hundred pounds. Behind the drill would be a forty-two-foot-long cylinder called a stem, which weighed 2,800 pounds. The bit and stem would be lifted and dropped by a four-and-a-half-inch-thick "bull rope," which was lifted and lowered by a wooden beam on a pivot. The beam was moved up and down by a flywheel driven by a steam engine and in later years by a four-cylinder internal combustion engine called a Buffalo Drilling Engine.

It's all very ingenious and Rube Goldberg–looking, but it did the job. The sharpened drill bit would drop, pulverizing the bedrock. The tiny bits were then scooped up into a hollow thirty-foot-long wrought iron cylinder called a bailer. When the bailer was full, it would be lifted out of the hole by the bull rope and its contents would be inspected and discarded. The drilling was done in twelve-hour shifts by two-man crews who were paid by the foot. When the contents of the bailer revealed slurry, oil mixed with rock, they had reached the oil sand located between two layers of bedrock. The drilling would continue until the next layer of bedrock was hit, letting the drillers know exactly how deep the oil sand reached. Then it was the shooter's turn.

Shooters had the most dangerous job of all. They drove mule-drawn wagons filled with nitroglycerine and dynamite, the tools of their trade. Two gallons of nitroglycerine, enough to level a city block, would be lowered into the drill hole and then dynamite would be packed on top of that. The dynamite and nitro would be detonated by a heavy iron weight called a go-devil that would be dropped down the well hole. Needless to say, go-devils were good for one time only. The explosion 1,600 feet under the ground would create a porous crater maybe six feet in diameter, and into this crater would seep crude oil being squeezed from the surrounding oil sand by millions of tons of pressure. A pumping jack would be installed at the top of the well and crude oil would begin to flow.

Oil wells are now drilled by portable rotary drills, six or seven of which are still in operation by independent contractors in McKean County. Since 1871 a total of ninety thousand oil wells have been drilled in the Bradford Oil District. The Penn-Brad Historical Oil Well Park and Museum is open from Memorial Day to Labor Day or by appointment. Call (814) 368-5574 or visit http://visitanf.com/penn-brad-oil-museum.

Hannibal Lecter, Meet Mad Anthony
Erie

During my travels around Pennsylvania, I found that listening to books on tape was a good way of avoiding local radio stations, both good and bad. The trouble with listening to radio on long trips through unfamiliar territory is that the worst stations tend to have the most powerful signals. And as soon as you find a station you like, you drive out of range, or a mountain interferes so that you're alternating between two stations, both of which are lousy.

I've listened to all kinds of books on tape—novels, histories, biographies—but during my trip to Erie, I happened to be listening to Thomas Harris's sequel to *Silence of the Lambs.* Hannibal turned out to be the perfect companion on a stop at the Erie Historical Museum, where I found a kettle that had been used to boil the meat off the bones of Revolutionary War hero "Mad Anthony" Wayne. Wayne wasn't mad when he found himself in a stew pot on the shores of Lake Erie. In fact, he'd been dead thirteen years when his body was exhumed at the request of his son Isaac, who wanted his father's skeletal remains shipped home for burial at St. David's Church in Radnor, about fifteen miles west of Philadelphia.

Well, sir, "Mad Anthony" Wayne was ornery in life and he proved to be just as uncooperative in death. Wayne died on December 15,

1796, two years after one of his greatest military victories, this time leading US troops against hostile Indian tribes trying to stop westward expansion. The Battle of Fallen Timbers near Toledo, Ohio, in 1794 was another in a disastrous series of defeats suffered by Native Americans trying to hold on to their land. General Wayne's victory opened up the Northwest Territory to Euro-American settlers. Wayne was commanding the American troops manning the garrisons in the new territory (including Fort Wayne, Indiana) at the time of his death. He was buried in a plain pine coffin in Erie, the largest town in the region.

Which brings us back to that kettle. When Wayne's body was unearthed more than a decade after his death, it was so perfectly preserved that it looked like he could have gone out to dinner that night. Because the trip to Philadelphia was almost four hundred miles over rough roads, and because his son Isaac had arrived to claim the body in a small sulky, there was no way to transport the entire body. So the great general's carcass was butchered, with great respect, of course. His flesh was removed from the bones, and the bones were boiled white in the kettle on display in the Erie Historical Museum, next to the fava beans and a nice bottle of Chianti.

The museum, at 356 West Sixth Street, is open year-round Tuesday through Friday from 10:00 a.m. to 5:00 p.m., Saturday and Sunday from 1:00 to 5:00 p.m. Admission charged. For more information visit www.eriecountyhistory.org.

What's Up with Erie?

Erie

Pennsylvania's water boundary with Canada extends for thirty-six miles along Lake Erie at the northwestern tip of the commonwealth. At its greatest width this little wedge of land reaches sixteen miles north of Pennsylvania's otherwise straight-edge boundary with New York. The wedge tapers like an axe blade to the southwest until it meets the Ohio state line almost exactly where New York's southern boundary would extend. In fact, if it weren't for this little northern appendage of land that meets one of the Great Lakes, the western boundaries of Pennsylvania would be perfectly rectangular.

Originally, five states claimed ownership of the wedge of land called the Erie Triangle, including New York, Virginia, Connecticut, and Massachusetts, all basing their claims on land grants from the king of England. Following the Revolution, the five states were persuaded to turn ownership of the land over to the new federal government of the United States, and in 1788 Pennsylvania offered to buy the land for seventy-five cents an acre. Andrew Ellicott, who would later become famous for surveying the street plan for Washington, DC, surveyed the land to be purchased and reported a total of 202,187 acres. On April 23, 1792, Pennsylvania paid the federal government $151,640.25 for the lakefront property, which may have been the best real estate deal of the eighteenth century.

Trivia

Where's Le Boef?

Erie takes its name from an Indian tribe that lived on the shores of the Great Lake until they were displaced by the Senecas in 1654. Erie County is the only part of Pennsylvania that shares a border with two states (New York and Ohio) and a foreign country (Canada). The French were the first white settlers and they named the nearby creek Le Boef (beef, in English) because of the large herds of bison were found in the area. Even today, just south of the city of Erie, a commercial bison (beefalo?) herd can be seen to the west of Interstate 79. The English, who won the land from the French in warfare, renamed the waterway French Creek, obviously in anticipation of a joke inspired by a TV commercial 250 years later: "Where's Le Boef?"

Some Schools Get Snow Days

I met an old-timer at the Penn-Brad Historical Oil Well Park and Museum who told me the following story:

Back in the early 1900s when shooters, the men who "shot" oil wells by detonating nitroglycerine deep underground, still carried their combustibles in mule-drawn wagons, there were occasional accidents. An accident was generally fatal to the shooter, his mules, and any other living creatures within a quarter mile of the explosion. Shooters had to travel over rough ground every day in their dynamite- and nitro-filled wagons, and Custer City was in the middle of the activity.

The old-timer attended the white-clapboard one-room schoolhouse in Custer City, and at least twice a year, the windows of the school would be blown out by the concussion of a shooter's wagon blowing up. When the windows blew out, school was dismissed, but not only because of the drafty conditions. The schoolchildren then became members of a search party looking for any remains of the shooter, which could be scattered for miles. The children would find bloody bits of clothing hanging from trees and chunks of flesh (some human, some mule) lying on the ground. The children would gather these pieces, which would be buried, man and animal, in the same coffin.

James Bryner, founder of the Penn-Brad Oil Well Park and Museum, told me that he'd never heard that story. "We've got more than a hundred elderly volunteers who work here from time to time," he said, "and some of them are prone to exaggeration." There were shooter accidents, that's for sure. Bryner said that as recently as 1968, a shooter's truck exploded on the side of the road, leaving a crater in the highway twenty feet wide and five feet deep.

A Man Named Cornplanter

Erie

Pennsylvania owes a debt of thanks to a remarkable Indian leader named Cornplanter for its Canadian lakefront coastline. Cornplanter was a chief of the Senecas, one of the six Indian nations in the Iroquois Confederacy during the American Revolution. Cornplanter's mother was a pure-blooded Seneca and his father was a white trader, probably Dutch, named O'Beale or Abell. Despite his mixed heritage Cornplanter became chief of his people. They controlled the land in western New York and Pennsylvania, roughly the triangular area between Buffalo, Pittsburgh, and Cleveland.

The Seneca fought with the British during the American Revolution, and in 1779 General George Washington ordered a scorched-earth campaign against the Indian tribes of New York, partly in response to the Wyoming Massacre the year before in Wilkes-Barre. Washington ordered General John Sullivan to march north from Easton and link up with two other Continental Army brigades and then descend upon the Iroquois. The Father of Our Country ordered the "total destruction and devastation" of Indian villages and farms so "that the country may not merely be overrun but destroyed." "Our future security," Washington wrote to Sullivan, would depend on "terror." No peace negotiating, Washington ordered his commander, before "the total ruin of their settlements was effected."

Sullivan's Campaign, although a great success during the Revolution, is today little known and yet long remembered by the Indians. "Town Destroyer" was the name the Seneca gave Washington, whose name when spoken caused children to run to their mothers. Despite this, Cornplanter, the vanquished chief, learned to love his enemy.

In 1784, following the Revolution, the Six Nations of the Iroquois Federation signed a treaty with the new nation they called the Thirteen Fires at Fort Stanwix, New York. Six years later Cornplanter came to the nation's capital in Philadelphia to tell his story. His words, through a translator, were eloquent, measured, and heartbreaking. "Listen to me, Fathers of the Thirteen Fires, the Fathers of the Quaker State, O'Beale or Cornplanter, returns thanks to God for the pleasure he has in meeting you this . . . Fathers, six years ago I had the pleasure of making peace with you, and at that time a hole was dug in the Earth, and all contentions between my nation and you ceased and were buried there." At that treaty . . . three friends from the Quaker State came to me and treated with me for purchase of a large tract of land upon the Northern boundary of Pennsylvania, extending from Tioga to Lake Erie for the use of their warriors. I agreed to sale of same and sold it to them for four thousand dollars. I begged of them to take pity on my nation and not buy it forever. They said they would purchase it forever, but that they would give me one thousand dollars in goods when the leaves were ready to fall. . . . In former days, when you were young and weak, I used to call you brother, but now I call you father. Father, I hope you will take pity on your children, for now I inform you that I'll die on your side. Now, father, I hope you will make my bed strong."

What happened next in Cornplanter's story does not cover the Fathers of the Quaker State in glory. After negotiating rights to hunt and fish in the new lands acquired by Pennsylvania (actually a tract of land almost twice the size of the current Erie County wedge), Cornplanter and 170 men, women, and children walked to Fort Pitt (Pittsburgh) to take possession of the thousand dollars' worth of "prime goods" promised for the autumn. Cornplanter's people were robbed, shot at, and cheated during the long journey. "Fathers, upon my arrival I saw the goods which I had been informed of. . . . One hundred of the blankets were all moth eaten and good for nothing. . . . Feeling myself much hurt upon the occasion, I wrote a letter to you, Fathers of the Quaker State, complaining of the injury, but never received an answer."

Cornplanter's list of grievances, his dignity and eloquence, moved all who heard him. President George Washington, "Town Destroyer," treated Cornplanter with affection and respect, enlisting his friendship in further negotiations with native peoples. The Fathers of the Quaker

State, in the form of the Pennsylvania State Legislature, awarded Cornplanter lands along the upper Allegheny River in what is now Allegheny National Forest. Cornplanter died there in 1836 at the age of 101.

Don't Give Up the Ships
Erie

What Gettysburg was to the Civil War, what Valley Forge was to the Revolutionary War, Erie was to the War of 1812: a Pennsylvania symbol of American resolve and a turning point in a war that quietly celebrated its bicentennial during 2012, when most Americans concentrated on or were distracted by the presidential election year. Among American wars, the one in 1812 is treated like a footnote rather than an important chapter in the new nation's history. It was during this war that the capital of the United States in Washington, DC, was invaded by foreign troops and the White House was sacked and burned. It was during this war (after the peace treaty was signed) that Andrew Jackson won national fame and later the presidency by defeating the British in the Battle of New Orleans. And it was during this war that Francis Scott Key wrote the words to the poem that would later be put to music in a familiar English drinking song that was to become our national anthem. And during that war, little Erie represented the state of Pennsylvania.

At the start of the conflict the borough of Erie was a small lakeside town of five hundred people. Its shipbuilding industry shifted into high gear when the United States declared war on Great Britain, then the greatest naval power in the world. By the summer of 1813, Erie dry docks had completed six vessels for the war effort, and on September 10, 1813, a squadron of nine American warships under the command of Commodore Oliver Hazard Perry met the mighty British in the most famous naval battle of the war fought on an inland sea. During the Battle of Lake Erie, Perry's flagship, the *Lawrence*, was brutally battered by British cannons. Eighty percent of Perry's sailors were dead or wounded when he shifted his command to the smaller *Niagara*, taking

★ ★

with him the *Lawrence*'s battle flag. The flag bore the dying words of Captain James Lawrence, who had died in battle three months earlier: "Don't give up the ship!"

Aboard the *Niagara,* Perry quickly turned defeat into victory. Fifteen minutes after giving up his flagship, Perry forced the British commander to surrender. In his report Perry penned words nearly as famous as Lawrence's dying command. He wrote, "We have met the enemy and they are ours."

The city of Erie never did give up the ship. Or ships. Although the *Niagara* was decommissioned and scuttled offshore in 1820, its hulk was raised in 1913 on the one-hundredth anniversary of the Battle of Lake Erie. Painstaking restoration took more than thirty years to complete, but by the 1980s the *Niagara* was beyond saving and it was finally dismantled. An exact replica was built and the new *Niagara* was launched from Erie on September 10, 1988. Today the US Brig *Niagara* is one of Erie's biggest attractions, at dock or in full sail. The *Niagara* has been designated the Official Flagship of the Commonwealth of Pennsylvania; Erie is the Flagship City.

Meanwhile, a replica of the real hero ship of the epic battle, the *Lawrence,* was also reconstructed by the Pennsylvania Historical and Museum Commission and then, during a controlled experiment at a gunnery range, fired upon with cannon from the *Niagara* to replicate the actual damage caused by twenty-four- and thirty-two-pound cannonballs. The damaged midsection of the *Lawrence* replica is on display at the Erie Maritime Museum at 150 East Front Street. Phone (814) 452-BRIG (2744) or see it at www.brigniagara.org.

These Fish Were Made for Walking
Linesville

WELCOME TO LINESVILLE reads the sign outside this Crawford County town near the Ohio state line, WHERE THE DUCKS WALK ON THE FISH. More than one visitor has quacked up after reading that sign, but there's nothing fishy about it. Or should I say, it's very fishy? Chances are you'll see more fish in five minutes at Linesville than during a full day at the National Aquarium. The difference is that the fish at Linesville come to see people as much as people come to see them.

Just outside of town is the spillway that separates the Pymatuning Reservoir into two bodies of water, and it is along the spillway that people gather to feed the fish and the fish gather to be fed. It is, quite frankly, the darnedest thing you've ever seen. Hundreds . . . no, thousands . . . no, *gazillions* of fish swarm to the concrete edge of the spillway waiting for people to toss bread into the water. The bread is devoured in a feeding frenzy by huge-mouthed carp as big as a man's forearm fighting one another for every morsel. An entire loaf of bread is gone in seconds, like a cow among piranha. It's more than a little spooky. The fish literally come out of the water and climb over each other's backs like a churning carpet of carp. Forget the ducks— a *human* could walk on the fish. Besides, all the ducks I observed remained on the edges, away from the fray.

I bought two loaves of day-old "fish bread" from the convenient souvenir concession stand next to the spillway parking lot, and every-where I tossed the bread, the cagey carp seemed to anticipate it like a dog chasing a stick. They gathered in thick clumps six feet below the spillway railing, their mouths undulating like huge toothless *O*s getting larger then smaller then larger again. My advice: Hold your children tight when they feed the fish.

A couple of hundred yards away from the spillway is the Pymatuning Visitor Center, run by the Pennsylvania Game Commission. Inside you'll find lots of information about raccoons and deer and other wild-life, but nothing about Pymatuning's biggest tourist attraction. When I asked a uniformed Game Commission guard about the carp, he grum-bled, "Ah, you'll have to ask the Department of Fish." Then he added, "They're the biggest welfare recipients in Crawford County."

He's not far from wrong. It's hard to say which came first, the people or the fish. But certainly the fish only come in large numbers because of the people bearing bread. The carp go away when the people do during the winter, and they return with the people in the spring. The biggest welfare recipients are also the biggest tourist attraction in Crawford County, a large but thinly populated area of fewer than 90,000 residents. In a town of 1,100 humans, it is the fish that draw more than 500,000 visitors each year to the spillway in Linesville. The town's other claim to fame is at the main intersection with the only traffic light for miles around. There's a sign mounted on the side of the only hotel in town that has arrows pointing east and west. To the west it says CHICAGO 500 MILES, and to the east it says NEW YORK 500 MILES. Little Linesville is obviously torn between its middling loyalties to its two neighboring metropolises.

In 2008 the feed-the-fish frenzy at Linesville nearly resulted in a ban on feeding bread to the hungry hippo-sized carp. State officials were about to enact rules that would prevent people from tossing anything but approved aquatically nutritional fish pellets into the gaping maws of those monster mouths. Try to imagine the appeal of throwing cupfuls of kibbles and bits into a ring full of ravenous pit bulls. It's just not the same. The bread ban was cancelled once the real reason for it leaked out. The bathing beaches along the Pymatuning tourist areas were being increasingly fouled by unpleasant deposits made by wildlife gathering around the bread feed. No, not the fish. Not the ducks. It was the Canada geese that gathered on the fringes of the daily carp scrum that were causing the problem. In a word the issue was—two words, actually—goose poop. The state's case against the bottom-dwelling bread eaters was dismissed.

The Pymatuning Reservoir was built as a public works project during the Depression. Its 17,088 acres make it the largest body of water in Pennsylvania, even though almost half of it is in Ohio. The word *Pymatuning* is of Indian origin, meaning "dwelling place of the crooked-mouth man." In modern American English this might translate simply as "Congress."

Has Punxsutawney Gone Hollywood?

Punxsutawney

> Once again the eyes of the nation have turned here to this tiny village in western Pennsylvania, blah, blah, blah, blah, blah. —Phil Connors (Bill Murray) in the 1993 movie *Groundhog Day*

Much has changed in Punxsutawney, Pennsylvania, since the first time I visited on February 2, 1983. Thirty years ago Groundhog Day in Punxsutawney was a strictly local event with perhaps a few invited out-of-town guests. The wire service reports on what the groundhog did or didn't see spread to newspapers around the world. But the event itself was more of a mom-and-pop holiday. The first time I traveled to Punxsutawney as a Philadelphia newspaper columnist to attend the sunrise ceremony at Gobbler's Knob, a clearing about three miles outside downtown, a crowd of maybe two hundred people gathered to see if Punxsutawney Phil, the prognosticating groundhog, would or would not see his shadow and therefore predict an early spring. Among those present was a high school exchange student from Montevideo, Uruguay. I asked her if they had any similarly unique ethnic customs where she came from. She replied, "No, we do not have winter in my country." The Groundhog Day custom was imported by German immigrants, who celebrated February 2 at Candlemas, a Christian holiday, the date of which coincides with a pagan "return of light" festival, much like Christmas coincides with pagan winter solstice rites. I leave to your imagination the answer to the question of whether the Christian or pagan significance of February 2 was successfully imported. However, I will point out that these superstitious German farmers believed that a groundhog could predict the length of winter based on his shadow. Whatever, Punxsutawney, Pennsylvania, has become the American capital of this groundhog weather cult, probably because their groundhog wears a hat.

When Molly and I arrived in Punxsutawney in the summer of 2007, the first thing we noticed was a twelve-foot-tall wooden cutout of a

★ ★

Molly and Phil pose for the third edition of *Pennsylvania Curiosities*.

groundhog in a top hat standing—almost comically—at the end of a runaway-truck ramp at the bottom of a long hill on Route 119 leading into town. This was the first of dozens of Punxsutawney Phils we saw—images painted on the sides of buildings, carved from logs, painted on the front of T-shirts, and printed on postcards, along with statues, billboards, gimcracks, knickknacks, and geegaws. Punxsutawney Phil was no longer a local secret, or Groundhog Day a seasonal occasion to celebrate. Punxsutawney Phil was now a major industry. And it was all because of a day that would not end in Punxsutawney, Pennsylvania, and a top-grossing movie made about that day in 1993 starring Bill Murray. The success of the movie *Groundhog Day* turned tiny Punxsutawney (population 6,200) into the one-day mid-winter-break Ft. Lauderdale for college students in the years that followed its release. Depending on the day of the week Groundhog Day fell (Wednesday, Thursday, and Friday were best), the mostly college-age crowds that descended on Gobbler's Knob approached fifty thousand at their peak. The continued success of the *Groundhog Day* movie on videotape and DVD meant that Punxsutawney would remain some-thing that most people in town had never imagined before—a genuine tourist destination. And what could attract groundhog-happy tourists to a particular business or cultural institution better than a larger-than-life-size fiberglass sculpture of Punxsutawney Phil?

These sculptures, called "Phantastic Phils," are three feet tall, three and a half feet wide, and delightful. To me the Phil template in these sculptures more closely resembles Rocky "the flying squirrel" from the *Rocky and Bullwinkle* cartoon show—a happy bucktoothed character, usually with his right hand on his hip and his left hand waving, but every Phantastic Phil is different. There's the greenbacks-painted "One Dollar Phil" in front of the bank. There's the coal miner "Philtuminous: The Heritage Hog" in front of a furniture store. There's a kilt-clad, bagpipe-playing "Presby MacPhil" in front of the Punxsutawney Pres-byterian Church. There's a pharmacist "Phil My Prescription, Please" Phil in front of a drugstore. There's even a bellhop "Phil'd with Ser-vice" Phil in front of the Pantall Hotel, where Bill Murray stayed when he visited Punxsutawny before filming started on *Groundhog Day* (which was actually shot in the town of Woodstock, Illinois). In fact, there are so many Phantastic Phil sculptures around town (thirty-two at last count) some residents began to complain to the chamber of commerce: "You've got to stop before there are more Phantastic Phils than people in Punxsutawney."

You can see the real live Phil (who must be well over 120 years old since "officially" there has only been one Phil and the first recorded Punxsutawney groundhog ceremony took place in 1886) in a glass enclosure inside the Groundhog Zoo on the first floor of the Punx-sutawney Library off Barclay Square downtown. On the day we visited,

Here's Looking at Chew

The last of a breed of realist painters died in Wheeling, West Virginia, on November 24, 2000, and with him passed a piece of Pennsylvania history. His name was Harley Warrick and you've probably seen his handiwork while driving along backroads or highways, along Route 30 between Gettysburg and Chambersburg, or Route 255 between DuBois and St. Mary's, or several places along the Pennsylvania Turnpike between Lancaster and Somerset Counties. Wherever you've seen a CHEW MAIL POUCH TOBACCO sign on the side of a barn, you've probably seen Warrick's brushstrokes.

Harley Warrick wasn't the only man to paint Mail Pouch ads on barns throughout Pennsylvania and the Midwest, but by his reckoning, at the time of his death at the age of seventy-six, he had painted or repainted twenty thousand barns with the famous black, white, and yellow message CHEW MAIL POUCH TOBACCO. TREAT YOURSELF TO THE BEST. In the process he helped create and preserve a piece of vanishing Americana that is going the way of the dodo and Burma-Shave signs. Mail Pouch barns used to be as common as Sheetz convenience stores throughout Pennsylvania, but now you've got to keep your eyes peeled or you could miss the faded lettering on the side of the barn on Route 309 between Hazleton and Tamaqua. "The first thousand were a little rough, and after that you got the hang of it," Warrick said in a 1997 interview, recounting his fifty-plus years painting Mail Pouch barns. He started working for Mail Pouch as a painter fresh out of the Army in 1946. He and a helper would travel the countryside, painting two barns a day, six days a week for a weekly salary of thirty-two dollars.

Mail Pouch Tobacco company started advertising on the sides of barns and other high-visibility buildings in the late 1800s. The original slogan was "Clean Lasting Chew" rather than "Treat Yourself to

Mail Pouch Tobacco barns can still be seen along the Pennsylvania Turnpike and along backroads and highways in various parts of the state.

the Best." Thousands of barns were painted, from Pennsylvania to Oregon.

The beginning of the end for Mail Pouch signs was the 1965 highway beautification act, which prohibited advertising within 660 feet of federal highways. Then came bans on tobacco advertising. In 1969 the company discontinued the barn-painting program, but they kept Warrick working repainting existing barns. By the time Mail Pouch barns achieved historic landmark status, Warrick was something of a historic landmark himself. He worked for Mail Pouch full-time until 1992; in his retirement he built and painted Mail Pouch barn birdhouses, bird feeders, and mailboxes.

Today "Chew Mail Pouch" barns are becoming as rare as brass spittoons or smoking sections in restaurants. There are still perhaps a hundred in Pennsylvania, but fewer each year as time and progress take their toll.

Phil was not his usual charming self, preferring instead to sleep behind a rock away from the direct late-afternoon sunlight streaming into his enclosure. I chatted up the two librarians on duty about the impact the movie *Groundhog Day* has had on Punxsutawney. One of them confided, "That was the most boring movie I ever sat through. I fell asleep." Spoken by someone who lives it every day.

To see it for yourself, check www.groundhog.org and www.punxsutawneyphil.com.

Trivia

It's Erie, Ain't It?

Erie sports fans are trapped between two foreign powers—the Buffalo Bills and the Cleveland Indians—and their loyalties to Pennsylvania teams are suspect. Erie is such a foreign outpost in the minds of most Pennsylvanians that you almost expect someone from Erie to say, "How aboot a beer, eh?" like their across-the-lake Canadian brethren.

Former US Secretary of Homeland Security Tom Ridge was the first Pennsylvania governor to hail from Erie, and he charmed the rest of Pennsylvania with self-deprecating jokes about his hometown's relative obscurity. After he announced he was running for governor, Ridge described himself as "the guy nobody has ever heard of from the place nobody has ever been."

index

index

★ ★

★ ★

Clark DeLeon is an award-winning columnist for the *Philadelphia Inquirer*, grandfather, rugby coach, photographer, mummer, college professor, pool shooter, and Philadelphia tour guide. He has traveled the world but never lived more than ten miles away from his birthplace, the hospital founded by Benjamin Franklin. After ten years as a columnist for another Philadelphia daily newspaper, *Metro,* DeLeon returned to *the Inquirer* where he writes a column called "Clark's Park." In addition he teaches English and journalism at Montgomery County Community College. DeLeon lives in West Philadelphia with Sara, his wife of more than forty years, and Molly, the youngest of their three children.

Clark and Molly DeLeon in front of a mural of the ubiquitous Benjamin Franklin outside Dirty Frank's, Center City Philadelphia's legendary dive bar at 13th and Pine Streets.